D0390023

PRAISE FOR *FUTURE PERFECT*

"This book is not what you think it is. What this book is is Victoria Loustalot reaching into my mind and sorting out my eternal struggles. Here's the thing: as much as it pains me to say so, my struggles are not all that unique. I wonder about my future, I ponder the mysteries and beauties and great pains of love, I wonder what's out there that might be greater than me. In navigating the realms of psychics and healers with a skeptic's eye and an open heart, Loustalot moves toward meaning in a way that is deeply resonant."

—Elizabeth Crane, author of *We Only Know So Much*, *The History of Great Things*, and *Turf*

"Writing from an anxious, impatient, image-driven, data- and option-overloaded generation, Victoria Loustalot looks at our longings and the sources from whom we seek answers. *Future Perfect* is about the psychics and mystics we either adore or are skeptical about, and the science that supports or debunks their syntheses and claims. But this book is also about us—thirtysomethings, women, memoirists, Instagrammers—what we yearn for, why we search, how badly we want to be found. In reading about Loustalot's journey, in research and in life, we might just feel a little less lost and a little less alone, and that the future, while imperfect, can be a breeding ground for magic and kindness and empathy. Whether she embraces the scientific or the spiritual, in the end, and certainly evermore, Loustalot embraces herself."

—Cinelle Barnes, author of *Monsoon Mansion: A Memoir*

Previous Praise for *This Is How You Say Goodbye*

"Moves between past and present and is told in frank, detailed narrative marked by irony, heartache and some humor."

—*The Sacramento Bee*

"In this moving memoir, her first book, Loustalot paints a portrait of a man stoic in the face of quiet suffering. By turns sweet and heart-wrenching, she writes with courage and candor about bidding her beloved father a final farewell."

—*Booklist*

"Eloquent . . . gently probing . . . Loustalot's careful, deliberative prose delineates a young woman's arduous passage to self-realization."

—*Publishers Weekly*

"[Loustalot's] adventure makes for compelling reading . . . An intimate portrait of a bittersweet father-daughter relationship."

—*Kirkus Reviews*

"Victoria Loustalot's memoir will resonate with anyone who has ever tried to resolve the complexities of an enigmatic parent, or plumb what lies at the heart of the filial bond. Her uncommon intelligence, wit, and compassion shine through in this beautifully realized memoir. Loustalot is a beguiling writer and *This Is How You Say Goodbye* a smashing debut."

—Alexandra Styron, author of *Reading My Father*

"*This Is How You Say Goodbye* is a remarkable accomplishment. A riveting narrative that lays bare how important it is to come to terms with the past, this honest and heartrending memoir is for everybody who has ever tried to find his or her place in their family—and in the world."

—Julie Klam, *New York Times* bestselling author of *You Had Me at Woof* and *Friendkeeping*

"In lyrical, thoughtful, often humorous prose, Victoria Loustalot searches for her father, who came out as gay when Victoria was only seven and died from AIDS too young. Her search takes her to many continents and lovers, all as she attempts to understand her own relationship to intimacy. What Loustalot has written is a love story—a moving, aching love story to the father she never knew. It will resonate for all who have loved and lost, and who wish to heal."

—Kerry Cohen, author of *Loose Girl: A Memoir of Promiscuity*

Future Perfect

ALSO BY VICTORIA LOUSTALOT

Living Like Audrey: Life Lessons from the Fairest Lady of All

This Is How You Say Goodbye

Future Perfect

A Skeptic's Search for an Honest Mystic

Victoria Loustalot

Note to the reader: the names and personal details of a few individuals depicted
herein have been changed in order to respect and preserve their privacy.

Published by Little A, New York

www.apub.com

Amazon, the Amazon logo, and Little A are trademarks of Amazon.com, Inc., or its
affiliates.

ISBN-13: 9781503903654 (hardcover)
ISBN-10: 1503903656 (hardcover)
ISBN-13: 9781503903647 (paperback)
ISBN-10: 1503903648 (paperback)

Cover design by Laywan Kwan

Printed in the United States of America

First edition

For my godmother,
who has never stopped praying for me

The worse the state of the world grows, the more intensely I try for inner perfection and power. I fight for a small world of humanity and tenderness. —Anaïs Nin, June 1942

In the bigger scheme of things the universe is not asking us to do something, the universe is asking us to be something. And that's a whole different thing. —Lucille Clifton

CHAPTER ONE

My first encounter with a psychic was Miss Cleo. Her TV commercials aired during the talk show *Ricki Lake*, which I watched religiously after school in the late 1990s. Miss Cleo's ads featured snippets of what were supposed to be real phone sessions. The callers wanted to know things like who the father of their baby was and if their girlfriend was cheating. Miss Cleo, almost always in a loose-fitting top some bright shade of saccharine pink or orange and a matching necklace of chunky stone, would shuffle her tarot deck and lay rows of upturned cards on the table before announcing, in her intermittent Jamaican accent, that the father was "the unpleasant one" and that, yes, the girlfriend was cheating. She mostly gave predictions about the present, mentioning the future only vaguely, if at all. Her cards exposed critical revelations about things that had already happened and events that were causing drama in the now. No one ever seemed to ask about the future. It's hard to worry about tomorrow when you don't know if you can make it through today.

When Ricki broke for commercial and Miss Cleo appeared and her callers' voices came on the line, I pictured Ricki's guests on the other end, as if they were using the break to call Miss Cleo for a second opinion. Ricki and Miss Cleo bleed together in my mind, offering the same sassy advice to the same beleaguered guests day after day: that man is no good, that woman is up to no good. But the only real sorcery involved was how they got hundreds of thousands of us to tune in every afternoon. Even as a kid I knew this was so-called trashy TV and that it was make believe. I wasn't watching because I was a believer. I was watching because I wasn't. The fun in both Ricki and Miss Cleo was the foreignness of the situations and the extremity of the behavior, precisely the utter lack of believability. And that, for decades, was the entirety of what I knew and thought about psychics. I might have kept on that way through my whole life and quite happily, too. But beware what you don't believe.

CHAPTER TWO

I had my first real experience with a psychic twenty years later. We met in Montreal. Her name was Catharine River-Rain, and she considered herself a clairvoyant medium and spiritual life coach. And meeting her led me on to a wild, bumpy ride, like Alice tumbling down the rabbit hole, a very long fall that ends with a beginning. See, I'd been wearing my skepticism with excessive pride for most of my life, so I didn't meet Catharine with any kind of enthusiasm, despite having sought her out myself. On the internet. In the middle of the night. Naturally.

I found her website when I was in Tokyo, jet-lagged and sweaty, trying to catch a breeze on a hotel balcony that overlooked the bay. It happened to be the week the cherry blossoms came into their full exquisite bloom, and beneath my room and the hotel's lanterns a thick ribbon of pink branches lined the water's edge. The company I was working for at the time had sent me to Japan for a project, but that night I was deep in bachelorette-party planning mode, thinking only about home and my best friend, Jane. She was getting married at the end of the summer, and her one request was that we say goodbye to her single past by taking a psychic peek into her married future.

Jane and I had met when I was eighteen and a New York City newbie. She was twenty, had a full-time job, and had already been living in New York for more than a year. She knew all the things I wanted to know. We solidified our friendship over a shared love of books and an up-for-anything-what-else-can-we-make-happen approach to being young and living in Manhattan.

Only now, twelve years into our once-inconceivable futures, Jane was preparing to make a lifelong commitment to a good man, while my own boyfriend of nearly seven years, B., was moving out of my New York apartment, because I had asked him to. Between me and Jane, if either of our futures needed demystifying, it was mine.

Jane's bachelorette-party weekend was to be in Montreal, and Catharine was not the first clairvoyant in Quebec I had contacted. The others had proven to be uncooperative and noncommittal, upholding nothing other than my assumptions about so-called mystics. Not Catharine. In her emails, she was friendly but all business. My kind of stranger. She confirmed my appointment request and deposit within minutes, and I was relieved to be able to cross this task off my to-do list, though it did briefly cross my mind that if a genuine psychic should ever exist, they would not be this efficient. No matter. Jane only wanted us to have a little fun. We weren't looking for anything real.

I shut my laptop and stood to lean out over the balcony. It was the dregs of the night, and I was finally starting to tire. There was no one walking along the path by the bay, and the only sound was the lapping water. The cherry blossoms were fat and hung heavy on their branches, and I could not quite believe, for all of their hype, for all of the incessant chatter about them, they were not a letdown. The minimalism of their beauty was irrefutable, but what stunned me, what filled me with reverence, was their unexpected warmth. Tokyo is a beautiful, stark city, but when the cherry blossoms come into full bloom, it becomes a warm city, too. The fine tension between that starkness and that warmth is what made me fall in love with Japan's capital. I had not believed such delicate duality was possible.

When the May morning of our appointment arrived, our party of four woke up queasy, with the chalkiness of the previous night's overindulgence thick on our tongues. The Montreal apartment we had rented had glossy furnishings and oversized lighting and had looked chic in the night, but in the morning light and out from under our newly hungover point of view, it appeared shoddy and cramped. But never mind. We had a long itinerary for our Saturday, and I was focused on our schedule and how we were to get from one activity to the next in a city none of us knew well. Catharine River-Rain was just the first stop, the errand topping our list.

We took a cab to her neighborhood, which turned out to be mostly warehouses where the most neglected ones were also the most charming. Each block was more unpeopled than the one before in that almost-trendy, almost-affluent way where the residents think they're too good to be seen. You sense their presence, but you can't prove it. No one here would be caught dead loitering. I couldn't help but think of New York City's Tribeca. Only back when Tribeca was newly gentrifying, not the way it is today, one-too-many face-lifts later, gentrified beyond recognition and so entirely devoid of expression that even rich people are tired of living there.

But all that was still ahead for this neighborhood, written but not yet borne out. For the moment, we were just looking for coffee, and we found it in a shop that continued to cling to the days when you knew a coffee spot was decent if it was a little dirty and if, in the back, there was a faded orange couch, and it was good that the ceiling was low, the windows small, and the lights half-out, because you wouldn't want to see the state of that couch too well anyway.

A woman at the counter held a paper cup of coffee and spoke to the clerk at the register like she knew him. We held the door for her, and she smiled as she walked by. She had porcelain skin, bottle-red hair, and a sensible smile that suggested she might have been a wonderful nursery-school teacher in a past life. Maybe it was the sense of innate kindness she radiated, but something about her made me turn and watch as she continued to the sidewalk and stepped off the curb. Ten minutes later, our own hot coffees in hand, we entered the warehouse labyrinth of the address Catharine had given me. The stairway was cement and windowless, and the stairs looked like those we had climbed in our midtwenties when we had lived perpetually en route to some party or the next that a friend's roommate's coworker's boyfriend's bandmate was throwing. *The kind of parties people eventually get married just to escape,* I thought, as we curled around and up to the third floor.

The woman who opened the door was holding a paper cup. "We just saw you across the street," I said, in place of hello, to which she replied sanguinely, "Oh, I know." Like she had always known. Sure.

This time she held the door for us, and we filed into the small, open loft. Catharine's apartment was not technically hers. It belonged to a friend, but with its brightly painted walls, draped tapestries, hanging plants, and faded, multicolored rugs, it was clear the friend was also of the psychic persuasion. Or had modeled her decor on literally any season of *The Real World.* If I'd ever stopped to consider where and how Miss Cleo had lived, this apartment would have come pretty close to anything I would have imagined. We sat on the first available seating we saw, a beat-up Victorian settee pushed against a wall.

Catharine called us up one by one and led each of us to the round kitchen table placed at a slight remove, giving the impression, at least, that our readings were more private than public. Jane went first and then Cara. Amanda and I played a silent, unacknowledged game of chicken to determine which of us would get to go last. I won. But it was a sorry victory. I did not want to go at all. In fact, I almost didn't. Catharine was generous and ran over time with everyone, so that when it was finally my turn, we were already running late to our next activity, a biking-and-brewery tour I did not want to miss. She insisted there was just enough time left for a quick reading, and I took my place at the kitchen table while the others waited outside. Catharine wanted her money from all four of us. I got it.

She asked me to say and spell my first and last names and wrote down each letter as I ticked them off. I was suddenly self-conscious that the way I naturally stated my identity, a name I'd always rattled off with very little, if any, thought, would inadvertently reveal something I might not want revealed, something just a little too helpful to Ms. River-Rain. So I said the letters of my name loudly and robotically, as if she were an automated operating system and I were just trying to reach a live customer service representative. (*Operator. No, I said Operator!*)

She underlined my name and then asked if there was anything in particular I needed to discuss with her. And even though I had just turned thirty and ended my long relationship with B., I crossed my arms and told her I couldn't think of anything special.

She looked me right in the eye and said, "Well, I hope you're willing to talk about your love life, because I have some things to tell you."

What I thought was, *Gee, lady, I'm thirty years old and not wearing a wedding ring, wonder where you got the idea I might want to discuss my love life.* What I said aloud was, "Okay." I kept my arms pressed into my chest and reminded myself not to give anything away.

Catharine sat slightly back, her shoulders relaxed, and kept her hands in her lap. She might as well have been watching television if on every channel was the same program: my stony, disbelieving face. The first thing she told me was that I had just ended a serious relationship and my ex was still holding on to the possibility that we would get back together. "But the relationship is done and in the past now," she said. "I see finality and that you're both going to be fine."

Heat spread down my neck and across my collarbone, down my arms, and into my fingertips, and I almost certainly nodded, jarred into sitting up a little straighter and also steeling myself to acknowledge the realization that I had needed to hear a neutral third party say exactly those words. For months, I'd been telling myself some version of that idea and even repeating it aloud to friends as part of my breakup narrative, but it was clear I hadn't entirely convinced myself of it. This was like therapy but without the annoying insistence that the patient work out their answers for themselves. Here, instead, Catharine appeared to be serving me answers on an expensive silver platter of dubious authenticity. That they were probably just the old standby reassurances dressed up as answers suddenly felt like an inconvenient truth worth ignoring.

With a fluttery sigh, she continued, "Now don't take this too literally."

Um, Catharine. That sounds exactly like the kind of free pass psychics aren't supposed to get.

"You're going to meet a Prince Harry type."

Okay. Time out. Here's the thing about this. I've had a crush on Prince Harry since the late 1990s, when I was in middle school and he seemed like just the sophisticated, international celebrity crush I was looking for. I liked his thick, wavy hair, the twinkle in his blue eyes, that devilish up-to-no-good grin, and the way he hammed it up for the cameras. All charisma, all easy times. Fifteen years later I even made a particularly smoldering Harry photo my avatar on my company's internal group-chat software, so my Prince Harry crush became something of a joke among my coworkers.

And, now, of all the celebrities she could have named, Catharine was talking about Harry. Yes, she'd cautioned me not to take this too literally, and, yes, I was still highly skeptical. It was just a coincidence. I knew that. Prince Harry is only a year older than I am, and it makes sense she would choose an attractive male celebrity specifically of my generation. She certainly knew her demographic. Still. You can reason away a lot, but I couldn't deny that for all of my attempts at rationalization, she had captured my full attention.

We weren't even to the good part yet.

"This man, he's going to be a lot taller than Harry. With much curlier hair. And he works in comedy. But he's very charming and social and good-natured, like Prince Harry. I see you two walking. A lot of walking. All over New York City. And you're going to be like this as soon as you meet."

She wrapped her middle finger over her index finger and held it up to me, and I think I may have nodded, but I did not speak.

"Do you have any questions you want to ask?"

"When? Am I going to meet this guy soon? Or not for a few years?"

Her answer came without hesitation and with conviction: "Oh, no, soon. The very beginning of the summer."

I had assumed she'd buy herself a year or two, give herself a buffer between the hope she was selling and the inevitable disappointment of reality. But her answer sandwiched expectation and fruition too closely together and belied the doubts I suspected her of harboring. Was it possible that one of us actually believed in this stuff? This, more than anything else that day, gave me pause. I had assumed Catharine made her living as more or less a con artist. A well-intentioned, nice-enough woman who told herself she was in the business of making people feel better about themselves and their predicaments. But a con artist all the same. I knew it, and Catharine knew it, and she knew I knew it: we were both complicit and had gamely accepted the terms of the arrangement. Yet, her swift and steadfast answer that I would meet my Prince Harry in a matter of weeks made me wonder if perhaps I was wrong. Perhaps Catharine wasn't in on the joke. For the first time, it occurred to me that Ms. River-Rain here might believe all of this was real.

"But you have to get out there. You need to make the effort. You won't meet him if you don't try."

Ah. There it was: the asterisk. A clairvoyant's insurance. If I didn't meet this man, it would be because I hadn't tried hard enough.

Catharine let her arms fall to her sides, her body seeming to deflate before my eyes. Her head and neck sunk into her shoulders and chest, compressing her physicality the way a Slinky collapses into itself when you let go. She could have been anyone near the end of a long day's work who wanted nothing more than to put her feet up and pour herself a drink. I was still here, though, and her work wasn't quite done. She mentioned now, half-heartedly and practically in passing, that my mom was very healthy and was basically going to live forever, which sounded cool but expensive. Speaking of which, I was paying for this, not my mother, so could we focus on the subject at hand, please? My mom could get her own psychic.

Catharine asked once more if I had any other questions, anything else I wanted to address or to clarify. But I couldn't think of anything. I suppose, if I'd tried, I could have come up with something, but the truth is more likely that I didn't really want to. Everything we had discussed so far had been positive; why push my luck? I shook my head, *No, no, I don't think so.* By that point, I was already half-gone, wondering where my friends were, thinking about what lay ahead.

We walked to the door, and she said, "I really hope you come back." I nodded and replied "Yes" with a tremendous amount of enthusiasm, because hell yeah, why wouldn't I come back? This had been *great.* But, really, all I cared about in that moment was that I was going to meet a Prince Harry look-alike. That's exactly what she'd said, right? She closed the door behind me, and I walked down the hallway giddy. *Super, embarrassingly* giddy. I finally recognized the appeal of it. Even if I never met my Prince Harry, I'd just left the best therapy session I'd ever had, and I felt excited for the future for the first time in a long time. No wonder two-thirds of Americans believe in the paranormal.

I hurried down the stairs to meet my friends, but on the second-floor landing I stopped short and looked back up the way I had come. Catharine had asked if I had any questions, and moments ago I'd been so certain that I did not. This was my first experience with a psychic, and she was clearly a good one, by which I don't necessarily mean a real one but rather one who is good at her job, who knows how to make you feel as though you're getting all of the answers you could possibly ever need, possibly ever want. Everything had felt so clear during our session, but already the positive effect was wearing thin, like it only worked in her presence. It hadn't occurred to me to ask her if this Prince Harry she saw was going to be my rebound relationship or my marrying man. I didn't really have time, but I considered running back up the stairs and asking her real quick, *Is this guy my guy? Or maybe just my first husband?*

My hand midair, one foot on the landing and the other a step below, I thought about how emphatic she'd been that if I didn't get out there, if I didn't make an effort, I wouldn't meet this man. The implication being that I was *supposed* to meet him, that I *should* meet him, that I would be better off meeting him than not. That seemed answer enough. I told myself that, either way, it didn't matter. I was just coming off a serious relationship; I didn't need to be thinking about marriage just because it felt like everyone else I knew was or because I happened to be at a bachelorette party. I didn't go back. I kept running down. But, in the year to come, I often found myself wondering what she would have said if I had run the other way, knocked on her door, and asked.

In the cab, my friends and I swapped the predictions Catharine had given each of us. That's what they felt like. Not predictions predestined by the universe, but cute little souvenirs she gave to us from our trip to Canada. The postsession analysis was even more fun than the psychic session itself. The energy among the four of us seemed to me to suddenly carry a new symbiosis. We had woken up tired and hungover, a bit shy even. We weren't twenty-two years old anymore, and a four-woman slumber party in a one-bedroom apartment with a single bathroom wasn't as cute and charming as our memories had led us to believe. Such sleepovers weren't part of our wheelhouse anymore. Two of us were married. One of us had a couple of children. None of us were accustomed to seeing each other barefoot and braless in threadbare T-shirts and boxer shorts, our eyelashes coated in sleep crust. It was the kind of intimacy among girlfriends that you take for granted in college but that fades every year thereafter until it's overtaken completely by the intimacy of spouses, children, and even just that of being thirty and single and protective of your nighttime and morning eye-cream ritual. But we had been a little undone by seeing Catharine. This woman had looked at us and seemingly seen us. And look how fantastic we were, even, especially, at our most raw. The real souvenir she'd imparted to us was a jolt of renewed self-confidence, which I could already tell we wore well. Then again, it was also possible that I was guilty of imposing my impressions of Catharine onto my friends, who had had their own unique experiences that had nothing to do with me.

For Jane, Catharine had brought out a tarot deck. She had barely touched it for my reading, but Catharine knew we were there at the bride's behest and must have wanted to give her some extra dramatic flair. She knew to give the people what they wanted. Near the end of Jane's reading, Catharine had her pick from the deck one last time, and Jane drew the Lovers card. Of course she did. Catharine could see that Jane was going to be very happy in her marriage. Pure rocket science, this psychic racket. What else would you tell a bride? It was a lovely thing for my friend to hear, but it was mere pleasantry, like the nauseating "I hope you're well" salutation that kicks off all those business emails from people you don't really know and who don't actually care whether or not you are in fact well.

But Catharine wasn't specific only on the topic of Prince Harry and me. She gave our bride details, too: Jane and her husband were going to leave the Northeast for someplace warmer and would have a baby girl in about a year's time. She also predicted more professional success for Jane, a literary agent, in the form of a significant biography or autobiography of a famous person. And Jane's female boss was going to be tough on her in the coming months.

That afternoon we talked mostly about the happy marriage, the sunny move, and the baby in Jane's predicted future. We glossed over the career details of her reading, because those didn't immediately resonate. Jane didn't typically represent celebrity memoirs or biographies, so it struck her as less likely that she'd see big success with such a book.

And she didn't want to linger on the idea that her usually kind and supportive boss was going to be tough on her. Without even realizing we were doing it, we let the negative predictions and the less meaningful ones slip conveniently away, until we were left with the futures we were excited to envision.

Or, if not excited about exactly, then at least those that we expected.

During Cara's reading, Catharine told her that her husband's grandmother was about to die. The family already knew the older woman was sick and that her prognosis was not good, so Cara wasn't surprised to hear that she was not going to make it through the summer. Catharine spoke to Cara's career, too, and revealed that an ongoing issue between Cara and a male colleague would come to a peaceful resolution and that they would be able to successfully work through it together.

Our friend Amanda listened without reaction to each of our retellings but shared little of her own reading. She mollified us with some general career advice Catharine had given her and a few details about a hobby we knew she had considered taking more seriously. Catharine predicted that she was going to start working in catering, which, if you knew Amanda, you would realize was exceedingly unlikely. Amanda wasn't nearly as charmed by Catharine as the rest of us had been, or rather as Jane and I had been. (In the hours after our readings, Cara played the part of Switzerland, as she so often did.) Amanda had never wanted to meet Catharine, and her resistance had been palpable as soon as I'd told her of Jane's request. She agreed to participate because she's a good friend, but she had still arrived determined not to be impressed. Then again, so had I. Amanda had remained unyielding, whereas I had folded at the first mention of royalty.

Many weeks later, after we had left Montreal and all gone our separate ways, I called Amanda. She was in the car driving from Washington, DC, to Philadelphia, and I was in California, where I found myself grateful for the physical distance between us; Amanda is one of my most private friends, and even just dialing her number felt like an invasion of the boundaries of our friendship. In fact, this call was only happening because of something Amanda's husband had mentioned to me in passing late one evening when we were all about one drink drunker than we needed to be. He had told me how upset Amanda was that the rest of our readings had gone so well compared to hers. By then, Jane's boss had proven herself to be as supportive as ever, the opposite of the tough critic Catharine had foretold. And Cara's colleague—the one whom she was supposedly going to work things out with—had been let go from the firm. So I wondered what Amanda had told him, because clearly there were holes in Catharine's story.

On the phone I asked her what she had really thought of our psychic experience. She answered not by addressing Catharine, but by talking about her dad, from whom she had been estranged for many years. She admitted that for most of the previous winter and spring she had been haunted by the news that he was very sick. Her brother had told her their father was dying, and when we went to Montreal that was still all that she knew. She hadn't told any of us about his illness, but she'd told Catharine. Despite her misgivings about the whole charade, she'd shown up with a very specific question: "When is my dad going to die?"

Catharine had replied that he was going to take his time and do it on his own terms. From Amanda's point of view, this was a nonanswer, a cop-out, made even more painful when her father died a couple of months later, because it had seemed to her that if any conclusion could potentially be drawn from Catharine's vague answer, it was that he was not going to die soon. But then he hadn't even made it to autumn.

Amanda also told me that she had liked Catharine. This surprised me. Catharine hadn't talked about herself with any of the rest of us, but she had confided in Amanda. She admitted that she didn't talk to her own father, either, and hadn't for a long time. Amanda had asked if she ever regretted that decision, and as swiftly as she had told me I would meet my Prince Harry soon, Catharine told Amanda that no, she never regretted her choice to distance herself from her dad. "I was very skeptical, but I still felt close to her," Amanda admitted. "It was like therapy but also not like therapy. With therapists, it takes me a long time to open up. But I got comfortable very quickly."

Later, after Amanda and I had hung up, it occurred to me that the difference might be precisely that Catharine wasn't a therapist. She wasn't a certified professional with an accredited degree looking to make a diagnosis and with whom Amanda would be building a relationship. In fact, if there was one thing Amanda knew about the future, it was that she was almost certainly never going to see Catharine again. There was liberation in that, maybe even enough to make Amanda feel momentarily and uncharacteristically unguarded. That was something real all right.

But was that the only thing real about the experience?

If psychic ability is pure conjecture, mere coincidence, does that mean it is also without value? If it is fake, does that mean it is also full of harm? If it is real, does its truth necessitate that it is also valuable? What if Catharine's predictions did eventually all come true? Would knowing about them in advance be helpful? Maybe psychic ability does exist, and that's the most harmful possibility of all. Or maybe it is fake, and that's what's harmful. Maybe we have no idea what's possible. Maybe we have everything backward. It wouldn't be the first time.

CHAPTER THREE

I've been consistently uncertain about online dating since the days when it happened on a desktop and not on a smartphone. I haven't made it a habit, though, to go around proclaiming my doubts about dating off of a screen. Not these days, when most of the weddings I'm invited to now are couples who met through an app. My party line is that of course meeting someone digitally is fine, great even. Totally for it. For lots of people. Just not for myself. I'd rather meet someone the old-fashioned way—drunk in a bar.

The last time I'd been single, digital dating happened on a web browser and was limited to Jdate, eHarmony, Match.com, or, the newest kid on the block, OkCupid. These sites catered to the religious; to the thirtysomethings with neither the time nor the inclination to shut down the bar; and to the late twentysomethings, who were too young for Match but not cool enough for an organic relationship. Or so went my narrow-minded assumptions. Twenty-four years old at the time, I believed I had no such limitations. But spending the second half of my twenties with one man and then breaking up just when all of my friends decided to get married and make some babies changed the landscape of things I was willing to consider in the name of love.

A couple of weeks after we got home from Montreal, I still hadn't met my Prince Harry. I was looking, though mainly from afar. On my walk to and from work each day, I scouted my fellow commuters for a tall, curly-haired Harry look-alike with a charming smile and a lighthearted, come-what-may attitude; I wasn't sure exactly what that meant or what it would look like, but I figured, like Justice Potter Stewart, I'd know it when I saw it. Every guy who could be said to resemble Harry, even fleetingly—or, as the days wore on, even those who really couldn't—got a once-over: Are you my prince? No. Nope. God, I hope not.

I also couldn't shake the notion that this was going to require more effort than I typically gave dating. Walking to work probably didn't count. But joining Tinder and Bumble, the de rigueur dating apps, definitely did. Everyone was on Tinder, which seemed like a liability to me but which a colleague insisted was a perk. Tinder was noisy, aggressive, and crass, with too many messages from too many men who erroneously assumed they were shooting fish in a barrel. On the other hand, on Bumble, the women were responsible for initiating contact. A man couldn't reach out unless a woman did so first. Little wonder then that Bumble felt classy and calm. I've always preferred driving to being driven. Not that I didn't also hate Bumble, because I did. I worked in tech and in media, which meant I spent all day using and thinking about apps and social media. Now I was supposed to spend my nights thinking about more apps.

Catharine's maddening admonishment that I had to *try* proved to be impossible to ignore.

So I deleted Tinder and focused on Bumble. In most ways, it continued to feel dispiritingly disconnected from reality. There was no getting around the fact that I was literally shopping for men, and it was unnerving how quickly that came to feel like a game. I started to forget that there were real people on the other end of all these headshots and pithy bios. In other ways, though, Bumble shed a very real light on my tastes and my instincts such as I had never before examined. I preferred men who were dark-haired, clean-shaven, broad (if there's a chance we could share pants, hard pass), and dark-skinned, or at least tan (I'm pale enough for the both of us). There were exceptions, but that was the general theme.

Seventy-two hours in, I'd managed to set up six Bumble dates for the upcoming weekend. I hadn't been on a first date in almost seven years, and I wanted to get the rocky reentry over with as soon as possible. (My schedule was Friday evening drinks, Saturday morning coffee, Saturday late-afternoon walk, Saturday evening drinks, Sunday midday coffee, Sunday evening drinks. And, between Saturday dates, I, of course, had a baby shower to attend on the far Upper East Side of Manhattan, about as far from my apartment as you could get without falling into the East River.)

Of the six dates, however, I only really cared about one.

M. looked entertaining and a bit goofy in his profile photos, like he wasn't going to let anybody bring him down, and his bio made me smile: "I'm super tall and sorta funny. I do yoga, and read books, and eat food and all that. Just moved to New York for work. Hoping to find bagels or pizza as good as what I left behind in Los Angeles."

I had swiped right, and so had he. We began to chat, texting back and forth, all that day and the next and the day after that. He was funny, yes, but I had also never had such a good time just texting with someone. It didn't matter what we were talking about; it was always fun. Our banter and conversation came so effortlessly that when he suggested we meet, I almost didn't want to. We were too good over text. What were the chances we'd be even half as good in person? But there was no point if we didn't meet, so we set a date and a time: three days later on Friday night, eight o'clock. Prime time. He was to be the first of my six dates that weekend. I wasn't sure I knew at all what I was doing, which was evident when I only half-kiddingly suggested that for our date we split a forty on a bench along the Hudson River. Fortunately, because one of us had an ounce of finesse, he demurred, and I came up with another suggestion: a quiet bar tucked inside a boutique hotel along the far west side of Manhattan on a block of Jane Street that didn't make the cut for the Meatpacking District but didn't feel quite like the rest of the West Village, either.

On Friday night, I arrived first. I sat in the corner, ordered a cocktail, and pretended to read the novel I had tucked in my bag, *Skinny Legs and All* by Tom Robbins. I was attempting, without much success, to reread it, because it had been so long since I'd read it the first time I didn't remember the middle. And because, even working in the tech industry and being attached at the hip to my phone, I can't seem to break the habit of also carrying a story, a real story on real paper, wherever I go. But I couldn't concentrate on the words on the page. I was too busy thinking about the story unfolding in the present. I smoothed the skirt of my summer dress and told myself that certainly we would be able to have a nice conversation. And if there was no physical chemistry after all, so be it. Maybe we could just be friends. That could be nice. Friends are cool.

This was my first real date back in the game, and I just needed to get it over with. Only that was starting to seem trickier to accomplish than I had imagined, because 8:00 p.m. had come and gone, and M. still hadn't arrived. It was 8:30, and I'd been nursing my drink so slowly it tasted now mostly of melted ice. M. texted that his Uber was stuck in traffic, so I knew he was on his way, but I hesitated to order another drink. I did not want to be two drinks already down on an empty stomach when we met. That kind of beginning had the makings for a good story but a bad romance—something I understood this dating round. That was the kind of mistake I would have made seven years ago. But no longer. There were too many new mistakes to be made!

I had started wondering where his Uber could have possibly been coming from when M. walked in, at last, all 6′5″ skinny legs of him, as supertall as his bio had claimed, wearing a thin black sweater that hinted at what I would come to know were taut swimmer's arms beneath. In his photos, his hair had looked merely wavy, but in person he had a mass of thick curls, and there was a twinkle in his dark-blue eyes that Bumble had entirely failed to capture. Suddenly, I did not hate Bumble. My only thoughts were, *Um, hello.* And, *hell no, I do not want to be friends with this man. Fuck friends.*

Our conversation picked up right where we'd last left it over text, and sitting across from him and talking in person was better even than all the days leading up to this moment combined. I loved finally knowing what his voice sounded like, his inflections, and the way certain words slipped off his tongue and into my ear. He was silly, goofy, in a way that was somehow both innocent and sophisticated. I had never been on a date with someone who led with their goofiness. Funny, yes, but not silly. I liked it.

There was a lot of talking. Mostly because M. talked. A lot. And superfast. He was energizing. He woke me up. If Joan Didion wrote to understand what she thought, then it seemed to me that M. spoke to understand what he thought. Not for a moment did I wonder what might be on his mind. I had never met anyone like that. It was exhilarating to talk to such a person. It was also comforting. There was nothing to second-guess, nothing to worry might have been misinterpreted. He left no stone unturned. So when he mentioned that his Uber had actually been an *Uberpool that he took from Fourteenth Street*—a pitiful five blocks away—I dismissed the absurdity of such logistics, laughing without questioning.

He hadn't even finished his drink when he suggested we find the lines of poetry by Frank O'Hara and Walt Whitman displayed in bronze somewhere along the Hudson River. I thought they were near Battery Park City, which was some two miles south of us. We rose from our seats, and M. went to the bar to settle up. When he realized I had already paid for my drink, he made a joke about how this was really turning out to be the perfect date—"I didn't even have to treat you!" I laughed again. This I was used to. I enter most every situation assuming I will pay my own way. I also have only ever seriously dated men who were not in a position to treat me, so there was never the chance to learn whether they might, on occasion, have wanted to. Maybe I didn't want to find out.

We left the bar and walked into the Hudson's light air, and its waft cooled our exposed summer skin. M. put his arm around my bare shoulders, which was sweet, while I cupped his right butt cheek because I'm not sweet and because, well, heightwise, that's basically what I could reach. We kept on talking, and M.'s long neck curved down so that his words fell from his mouth right into my ear.

And because it was a night somehow outside of logic, before we found the poems, we found a strange, stirring memorial.

M. spotted it just east of the river walk, tucked between two high-rise apartment buildings. The security lights, soft and surprisingly sensitive to the nature of the exhibit, illuminated its grassy green landscape despite the darkness. Neither of us knew what it was exactly, but it seemed to be a small, elevated park. It sloped east, down and away from the water, and had wrought-iron gates at either end, blocking off the tunnel that ran through its center. The grass wasn't a manicured lawn, but a green field, harsh and tangled, lush. The ruins of a stone cottage stood at the center surrounded by a winding fence made of stones, which we would later learn had been imported from each of Ireland's thirty-two counties. The plinth of the memorial was limestone and covered in text that interspersed the story of Ireland's nineteenth-century potato famine with quotes about world hunger in the twenty-first century.

If it sounds straightforward, it wasn't. It was an Irish field on a steep incline held aloft by an illuminated limestone structure with a tunnel beneath and an absurdly unobtrusive sign that merely suggested it was a memorial for hunger. There was no plaque of explanation or context. It was all wild nature party on the top and all midcentury modern sharp edges on the bottom. And it was in downtown Manhattan, surrounded by the uniform gray skyscrapers of an Ayn Rand wet dream. It didn't make any sense at all, but it was magnificent and moving and reminded me I was a part of something bigger, which was also how I was beginning to feel about this man and his ass, which I was still cupping.

We continued south, and after walking right by them and then circling back, we finally found Whitman and O'Hara shortly before midnight. We read their words aloud and to each other, which, had I been an observer and not a participant, would have made me roll my eyes and think, *Oh, my god, get a room.* But from inside, the moment was pretty damn great.

"CITY OF THE SEA! . . . CITY OF WHARVES AND STORES—CITY OF TALL FACADES OF MARBLE AND IRON! PROUD AND PASSIONATE CITY!"
—"CITY OF SHIPS," WALT WHITMAN

It's a good line. We don't think of New York City as made up of islands, truly a city of the sea. We don't always see things for what they really are, or can be, or never will be. We think we do, but we are sometimes blinded by our pride, sometimes by our passion, and sometimes, when it's bad, by the pair of 'em together.

"ONE NEED NEVER LEAVE THE CONFINES OF NEW YORK TO GET ALL THE GREENERY ONE WISHES—I CAN'T EVEN ENJOY A BLADE OF GRASS UNLESS I KNOW THERE'S A SUBWAY HANDY, OR A RECORD STORE OR SOME OTHER SIGN THAT PEOPLE DO NOT TOTALLY REGRET LIFE."
—"MEDITATIONS IN AN EMERGENCY," FRANK O'HARA

We headed even farther south, and I kept thinking about O'Hara and his "Meditations in an Emergency." There is a line that comes before the bit about New York, near the beginning. It's the only line of the poem I can ever quote from memory, and it goes, "Each time my heart is broken it makes me feel more adventurous." My heart was still a little broken from all the sadness and disappointment of ending my last relationship. I may have been the one to end things with B., but the truth is that we broke our relationship together, painstakingly, over a period of years. The reason it took so long was because it was the only thing we had ever done as a team. We had felt our closest, our most intertwined, when we were pushing and pulling toward and away from one another, and it took me a very long time to realize it didn't have to be—should not be—that way. I still didn't know if my heart would ever not be tender to the touch, and I didn't know M. at all, but when I looked at him, I knew what I saw: adventure.

About another mile down the river, past Saint Joseph's Chapel and just before the Museum of Jewish Heritage and Manhattan's very tip, we found ourselves beneath Mary Miss's South Cove sculpture and architectural installation, a pair of curving staircases that came together to form a viewing platform with a bench at its center and apex. M. and I climbed these stairs and looked out over the harbor. It was a flawless summer night with the kind of mild, breezy weather that dulls the memory of how shitty New York City temperatures usually are. The Statue of Liberty was lit and regal, looking just as the French must have envisioned she would. We leaned in so close to a first kiss, I could feel his breath hot on my bottom lip, but at the last possible split second, M. pulled back and wondered aloud, "What if it's bad? What if this is our record scratch?" And then he pressed my body against his and kissed me long and open and hard, and when we finally separated, he said, his eyes never leaving my lips, "No scratches there."

Hope. There is hope in those Whitman and O'Hara poems—"City of Ships" and "Meditations in an Emergency." I hadn't read them in their entirety in years, but I reread them after M. walked me home that night, and it was their hopefulness that struck me. Hope, that feeling I'd rediscovered at Catharine's. But that night I wasn't thinking about her or even hope really. I was thinking about M. and our date, which had been sprinkled with pixie dust from the moment he walked into the bar, or, maybe, well before.

Months later, after Jane had been successfully married and the East Coast's summer had begun its cutting fade into fall, Jane's own reading was buoyed anew by the announcement that her husband had been offered a job down south and that they were expecting a child—a baby girl. Here was both the big move from the Northeast to someplace warmer and the daughter Catharine had foreseen. Before that, Jane had also sold a big biography of a high-profile politician. At the height of the summer, too, Cara's husband's grandmother had passed away. Even earlier still, a couple of weeks into dating, I realized that M. and I had matched and started chatting on Bumble on June 21, the first official day of summer. And while he looked nothing like Prince Harry, he was tall and had curly hair, and, before I even knew he worked in comedy, M. had suggested we walk, and so we had and had been, middle finger over index, like this, ever since. Exactly as Ms. River-Rain had predicted. Now it wasn't just she who had my attention but her entire industry.

CHAPTER FOUR

2017 was a year of trauma, a fact that sometimes feels like the only thing left uniting us. Bombs: in a Pakistani shrine, at an Ariana Grande concert in Manchester. Shootings: in a Texas church, on the Vegas Strip. The inauguration of Donald Trump as the forty-fifth president of the United States. Fires of man and nature: Grenfell Tower fire in West London, wildfires in Southern California. Hurricanes: Harvey, Irma, Maria. Trump's withdrawal from the Paris Agreement. The riots in Charlottesville. The persecution of Myanmar's Rohingya minority.

Harvey Weinstein *et fucking al*.

Between January 1, 2017, and December 31, 2017, these and other horrific events took place, and we failed to foresee them. There could be no denying the reality that millions, truly, of us had been wrong about so much more than we'd ever been right about. The world felt senseless. I felt helpless. I was scared. I had been extraordinarily privileged to have ever felt otherwise. There were those who had felt helpless and scared for a long time coming, and I had ignored them. What I had believed was far in the past behind us no longer seemed any time ago at all. What I had believed was in the present, the ground solid beneath us, no longer held. What I had believed was in our future ahead of us no longer felt attainable. 2017 became a year that called into question everything. Including what I had presumed to know about psychics.

Nor was I alone. I certainly wasn't keeping the psychic industry's annual $2 billion revenue afloat on my own.

When the New Age trend and its zeal for psychics, shamans, and astrologers, which had last peaked in popularity during the Reagan administration, dimmed in the nineties and early aughts, the mystical went underground. The belief persisted, but if you had it, it became one of your dirty little secrets. A lot of us weren't wild about admitting that we read our daily horoscope or saw a psychic once or regularly. People still did it; they just weren't posting about it on Instagram—and that's only partially because Instagram hadn't been invented yet.

In the last decade, however, the pendulum has slowly but steadily been swinging back, especially as interest has soared in exploring alternative remedies for all that ails us not only mentally but physically—everything from organic, all-natural herbs and tinctures to meditation, yoga, and daily mindfulness rituals. Young, educated professionals, who pride themselves on their savvy, their sophistication, and their skepticism, happily pay out of pocket for herbalists, acupuncturists, Ayurvedic nutritionists, and manifestation guides, and they spend less time trying to get in to see their general practitioners, if they even have one. After all, if you can avoid becoming entangled in the maze of red tape patching the current American health-care system, why on earth wouldn't you?

Many of these same young, educated professionals were blindsided by Donald Trump's presidential victory. Where did we go wrong? Could we, had we done things differently, have prevented it? The brilliant political strategists with their polls and the rigorous academics with their editorials were wrong. Suddenly, it didn't seem implausible that maybe psychics weren't the crazy ones in the room. In 2010, 62 percent of Americans believed astrology was ludicrous. Today, the majority of eighteen-to-twenty-four-year-olds in the United States believe that astrology is based, at least in part, on sound science. (It's not, but that is also not the point.)

In 2017, Susan Miller's monthly horoscopes reached more than six and a half million readers, and her site averaged more than twenty million page views every month. Ophira and Tali Edut, the AstroTwins, saw traffic on their astrology website, AstroStyle, double that same year, while the average horoscope post on *New York* magazine's The Cut got 150 percent more traffic in 2017 than it did in 2016. The Conscious Life Expo, which is held every February in Los Angeles (of course it is), has seen attendance triple in the last decade. Even Chaz Ebert, the former civil rights activist and trial lawyer who made her career at the Environmental Protection Agency and the Equal Employment Opportunity Commission, believes we can talk to our dead. She has gone on record about communicating with her late husband, the famed film critic Roger Ebert.

The public embracing of these beliefs and the rise in their acceptance correspond with a drastic dip in religious faith. Year after year, fewer and fewer of us attend religious services regularly, if ever, and millennials are statistically far less religious than either their parents' or grandparents' generation.

We still want purpose. We still need meaning. But we're no longer looking for them in houses of worship but the houses of the zodiac.

Seeing Catharine and meeting M. had given me neither purpose nor meaning, but the experience had lent itself to self-reflection, which is another component of religious faith, of investing in a belief system. In the weeks before I met M. and then in the months after, while he and I familiarized ourselves with one another and the social and political worlds around us became increasingly unrecognizable, I thought more and more about the past, the present, and the future and how it was becoming difficult to tell them apart. I came to believe that reconciling with whatever I really thought of psychics would mean reconciling, too, with what had come before, was here, and might still be to come.

I was curious about this other, mystical world I had glimpsed. I wanted to see more of it. I didn't know what I was doing or where it would lead, but then, I never had. The only difference was that I was finally aware of how clueless I'd been all along. I hadn't understood it at the time, but when I broke up with my ex B., I'd been breaking up with certainty. Or, at least, the nearest thing I'd ever had to it. Now, the only certainty I had left was that I was not a victim. Nobody was forcing me to pony up the cash and hold out my palm. No matter what had happened, was happening, or was going to happen, I would have no one to blame but myself.

CHAPTER FIVE

Psychics began falling into my lap the way you learn a new word and then hear it everywhere. *Baader-Meinhof phenomenon* is the scientific term for it, and the research strongly suggests it's not nearly as magical as it feels. The far less sexy truth is that it has to do with both the biological necessity of our being able to quickly and reliably identify patterns as well as the cognitive bias known as the *recency effect*, which leads us to overemphasize the significance of the most recent knowledge we've acquired. Setting that inconvenient truth aside, I suddenly couldn't seem to escape psychics, so, obviously, this was all cosmically destined!

A couple of months into our relationship, M. mentioned that a colleague had told him about a teenage psychic who lived in New Jersey. Around the same time, an extremely tangential acquaintance of mine posted on Twitter about visiting her wife's psychic grandmother in California. I immediately slid into her DMs—the Direct (private) Message feature on Twitter—and asked if she might be willing to introduce me to Grandma. I put the same question to M.'s colleague, whom I did not know in the slightest. Both of them were not only willing but enthusiastic. (It never ceases to amaze me how receptive people are to brazen requests from virtual strangers; it might be my favorite thing about being a writer, other than the easy greenbacks, of course.)

I wanted to know a psychic's process. I had learned what it was like to sit on the receiving end of the crystal ball, but I wanted to understand what it was like to look into it.

Grandma Reesha and I chatted by phone, but because New Jersey is far more convenient to New York than California, I got to meet Andrea, the teenage psychic, in person.

Andrea is a triplet. She and her siblings live in Denville, New Jersey, and have spent their entire cognizant lives in that state. But there was a time before, occupying the gap from birth to their first tangible memories. They were born on the other side of the country on April 20, 1999, in the inner Sunset District of San Francisco, and took their earliest breaths just south and a hair west of the infamous intersection of Haight and Ashbury. They were still babies when their parents relocated their young family three thousand miles away to New Jersey, but their place of origin remains worthy of note.

Call it the gift of hindsight or, less generously, the desire to demystify the mysterious by any conceivable explanation. But Psychedelphia, as the neighborhood surrounding Haight and Ashbury was called for a brief spell in the 1960s, seems to have made a significant impression on Andrea, bypassing her siblings and leaving a kind of mark on her alone. She caught something in the air there, beginning as she did in a city where the wind smells of thousand-year-old redwoods, ancient ocean salts, and fresh cannabis. That must be why today she claims she can see the future and speak to Denville's dead.

Or not. But they don't tend to grow 'em like that in New Jersey.

There are barely seventeen thousand residents in Denville. The town, smack in the middle of northern New Jersey, is about an hour's drive from anything: the Jersey Shore, Philadelphia, New York City, the PEZ candy visitor center and museum in Connecticut. The community has a deep-seated habit of voting for Republican presidential candidates and has not given its support, in recent memory, to Al Gore, John Kerry, Barack Obama, or Hillary Clinton. They also liked Chris Christie enough to help vote him into the governor's office twice. Rumor has it that the very first game ever played of American flag rugby—a soft, no-contact version of rugby designed specifically for children—was on a field in Denville.

Officially, the town has two Starbucks locations. There's one along Route 10 West in a shopping complex on the outermost edge of Denville's limits. But when Denvilleans talk about going to Starbucks, they mean the other one, which sits near the end of a strip mall in the center of downtown and faces the precise point where Main Street turns into Broadway. A Great Clips hair salon is next door, and Denville Pizzeria across the street still sees a steady stream of customers, even though most everyone seems to agree that removing the arcade machine was probably for the worst.

Andrea grew up on those pizza slices but has no opinion on the arcade machine. A single semester stands between her and high school graduation, and she intends to move to New York City as soon as possible. She will study at the John Jay College of Criminal Justice, which, tucked back a block off the Hudson River, between self-serious Columbus Circle and self-confident Lincoln Center, is about as far and otherworldly from Denville as you can get in roughly an hour. Should college Andrea ever want a Frappuccino, a branded travel mug, or a side gig, there are, at this writing, eighteen Starbucks locations within a mile of John Jay's campus.

That's the future.

For now, she spends the hours after school pulling espresso shots at the downtown Denville Starbucks, and none of her customers have any idea that how they take their coffee is the least of what she knows about them. That Andrea claims to have the "gift," though I will come to learn she does not like that term, was all I knew when I traveled out to Denville to meet her.

Just shy of sunrise on a dark January day in 2017, I boarded a surprisingly crowded Port Authority bus. My fellow passengers appeared to be mostly New Jersey residents who worked graveyard shifts in the city. Someone unwrapped his dinner as we made our way through the Lincoln Tunnel and wound around the Weehawken loop on the 495. The smell of a thick, steaming stew filled the back of the bus, and the teenage boy across the aisle from me, who appeared to have been up all night, though probably not on the job, looked worse for the aroma.

Several of the bus stops on our route were hardly stops at all; periodically, the driver would glide to the side of the highway and brake just long enough for a passenger to exit beside a post or faded sign I could not make out. We'd lurch back into traffic, while the disembarked walked into nothing but darkness. The trip took on a dreadful eeriness. It did not help that the only reading material I had brought along was Dion Fortune's unsettling *Psychic Self-Defense: The Classic Instruction Manual for Protecting Yourself against Paranormal Attack.*

As far as I was concerned, the paranormal attack in question was the still-raw inauguration of the forty-fifth president of the United States. For months, years even, it had been predicted, practically predestined, that we would inaugurate Hillary Clinton on January 20, 2017. I had been so confident we would ride jubilant into the New Year, high on having a Madame President newly elected to the Oval Office, but my confidence had been misplaced. Worse, it was my demographic who had done it—53 percent of white women voters had chosen Donald Trump. I hadn't. (Most of) the white women I knew and loved hadn't. But I am only one white woman, and, frankly, I don't have that many friends. I had spent much of 2016 questioning and redefining my romantic relationships and the kind of life partner I wanted to have and wanted to be—because, one, I had the luxury of those being my primary concerns, and two, I had foolishly let myself be lulled into the complacency of eight years of having my candidate of choice and confidence in the White House.

Now it seemed I would spend 2017 questioning and redefining everything else: that just because I had approved of two terms of an

Obama administration didn't mean other Americans felt the same; that the extreme whiteness inherent in my experience of feminism and the world at large is a much bigger part of multiple problems than I will ever be capable of understanding in its entirety; that under this new regime I find myself returning again and again to the Constitution, horrified and terrified that no one in this administration seems to care to familiarize themselves with the document and that I might be turning into much more of a constitutionalist than I ever could have imagined possible.

Within hours of the new president's arrival in Washington and his first jolting executive orders, a Carl Sagan quote had begun circulating across social media platforms. The suddenly popular passage is from his 1996 book *The Demon-Haunted World: Science as a Candle in the Dark*. Sagan died in 1996, but now his words had half the internet convinced he was psychic:

"Science is more than a body of knowledge; it is a way of thinking. I have a foreboding of an America in my children's or grandchildren's time—when the United States is a service and information economy; when nearly all the key manufacturing industries have slipped away to other countries; when awesome technological powers are in the hands of a very few, and no one representing the public interest can even grasp the issues; when the people have lost the ability to set their own agendas or knowledgeably question those in authority; when, clutching our crystals and nervously consulting our horoscopes, our critical faculties in decline, unable to distinguish between what feels good and what's true, we slide, almost without noticing, back into superstition and darkness."

I have never clutched a crystal. I have always just said no to the notion of ghosts. I have never been and am not now superstitious: I will open your umbrella indoors; I will walk under your ladder; I will pet your black cat every time he crosses my path. But 2017 was not 2016 or 1995 or 1981 or even 1939. When I rode out to New Jersey to meet Andrea, 2017 was still in its infancy, but we already knew it was something we had not entirely seen before, or, rather, that it was unseen among those of us born to the millennial generation. Sagan didn't live to see it, but both his children and his grandchildren did, and, almost immediately, 2017 laid bare a new, undeniable fact: what we thought in the past was working for our country politically, socially, and empathetically was not. Which meant the first step in this new reality needed to include the recognition that if we were wrong about that, we were probably wrong about a lot of other things, too. I entered 2017 uncertain and afraid but also humbled. The only thing left it seemed safe to assume was that all of your and my (and even Sagan's) assumptions were just that.

Sagan said it himself: "Science is more than a body of knowledge; it is a way of thinking." So I was thinking that it was time to think a new way. What if Sagan's assumption was wrong? What if crystals and horoscopes don't just feel good; what if they can also be a source of *not* science, *not* fact, but truth? (What is the appeal of great fiction, a great novel, if not truth?) What if sliding toward the mystical is actually sliding not away from but into the light? Or, better yet, a light, one of many lights? Like the loves of our lives, maybe it is not the one we should be looking for, but the ones, who will arrive (and perhaps depart) in their own time over the course of what will, ideally, be each of our long, rich existences.

Sagan was a lifelong advocate of both skepticism and wonder, and the two together propelled his prolific and varied career. So I decided to take a page from his book, though not, perhaps, in any way he would have imagined or endorsed: I decided to (skeptically) open myself up to the possibility of (wonder) magic. After all, if *Saturday Night Live* could become culturally relevant again, anything could happen.

I decided to open myself up—full stop—in every sense of the phrase. Open myself up to everything I had chosen not to think about, not to address, not to understand in myself and in my life and in the selves and lives of the people around me and in my community, both those I knew intimately and those I did not. Especially those I did not, whom I had been ignoring, who had different ideas from mine. And to open up to the possibility that the mystical and the numinous, unlike the political polls I had mistaken for fact, might be able to help me make better decisions about the future, sure, but might also be able to help me better embrace whatever the future brought. Help me better relax into what might come instead of strategizing in anticipation at every exhausting turn. Who am I to dismiss out of hand any potential navigational resource that might help guide me through this mapless existence? I want every imaginable apparatus in my toolbox. The jig is up. I need all the help I can get.

It was a relief to reach Denville and close Fortune's book. The suburban blankness of the low buildings and the businesses therein (a smoke shop, a Thai restaurant, a thrift store) was familiar and suggested order, even if the doors were still locked, not yet open for the customers the day would bring. It had been dark when I'd left the city, but now I wished somebody had told me it was going to be so sunny. I should have known. Northeastern winters come with the cruelest kind of sun: flagrant, unflinching, and without a trace of warmth. The better to see with, though.

Andrea and I hadn't even finished sitting down when she told me she was, officially, "a psychic-medium." We were across the table from one another inside a tiny independent coffee shop that may have been within spitting distance of the Starbucks where she worked but was altogether very different from that of her employer. She told me that because she could see the future as well as the dead, she preferred the term *psychic-medium* for its accuracy. Accuracy mattered to her. That was the second thing she told me. The third was that she was just a "teenager trying to get into college." By that point, regardless of what she could or could not do or see, I knew one thing: I liked her.

Andrea has startling blue eyes, a psychedelic shade of aquamarine unseen in nature outside of quarries and oceans—and, now, the

Cipriano triplets. You can look away from them, but you don't want to. Andrea's are accentuated by very dark, thick brows that look painted on but aren't. Her dark hair is shaved to a short, soft buzz on one side and left just long enough on the other to graze her earlobe. Her clothes, too, are dark, not in any kind of angst-riddled, dramatic way, but in a no-nonsense and sincere kind of way. She exudes tranquility. She is affable.

I read my first question off a page in my notebook: "When did you realize you had this gift?"

She smiled sweetly at me before offering a correction. "I call it a skill. When you say it's a gift, you exclude people. But everyone has this ability. Or can develop it."

I couldn't help but think of ninety-one-year-old Grandma Reesha, my Twitter acquaintance's Welsh tea-leaf-reading grandmother-in-law, whom I had spoken to just a couple of days earlier. I had called Reesha from New York City, and she had picked up from Santa Barbara. She told me she was at home, surrounded by the color red, because her house is decorated in shades of red—the color of energy, passion, danger. Red Bull. Advertisers use red, because it stimulates people to make quick decisions. *Click here! Buy now!*

Like Andrea, Reesha had also expressed the idea that people can be more intuitive than they realize. "Intuition, darling, is when you think something quickly. It's a little message that's coming to you. People get those, you know, but they don't listen to them. Of course, I hear them better than most."

If there are messages in the air for each of us, what's the difference, then, between someone who considers herself highly intuitive and someone who claims to be psychic? I posed the question to both my psychics; Andrea shrugged, and Reesha said a lot that basically boiled down to semantics. Could it possibly be that the only difference between the people who call themselves psychics and the people who don't is that some of us are paying attention and some of us aren't? There are messages in the air for each of us. *Click here! Buy now!*

Reesha has spent a lifetime listening. She grew up in Wales in a whole family of psychics. "My mother and my father, yes, and definitely my sister, too. The Welsh are all pretty much psychic, you know. Some people believe in the mysteries, and others discount them."

She told me that when she was very young, she would daydream during school and still know all of the answers. Her mother would start to say to her, "Would you . . ." and Reesha would already be running to retrieve whatever her mother had been about to request. I couldn't prove or disprove any of her stories, but it was clear she didn't much care whether I believed her or not. Which had the effect, intended or otherwise, of making me sit up a little taller and pay even closer attention. She was playing hard to get, and it was working. She seemed never to have questioned her ability or that it would be her path in life. Nor had she ever harnessed it or tried to direct it, only let it show up and be whatever it wanted to be. Reesha's been doing her thing for nine decades. She's outlived doubt.

She left Great Britain as a teenager, another young bride following her soldier husband home to the United States at the end of World War II. She was nineteen years old and had the good fortune of marrying an American from not only California but Santa Barbara. When Reesha left home, Santa Barbara was just the name on her ticket—she could have landed in Denville and been none the wiser. Denville and Santa Barbara may be on opposite sides of the country with opposing vistas, but there are similarities between the two. (Bear with me here.)

Santa Barbara's lone daily newspaper, the *Santa Barbara News-Press*, endorsed Donald Trump for president, and both towns are a pain to reach. Santa Barbara sits in the shadow of mountains and at the mercy of the sea. Its borders are the Pacific Ocean and the Santa Ynez mountain range, the foreboding entrance to the deep Los Padres National Forest. My French ancestors left France and came first to Santa Barbara. They stayed long enough to buy property on State Street, but within a few years, they sold everything and moved inland to Bakersfield. (If you're unfamiliar with Bakersfield, there's a reason for that.) Family lore has it that they left the coast because they felt suffocated in Santa Barbara, trapped between those dark mountains and angry waters. They felt liberated in Bakersfield, with its wide-open spaces. (I've never claimed to come from psychics.)

Since its first structures were built in the eighteenth century, Santa Barbara has survived repeated earthquakes, tsunamis, and wildfires. US Highway 101, which was built the same year Reesha was born, is the only direct route connecting Santa Barbara to Los Angeles (ninety-five miles south) and to San Francisco (three hundred and twenty-six miles north), which means reaching an international airport or a museum of any note is time-consuming. The cost of living in Santa Barbara is 94 percent higher than the rest of the nation, and the population is more than 70 percent white. Volatile. Isolated. Wealthy. White. If you've never been to Santa Barbara, you might be starting to imagine that, by this definition, the town is Donald Trump personified. And you might wonder why anyone stays. But if you've ever been to Santa Barbara, you don't wonder.

There's an area of town called Summerland. That's not a fluke. Every day looks like summer in Santa Barbara. Early in the morning and late in the evening, the breeze off the water picks up the scent of the native lilac and sage growing in wild spurts through the sidewalk cracks, and though cracks are few and far between, there are just enough to perfume downtown. State Street is lined with palm trees, and ivy vines lace the sides of the bright-white adobe buildings, each capped in sun-bleached terra-cotta tiles. Banks, grocery stores, and automotive repair shops have never looked so good. Residents like to say, usually while holding a margarita, that living here is like living on vacation every day of the year. Santa Barbara is the war-bride jackpot, and Reesha isn't leaving until her heart stops. Even then, she might stick around, she told me.

It is curious that in a small town that considers itself the American Riviera, Reesha can generate enough business to keep herself and her house in all those passionate and decisive shades of red. People don't tend to visit psychics when they're on vacation, after all. But everyone is afraid of something, and you can't buy fear off, never entirely, never forever—what is Donald Trump, if not terrified? Reesha claimed that the more money a client has, the more difficult it is for them to hear what the universe is trying to tell them. They've never been taught how to listen to it, never thought they needed to. But they can afford to be self-indulgent, both with their time and with their money, and for decades Reesha has made her living catering to them. Her Welsh family history and flair for the dramatic fit the mystic stereotype, and to the ears of Californians, her British accent makes her tony. It's a compelling combination, and Reesha knows her audience. She may not care whether or not I believe her exactly, but she is still a saleswoman. She needs return business. Her sales pitch sailed through the phone crystal clear, and, despite decades of use, it hadn't lost its shine. Unprompted, Reesha did a mini over-the-phone exercise with me.

"Hold your hand up. Do the tips of your fingers come to a point?"

I did as I was told, but it was hard to say for certain.

"Um, maybe?"

"Is the skin flat across?"

"No, it, uh, I guess it kind of curves a bit on each finger."

"I know," she replied, and while I still wasn't sure what direction, if any, my fingertips were pointing, I knew the sound of self-satisfaction when I heard it.

"People with flat fingertips don't like to be touched, but you need physical affection," Reesha concluded.

What I replied was, "Ha, okay. Now I feel like I need to go inspect my boyfriend's fingers!"

What I thought was, *Wait, doesn't literally everyone need physical affection?* Wasn't there a series of scientific studies done in the 1930s and 1940s, some more ethical than others, that concluded if you deprive infants of affection, their physical and mental development withers, possibly beyond repair?

In other words, Reesha, after talking to me for nearly an hour, correctly deduced I was more than likely human. She seemed to think she had offered me some sliver of soul illumination, but the exchange struck me as lame. This doesn't necessarily mean she is a scam artist. A slick sales angle doesn't automatically negate a product's value. Reesha may very well have psychic ability, but, as we continued to talk, her considerable charm, her considerable effort, did have the effect of giving me pause; there is such a thing as being too charming. Money changes everything. Even magic.

Andrea was different. As far back as she's been able to research and verify, no one on either her mother's or her father's side of the family has claimed psychic abilities. No, when all this began, Andrea and her siblings were in elementary school, and her family was afraid she was exhibiting signs of mental illness.

"I had imaginary friends. Like a lot of kids. Only all of mine were dead." For a long time, it didn't even occur to her to mention that salient detail. She just assumed everybody's imaginary friends were deceased. But by the time she was in the fifth grade, she was noticing other, scarier things. It was no longer just the lifeless company she was keeping. She was starting to feel things, too, and to know things she shouldn't have been able to know: that the teacher was going to give the class a pop quiz, that her best friend shouldn't get in the red car—never mind that her friend's family didn't have a red car and that Andrea had no idea which red car or where or when or why. But then the teacher did give a pop quiz, and her friend did come to school describing a strange red car that had followed her all the way home the day before.

So, Andrea started talking about what was happening to her, the way children tend to do when they're still young enough not to realize that sharing everything you're thinking and feeling almost always has consequences. Even now, she spoke to me openly and comfortably in a way that made me want to shield her, made me want to reach across the table and wrap my hands around her exposed vulnerability. The irony not being lost on me that I had an instinct to protect her from . . . me. Writers. Journalists. Exploiters. I felt the weight of responsibility for her naivete.

I also admired it, and I realized I was attempting to replicate it in my burgeoning relationship with M. When I talked about him with my friends, I saw the leery flash across their faces and heard it in the pause they took before they spoke, in the measured way they released their reply. They wondered if maybe it wouldn't be better to date a little more, to take a little longer for myself and to recover from the end of the life I had worked so hard to build with B. They worried M. was a rebound relationship and that I was taking him too seriously. Rebound or not, I am always all in or all out. As my very witty friend Meg put it, "It's either goodbye or good morning." I can't imagine being any other way. I don't want to be any other way. I wanted to be naïve with M. I wanted to trust someone. For the first time in my life, I wanted to feel young enough to blindly believe I could share everything I was thinking and feeling with someone and have the only consequence be more intimacy, more love.

My Pilates instructor will sometimes suggest that I adjust my position in certain exercises so as to "open the heart more." She means it in the physical, literal sense, opening the chest to expand the heart, but every time she says it, it feels like a reminder of the vulnerability I desire. All I have ever wanted is to be able to trust someone. All I have ever wanted is to be with someone who makes me feel safe.

I wanted to take a cue from Andrea, who had the naivete—no, the gumption—to start talking about what was happening to her on the cusp of sixth grade and puberty, which, of all the life moments, is right up there at the top of *this is awful, you have GOT to be kidding me.* I was unsurprised when she told me that, in response to the stories she told, her classmates bullied her and her family was alarmed. She may have been a triplet, but her brother and sister claimed not to be able to relate. "In sixth grade, I shut it down. I just ignored it." She tried to tune out her imaginary friends, which she now understood were not so imaginary. Sometimes ignoring worked well enough. Other times it failed spectacularly.

"When I was little and didn't know how to control it, I'd wake up with twenty people in my bedroom, all fighting for my attention. Like, shoving, and saying, 'No, I was here first.' It's always unfinished business. That's why they come. It just got really overwhelming."

I wrote "It's always unfinished business" in my notes and circled it. Thank god for unfinished business. Without it, we memoirists would be out of a job. Psychic-mediums, too, I see.

"Was it frightening?"

"Yes! It was terrifying!"

Sixth-grade bullies are a powerful silencing force. Andrea tried to tell herself she was just having nightmares, but she didn't actually believe that. She'd had nightmares before, and these weren't those. Her parents took her to a series of psychiatrists, worried their daughter was schizophrenic. Yes, she was hearing voices and having conversations with people no one else could see, but she wasn't exhibiting any of the other symptoms that could suggest schizophrenia: she was years younger than the typical diagnosis, which usually occurs, at the earliest, in the late teens or early twenties; she didn't have difficulty organizing her thoughts or concentrating; she wasn't struggling with memory loss; she wasn't jumpy or withdrawn. She was doing well in school and, once she stopped bragging about her dead groupies, had a dynamic circle of friends and was just as social as her outgoing brother and sister. Even if any of those symptoms had been evident, they could easily have been explained away as signs of typical teenage angst—or the completely rational reaction to the stress of being followed by dead people and discovering that you know impossible-to-know things before they happen. Because there's no chapter on that in *Our Bodies, Ourselves*.

The doctors didn't necessarily believe Andrea's version of events, but they also didn't believe she was schizophrenic. As long as she wasn't hurting herself or others, they decided it was safe to continue to monitor the situation without making any formal diagnosis or putting their young patient on any complicated prescription regimens, at least not yet. In this way, Andrea's timing was incredibly fortunate. The alarm bells had recently begun to sound loudly across the medical—and media—communities that we might be overmedicating our children, not to mention ourselves, our aging parents, even our pets. It seems plausible that, consciously or unconsciously, Andrea's doctors were influenced by that trend in their willingness to let her continue to explore the full breadth of this experience, whatever it was: mental illness, teenage dramatics, talent.

So it went for nearly a year, until halfway through seventh grade when Andrea received her "formal validation." She said this phrase to me, "the moment of my formal validation," and I stopped taking notes to look across the table at her. "Your formal validation?" She smiled and nodded. I'd never heard those two words linked together and certainly not in any comparable context. Not as anything official, the way Andrea had just said them, casually, as unremarkably as saying *official certification* or *confirmation hearing*.

What struck me, what made me put down my pen, was that this is exactly what all of us—the psychics, the teenagers, the mentally well, the mentally unwell—are seeking: some kind of formal validation we can trust.

This seventeen-year-old girl was telling me that not only did she find exactly that but that she found it five years ago when she was a child of twelve: "In seventh grade, there was this spirit named Kyle in my math class. He kept bothering me, telling me that he needed to talk to my teacher, Ms. Corforte. He was an adult, but young, and he wore a wet suit like he was dressed to go surfing. I kept trying to ignore him, but he would talk louder and louder. Finally, I told Ms. Corforte that I was having trouble hearing her, and she suggested I move up to the front. I told her that wouldn't help, which, you know, kind of got her concerned. I ended up having a meeting with her and my guidance counselor the next day. And I told them about Kyle. I almost didn't."

Kyle and one of Ms. Corforte's friends had grown up together. And they had loved to go surfing. But Kyle had died tragically and unexpectedly, and he wanted Andrea's teacher to tell his friends and family to stop blaming themselves. That he was okay now. After the meeting, Ms. Corforte called her friend and, according to Andrea, learned that everything Andrea was saying was true.

After that, things changed. Andrea still tried not to tell her classmates about the people she saw or the things she inexplicably knew. But her parents stopped dragging her to sessions with the psychiatrists and eventually even helped her find another kind of teacher, someone like her. They enrolled her in psychic school, which was where, when she described the incident with Ms. Corforte, she was told that the experience had been her formal validation. That every psychic had one. That it was a rite of passage.

What happened with Andrea's math teacher was one kind of formal validation. It was an external one, and it led to a significant turning point. Now, her teachers and family took her seriously and stopped the threat of medication and endless doctors' assessments. But it was psychic school that gave Andrea an arguably more important validation: an internal one. At a renowned East Coast psychic academy, she learned from her teacher and mentor, Lee Van Zyl, that what was happening to her had happened to other people, that she was not alone. Lee taught Andrea how to control her ability, to tap in and tap out, so that when twenty distraught people showed up in her bedroom in the middle of the night, she could send them away, ask them to come back another time. "Now I know I have to close my eyes and do a simple breathing meditation, exhale, and then explain to the spirit, or however many are there, that I need to tune out. That it's not a good time, because I'm trying to sleep or to study."

Meditation. Of course. These days, the answer is always meditation.

"That's it?" I asked. She nodded and smiled that smile again, the one that suggested I was a well-intentioned layperson, a sweet muggle.

"What happens when you see something in someone's future? What's it like?"

This was the question I'd been waiting to ask, the one I was most curious about. When I had posed this same question to Reesha, she had answered instantly: "Oh, darling, I don't know why I know anything. It just comes out. I don't think. Lots of times something will come out of my mouth, and I'm shocked! A true psychic never pauses. Their responses are quick and unthinking. A real psychic can't analyze, and we're not good with time." Red, the quick, energetic, decisive color.

Andrea's response was more measured. "I guess it's like everything gets finer. It's like when your ears pop coming out of a tunnel or off of a plane. Everything gets clearer. The fog lifts, and the world comes into focus."

"Does that mean when you're not seeing someone's future, like right now, the two of us just sitting here, the world is out of focus?"

She nodded and for once didn't smile. The "regular" world, the "normal" world, was the cloudy one. Andrea could only see clearly when she was looking ahead or behind. It sounded tiring, sad.

"Is it always the same? No matter whose future you're seeing?"

"Not really. It varies. Sometimes it feels like watching a reel of somebody's life. But psychics and mediums, we all experience it differently. Some hear things really well. For me, it's less about what I hear and more about what I see. I'm a clairvoyant type."

Reesha, on the other hand, told me she neither sees nor hears anything. She just knows. But she relies heavily on tea leaves. "I read tea leaves, which is quite unusual. Nobody does that anymore. A lot of psychics read palms now. People give me palmist books, and I can't understand them. I give them away to Planned Parenthood to sell."

Reesha doesn't read books on her craft. She's never been to school for it. She isn't interested in research and history or in the how and the why. For a psychic, she's surprisingly uninterested in either the past or the future. She cares only about the right now and the client presently sitting in front of her.

In her classes at her beloved psychic school, Andrea spent most of her time practicing, giving practice readings to other students to help her hone her skills and improve what she sees and how she interprets it. Not only do psychics experience and receive their skills differently, she explained, but they also all have their own language of symbols and signs they must learn to define. "I see certain images, but I still have to figure out whether or not they're symbols or meant to be interpreted literally. For me, a blue rose means that someone has recently died, and a blue dandelion floating above someone's head means they're psychic, too. But another medium or psychic will have totally different symbols for those things."

When a psychic makes a mistake during a reading, the fault is not with the vision itself or the message the psychic thinks they received, but with their interpretation of it, Andrea said. "One time during a reading, I saw Mount Katahdin in Maine, and I assumed it was just a symbol, that something significant had happened on a mountain somewhere. Which was true. Something significant had happened on a mountain." But not just any mountain—literally on Mount Katahdin. She had been more right than she had understood or assumed she could be.

Andrea never doubts the veracity of what she sees, but she does question the meaning behind what she sees constantly. Both Reesha and Andrea emphasized that they aren't ever given any context. "Oftentimes when I see something in someone's future, I won't know who or why or where or when. I may know that you shouldn't go on a trip, but I can't tell you if the trip you shouldn't take is next week or this summer or when you're eighty-five years old," Andrea said.

Like Reesha, she believes psychics aren't good with time. This is the part of her skill that frustrates Andrea and worries her. She has all these messages, these puzzle pieces, but can never put them together quite right—only the person for whom the messages are intended can do that. It's like poetry, I told her. She gave me a quizzical look. But it is.

Mary Oliver once said, "Almost anything is too much. I am trying in my poems to have the reader be the experiencer. I do not want to be there. It is not even a walk we take together." Your psychic is your poet. Both when we read poetry and when our future selves are read to us, we want to feel less alone, and we want to see the world and our lives from a new point of view. When we get even one of those rich pleasures from a poem and its poet, it's more than enough. But we hold our psychics to a different standard. We expect more. We expect proof.

As Andrea put it: "I feel pressure and a responsibility to give people irrefutable evidence. Human energy is the easiest to feel. So I can feel a person clearly, but it's a lot harder to feel the inanimate details of that person's life. Say I see your grandmother. I see her clearly and quickly, and I feel strongly she is your grandmother. But let's say she also owns a set of bright-yellow pots and pans that you gave her. That's something you and she would know, but how could I know that? So if I tell you that I see your grandmother, and she's standing by a set of yellow cookware, you're going to be excited, and you're going to be more likely to believe what I tell you. Unfortunately, picking up the energy of a pot is much harder than picking up the energy of a person."

I asked both Andrea and Reesha if they could read their own futures. Reesha told me she gets little messages, intuitions, that tell her what to do in the situations that crop up in her life. But Andrea has had a different experience. "I've tried, and I've done a couple of readings on myself. A little bit I see my future. But it's your own life, so it's really hard. Everything is inflated." Even if she can't see her own future with distinction, she said that she does sometimes get an instinct, a brief notion, of how things might go. Like balloons she can't quite catch.

"Do you think you'll always want to tap into your ability? Or do you think someday you might decide you were onto something back in sixth grade—that ignoring all this is better?"

Andrea didn't answer immediately, and I watched her silence. Whatever this is, whatever ability she has or thinks she has, it isn't easy for her. "When I do readings, I set an intention at the beginning. I ask for only good information. I want to spread positivity, and I don't think that will change. People should know that they have the power to put whatever they want out into the universe. They can set guidelines. They always have the free will to alter their future."

What Andrea sees can be changed. Maybe that's why she is supposed to convey a message in the first place, to encourage the recipient to make a needed adjustment.

Reesha has done thousands more readings and has never been tempted to stop. She has a peace that Andrea doesn't that can only come with the passing of much time.

"The most important thing is helping somebody to realize they don't have to be stuck. One of my clients used to whine every time she came to see me that she didn't like the future I saw. She had no self-esteem. I gave her the homework to change her karma. In Wales, we make a burning list on New Year's Eve. You write down all of the actions of other people that upset you that year and that you don't want them to continue doing in the New Year. Just the actions. Not the names of the people doing them. That's important to remember, because otherwise there could be bad consequences! Anyway, you make the list, and then you burn it. It works. Those behaviors just stop! I told this client to make a burning list, and then I told her, 'Every day for two weeks, write down all the things you are thankful for and all the things you love about yourself.' The assignments really helped. Actually, she's almost impossible to be with now. She loves herself too much," Reesha said and laughed (and laughed).

When we first started talking, Andrea was eager to tell me about her post–high school plans, how much she's looking forward to going to John Jay College, how much she wants to study criminal justice there. She mentioned it a few more times as we continued our discussion until I was compelled to ask, "Is your desire to study and work in criminal justice related to your psychic-medium abilities? To be able to see and communicate with dead people who are struggling?" She nodded and for the first time gave me a smile that wasn't gently patronizing.

"I'm actually about to start a psychic internship [with a nearby police department] in their cold cases department. The detective told me we have to be kind of quiet about it, because the department can't be thought to be endorsing the work of mediums, but they're going to give me photographs of victims, and I'll see what I see beyond the photos."

"Did the detective tell you anything else?"

Andrea started to shake her head but then stopped short and grinned. "Oh yeah, well, one thing. You know how if you ask cops about psychics helping them solve cases, they'll dismiss it as TV nonsense? The detectives I interviewed with said cops love psychics. They all see psychics on their own, like in their personal lives. We're really popular with cops."

Andrea's dad came to pick her up, and we said our goodbyes. I waited for my bus back to New York on the side of the highway and made a note to follow up with Andrea about her internship—and to track down some of these psychic-loving cops she claimed are all around. I also wanted to talk to her math teacher, Ms. Corforte. And I even admitted to myself that I was a little disappointed that in our morning together Andrea wasn't once overcome with an urgent message for me about my future or from someone in my past. But then I thought of Reesha and her fingertip exercise and chided myself for my puerility. I realized I was glad Andrea didn't press any kind of revelation on me. I believed her more for not doing it.

But I also didn't dismiss Reesha. She's been giving tea-leaf readings for more than seventy years; whether she's foretelling the future or scamming the present, she's doing something right. I scanned my notes from my conversations with both Reesha and Andrea and was struck by how often each of them returned to the idea that their ability is not so special, that everyone can access this skill if they want to. Where, precisely, in this world does such a notion come from? There must be communities and cultures out there that encourage and support mystics and their spiritual philosophies more readily than the one I come from. Reesha claimed Wales is such a place, but it can't be the only one.

And then, right as my bus came into view, it occurred to me to pull out my phone and google "Lee Van Zyl," Andrea's psychic teacher. I discovered there are two psychics named Lee Van Zyl, each of whom runs her own independent psychic school, completely unrelated to the other. Now *that* I had trouble believing.

CHAPTER SIX

Maybe it's because M. had only moved to New York a couple of weeks before we met and didn't know many people, hadn't yet had a chance to establish a life and a routine of which he was protective. Maybe it's because he was subletting a friend's apartment in Queens and had none of his own furniture and few belongings. Maybe it's because my apartment was just so dang close to both his office and his gym, the two places that thus far had made up his New York existence. Maybe it's because he was so effusively complimentary of me, so openly physically affectionate with me, and I had never dated anyone like that before. It was as if I were thirty-one years old and had just discovered that chocolate and peanut butter complement each other.

All this flattery was new to me, and while that says more about the people I had chosen to date in the past than it does about M., in those first heady months of our relationship, it felt entirely about him. It was like M. was auditioning for the male lead in a romantic comedy and was a natural on camera. Of course, there was also Catharine: "And you're going to be like this as soon as you meet."

Whatever the reasons, the morning after our first date and kiss, I canceled my other five Bumble dates, and that night M. came over and never left. And in no time at all, he had started talking about what our announcement in the Sunday *New York Times* Weddings section was going to say. At forty-two years old, M. was of a generation when, perhaps, those blurbs of wealth and social achievement and who's who of *Mayflower* descendants still meant something. For me, more than a decade his junior, the Style section of the newspaper was utterly passé.

For a certain segment of the American population, particularly those currently between the ages of twenty-five and forty, complaining about weddings is like complaining about traffic, another long-honored pastime of the elite. Every complaint that is made about weddings and the vast moneymaking industry behind them, not to mention the disturbing bridal complex behind it all, is essentially true. But, at this point, it's all been said ad nauseam, and it's just not that interesting.

We heathens born under the Reagan administration have largely chosen to marry by means very different from those of generations prior: Most of our parents did not have multiday weddings or even weddings lasting all of a full day; a few afternoon hours spent at the church or the temple and the adjoining community hall for cake and punch sealed the deal. Our moms and dads did not have live bands or DJs or, god forbid, both. Guests were not sent off into the night with personalized tote bags or midnight pizza slices.

There is nothing inherently wrong with caring about the details, about enjoying the process of brainstorming clever puns for your wedding hashtag or wanting to create a memorable experience for your friends and family. There are far too few occasions in life that bring together everyone you love under one roof (or one seven-thousand-dollar wedding tent), and I will never argue against grabbing ahold of an opportunity to celebrate and shaking it till the dance floor is resplendent with confetti and glitter. Because, otherwise, the scales would tip too far in favor of the other moments, those unavoidable occasions of loss and of sorrow. So, despite my prolific eye rolls, I do not judge how anyone ever chooses to take the leap into a lifelong commitment. Deciding to marry and staying married take a vagina of steel.

I also suspect my generation's approach to weddings is fleeting, and it seems an easy prediction that our children, who will be the inevitable outcome of these lavish ceremonies and receptions, are destined to wed very differently from us and from their grandparents. Should they choose to marry at all, they will do it their way. What is left, then, is to wait this out and take solace in the fact that the Sunday *New York Times* wedding announcements appear to be a dying breed. And while we are waiting and not reading the Style section, we might as well attend the required weekend-long bachelor and bachelorette parties that precede the actual wedding festivities.

Having my first psychic experience at a bachelorette party in Montreal clearly set off some kind of chain reaction in the universe, because it was not the last time I would see the bachelorette meet the mystic. At another bachelorette party, for another friend, I found myself in New Orleans. It was the first time M. and I had been apart since we started dating, and, as someone who has spent so much time alone, so many years doggedly asserting her independence, never more so than when I was with my ex B., it was an odd feeling realizing that it felt unfamiliar to be on my own again. I was a little awkward, a little shy with my friends, with myself, even with M. when we spoke by phone. We were shaping up to be an all-or-nothing kind of couple. The intensity was intoxicating, but it also meant that apart, even just for a long weekend, we floundered. I was uncomfortable and confused.

On my first morning in New Orleans, I woke before anyone else was up and walked to a nearby Pilates studio to take their sunrise class. Nobody else showed, so it was just the instructor and me, and it was only there in that small, bright room, forced to synchronize my mind and my body and to stretch my heart open a little farther than it was used to going, that I started to feel comfortable again.

That weekend, I took the occasion not only to celebrate my high school friend's love and happiness and impending union but also to spend more time alone than I ever thought I would at a bachelorette party. After my class and after the others had gone off on a swamp tour, I took the bus to the New Orleans Historic Voodoo Museum.

The voodoo museum is located in the middle of the French Quarter and is either entirely, or very nearly entirely, a tourist trap. I suspected this fact before I went, and I left swayed in neither one direction nor the other particularly. What I did learn was that, as places go, it is basically my personal worst nightmare of a physical space.

It's narrow, cramped, and low ceilinged, and some kind of drum chanting is played on a continuous loop through the dusty speaker hanging from a corner in every room. Every inch of wall space and much of the floor space is covered in stuff: never lit and previously lit cigarettes, unopened and half-empty bottles of Regal Apple rum, beer cozies (the camouflage variety being the most popular for no discernible reason), dollar bills out of place in their crisp newness, coins that I counted from half a dozen different countries before I lost interest, pocket lighters, snapshots of smiling people who were now almost certainly dead, Mardi Gras beads, beach shells, candy, gum, coconut water, business cards, Tic Tacs, glasses of water set out to absorb negative energy (if only it were that easy), and, last but certainly not least, two cockroaches very much alive, each seemingly unaware of the other, skittering across the floor of the largest, but still tiny, room.

Someone had left an opened plastic sleeve of bodega pound cake as an offering to Marie Catherine Laveau, and I watched the roaches circle it, having presumed it was for them. An honest mistake. Why leave an offering of pound cake, and specifically the lowest-caliber pound cake at that, I do not know. What I do know is that Marie Laveau, who was a devout Catholic from birth to death, was also the devoted Voodoo Queen in New Orleans from life well on into death and today. Her celebrated grave is a handful of blocks from the museum in the severe, tree-bare St. Louis Cemetery No. 1, where the tombs and vaults are built aboveground, stand crowded on named streets, and suggest a metropolis larger and taller than the city that lives on beyond its walls.

Where voodoo is just as much alive among the dead here as it is among the living there.

When I think of voodoo, I think first and foremost of the A Guy Called Gerald song "Voodoo Ray," which I dare you to listen to without shimmying. It was originally inspired by the phrase *voodoo rage*, but, in the recording studio, *rage* came out sounding like *ra*, which eventually improvised its way into *ray*. The majority of the lyrics consist of *ooh*s and *hey yeah*s, and if you can find any semblance of a narrative arc, I salute you. The entire song sums up what was long my woefully truncated understanding of voodoo: sweaty shimmying somewhere under a burning sun with a pulsing undercurrent of flight, not as in flying, but as in fleeing. The way it feels to dance to "Voodoo Ray" may rightly capture something of the emotion of voodoo, but its meaning and history are something else.

Voodoo, the roots of which can be traced back to a handful of West African religious traditions, is an Afro-Haitian religion. It is an oral tradition, but I think of it also as a tradition of the physical body, incorporating and celebrating not only song but head-to-toe shimmying; it is rhythmic, musical. Its priests and priestesses, alongside their congregants, may sing or chant or dance during rituals, and they may employ candles or oils or beads. In other words, voodoo rituals are not so unlike the rituals of many world religions, including Roman Catholicism. In fact, in Haiti, more than 50 percent of the population are practicing Catholics, and most of them also practice voodoo; they have harmonized the two faiths. And yet, there is something about the physicality, the interweaving of sight, sound, touch, and movement, in voodoo that feels somehow more human and more natural than the Catholic traditions I was raised on. Voodoo appears to me, as an outsider, to lack much of the shame and self-consciousness that weigh so heavily on the Catholicism of my own roots.

Those who do not practice it and know nothing about it sometimes associate it with witches. But there are no witches in voodoo. Where there are witches and witchcraft is in black magic, whose origins lie in the ancient Mediterranean world. Evil exists in voodoo only because people exist in life. According to voodoo doctrine, evil originates with individuals not with spirits.

People can do and be evil, but voodoo is not about and is not itself inherently evil. Religions, cultures, political parties, even *CSI: Name Literally Any City* spin-off series, for that matter, acknowledge and accept as fact the existence of evil. Religions have always been, in part, a reconciling, a finding a way to live with the reality of misfortune and evil.

Voodoo is about that reconciliation. It is also, as with all spirituality and religion, about connecting with our ancestors and with something, no matter what you name it, that is bigger than ourselves, our families, and our communities, yesterday, today, and tomorrow. This is the root, too, of every shamanic practice I have encountered: African, Peruvian, Mexican, Native American. Think of the Greeks, with Pythia, the priestess of Apollo at the Oracle of Delphi, whose future prophecies are said to have been foretold by distinctly shamanic means: the trance the priestess is documented to have fallen into, her distinct vocal sounds reminiscent of no identifiable words.

For all the ways in which these threads appear disparate from one another, for all the ways that a dank, dirty tourist trap, littered with what many of us would dismiss as trash, resembles nothing of a Jewish synagogue or a Protestant church or a shamanic drum circle or an ancient Greek shrine, each hopes to address the same pains of human nature. Follow the trails of pound cakes, of matzoh balls, of loaves and fishes, of ayahuasca, of Apollo's laurel branches, which begin in such far-flung and seemingly opposing corners of the earth. Keep going still, past the greed, past the power hungry, past the bloodshed, and you will find that the religious and spiritual paths end in the same place every time: gratitude, purpose, and compassion. No, I'm serious. On the other side of our worst qualities and deeds are our best: the desire to be loved and accepted and the desire to love and accept in return. (Our problem is that we want to be loved and then to love back. You first. No, you.)

Woven into historical records, this common thread of benign goodness emerges and remerges across landscapes and cultures throughout the long centuries when the idea of the world being small enough to fit on a screen the size of our palms would have been heretical. Here we are in this century, perpetually hunched over, having bent the round world to our will, having flattened it and slipped it into our butt pocket until we want it again (undoubtedly two seconds from now), and, still, most of us, despite our desire for gratitude, purpose, and compassion, remain no closer to embodying them than the oldest ancestor we can trace on Ancestry.com. I didn't know I was barreling through life parched for these most crucial, most human, of longings, living in a drought entirely of my own making, until an astrological hunter on the other side of the world spun me around and put me on the scent.

Hunter Reynolds was born in Illinois, has ties to California, and currently lives on an island in Indonesia. I found him where, apparently, these days, I find most people. On the internet. He self-identifies as both astrologer and poet. Every poet may not be an astrologer, but invite me to your dinner party, give me a glass of wine, and sit me at a table with a garrulous, contrarian-minded group, and I'll argue till you put me in an Uber that every astrologer is a poet. Which might suggest that an astrologer describing himself as also a poet is redundant, except it's not, because most people don't think of astrology as a form of poetry. That would be giving it too much credit. As it happens, Hunter is not the first astrologer I have found who thinks of himself as an astrological poet, and this form of résumé calls to my mind the old "If you want a puppy, ask first for a pony." If you want to be a poet, tell your parents first you want to be an astrologer.

Hunter and I have never met, and I suspect that the one black-and-white photo of him that dominates his Google image search results is at least a decade out of date. In it, his hair is long, his face is bearded, and he looks not at the camera but off, as if he hasn't yet realized that the photographer is there with him. His expression is intense, probing, which is appropriate enough. I realize that I have taken more than my own fair share of too-serious photographs, but when I look at his head-shot now, I find myself wishing he was smiling. I would like to know what he looks like when he smiles.

When I was in my twenties, I thought unsmiling faces were cool. I am far from suggesting that everyone should smile all of the time or any of the time they do not wish to, but what I am suggesting is that when I was younger, I was an idiot. Maybe it has something to do with the gratitude and compassion that Hunter would eventually try to show me how to cultivate, but these days I can't help wanting to know what everyone I speak to looks like when they smile. When they really smile, not a courtesy smile, not an absentminded "I'm listening to you, sure, it's just that I'm also thinking about what I shall have for lunch" kind of smile. No, I mean the kind of smile that even the smiler doesn't see coming. Lately, I have found myself prolonging conversations with people I don't particularly care to be talking to, in the hopes that they'll smile and then how I feel about them will change. I will probably never learn what Hunter looks like when he smiles, but I have heard his smile on the phone, and it sounds wide and plentiful.

On his website, Astro Dharma, in an article entitled "Astrology and the Middle Path: The Six Paired Lessons in Love," Hunter writes, "When we learn to love both aspects of a dichotomy, the dichotomy collapses and gratitude releases us into an all-embracing nondual dimension. Christians call this 'the descent of the Holy Spirit.' Buddhists call it 'enlightenment.'"

Hunter, whom I've grown to think of as perhaps most aptly an astrologer-poet-philosopher (the true trifecta of parental aspirations for their offspring), says that "the purpose of astrology is to help us define and make more conscious the polarities [or dichotomies] we are vibrating between so we can more discerningly meditate them back together—each side constantly pointing us back to the middle." The middle being, in Hunter speak, an "ego-dissolving center point." God, that sounds so smooth and sweet, like self-help candy (the way sucking on a butterscotch LifeSaver lessens the stress of waiting at the West Fourth Street subway station for that ever-elusive F train).

Should you choose to take this self-help candy and accept the twelve sun signs, these are the resulting six archetypal dualities or polarities as defined by Hunter's philosophy of astrological poetry:

- Independence/Intimacy (Aries/Libra)
- Stability/Metamorphosis (Taurus/Scorpio)
- Information/Synthesis (Gemini/Sagittarius)
- Nurture/Discipline (Cancer/Capricorn)
- Hierarchy/Equality (Leo/Aquarius)
- Discernment/Faith (Virgo/Pisces)

If you are at all like me, you scanned this list, first and foremost, for your own sun sign and have already considered whether or not the corresponding archetype resonates with you. The rest of the signs and their dualities are blurry, of far less interest. Except perhaps the sign of whomever you are currently dating. Beyond that, if you are a Scorpio, say, who gives a shit about Leo? But Hunter cannot emphasize enough that the qualities of all of the twelve sun signs exist in every last one of us. (How convenient.)

Take Hierarchy and Equality (Leo and Aquarius). We all struggle with Hierarchy and Equality. We can all, on occasion, go too far in the direction of one or the other or fail entirely to understand either of them. Hunter describes Hierarchy and Equality's ideal ego-dissolving center point just so: "Specialness and equality arise together as we realize that a good leader is one who makes the team think they did it themselves, and a good team is the one in which each person exercises superior leadership in the area of their expertise." Or let's take Discernment and Faith (Virgo and Pisces). Hunter writes that "Virgo/Pisces integration is achieved by becoming mystically realistic . . . It is this relaxed faith in the ultimate perfection of all worldly outcomes—be they chaotic or painful—that equips us with the relaxed, nurse-like focus needed to balance subjective intuition with diagnostically accurate analysis."

In her Dear Sugar column, Cheryl Strayed once advised a frazzled bride-to-be: "Let [your wedding] be what you can't yet imagine and wouldn't orchestrate even if you could. Remember why it is you've gone to so much trouble that you've been driven to anger and aggression and an online advice columnist. You're getting married, sweet pea! There's a day in July that's a shimmering slice of your mysterious destiny. All you've got to do is show up."

What we imagine and are capable of orchestrating will always fall short of what could be—for our weddings, sure, but, more importantly, for our communities, our jobs, our neighbors, our partners, our children, ourselves. How much better then to stop and let the wildest possibilities pass us, come into the lead, and guide us as they become whatever they may. Here's the kicker: showing all the way up, just to stop and be led by possibility, *by question marks?* That's tough. Especially for someone like me, especially when I am white-knuckling emotions of fear and insecurity and uncertainty, those pesky feelings that seem to have a knack for finding me on the days in which the sun has risen, *again.*

What Cheryl is suggesting to this bride is that she find her own unique balance between Virgo's discernment and Pisces's faith. If Hunter had replied to this bride, he might have quoted himself: "Straying too far into Virgo, our soul worships discrimination over flow and makes an identity out of efficiency, planning, and service . . . Our tidy Virgo facts and formulas are continuously undermined by unforeseen Piscean variables, causing us to become obsessive, anal, and perfectionistic."

When you put it like that, maybe we do sidle up to the bar and order a round of faith shots, after all—and make 'em doubles.

I can't stop thinking about Marie Laveau, that devout Catholic who reportedly attended Mass every day of her life, all while building a reputation as the Voodoo Queen of the French Quarter and becoming something like the nineteenth-century Cheryl Strayed of the eighteenth US state. Regardless of your feelings about the Catholic Church or voodoo or Cheryl Strayed and whether or not you believe Laveau had the ability to heal or to talk to God or spirits or to predict the future, it's undeniable that she sparked a persistent strand of devotion that hangs on still, nearly 140 years after her death.

I saw the crowded voodoo museum and the stacks of offerings at her tomb, and I've listened to the songs she inspired by artists as varied as Jimmy Buffett, Bobby Bare, Volbeat, Papa Celestin, Redbone, Shel Silverstein, Joe Sample, Grant Lee Buffalo, Tao of Sound, and Dr. John, among others. I've flipped through the pages of the Marvel comic books featuring a character based on Laveau, and I've seen snippets of the video game that makes liberal use of her story to propel the twists and turns of its challenges. And the novels. She has inspired characters and plot twists in books by Robert Tallant, Francine Prose, Neil Gaiman, Rick Riordan, and Charlaine Harris, whose True Blood Sookie Stackhouse novels feature Laveau's tomb. And does it get any better than having Angela Bassett portray you? It does not. Bassett played a memorable character based on Laveau in the third season, Coven, of the television series *American Horror Story*.

What is it about Laveau exactly? Especially when so little of her life can be substantiated in any meaningfully satisfactory way. Not all historians are even convinced she's actually buried in that decorated tomb in St. Louis Cemetery No. 1. Perhaps what she could or could not see and conjure have little to do with her legacy. Our best guess is that Laveau was a Creole born free in New Orleans sometime around 1800 to a mother of African and Native American descent and to a father who was part French and part African. And we think that just before her eighteenth birthday, she married a French Haitian refugee, a union that lasted barely a year because her husband died. Or because he left her and then town. It's real murky.

However it went down, it is believed that by her early twenties, Laveau was a single mother who had taken to calling herself Widow Paris (her married name) and fully embracing her independent, entrepreneurial selfhood. She took on work as a hairdresser, most likely styling the hair of local black servants but possibly doing the hair of the city's wealthy women as well. She became what today we might call something of a celebrity hair stylist. Eventually she took on a lover, who is believed to have been a white man. They had several children of their own and lived together for decades until he died (his death being much less murky).

All this in the first half of the nineteenth century. All this while dominating the voodoo scene, leading ceremonies of thousands of participants at Lake Pontchartrain and in the center of Congo Square, one of the few public spaces in the city where people of all different races and ethnicities came together in peace. She was the kind of woman I think Cheryl Strayed would have liked. I know I like her, and I knew it long before I read in her 1881 *New York Times* obituary that "she died without a struggle, with a smile lighting up her shriveled features." My god, may we all be so lucky to get a line like that in our obit.

On the second night of the bachelorette party in New Orleans, after I had been to the museum, the cemetery, and Congo Square, I decided to do that round of faith shots. I got the bride-to-be, whom I've been friends with since we were teenagers and so little of our lives and selves were known to us, to do a shot of rum with me at the back of a tiny, frill-less bar on Frenchmen Street in the Marigny District. I told her we should take the shots in Marie's honor. I told her Marie was beloved, that as the Widow Paris she worked as a hairdresser and that while she fixed her clients' hair, she listened to their secrets, well aware that what they were really sharing were their desires. The bride said she'd drink to that. She and I have certainly drunk to less.

So we did. The bride didn't know it, but as we threw back our heads and the glasses and the spice of the warm rum ran down our throats, we were drinking not just to Marie but to the seesaw of discernment (Virgo) and faith (Pisces) that my friend's approaching wedding represented, that enduring notion that the one we finally choose to say yes to is the right choice because we have discerned that he or she or they are and because we have faith that he or she or they will continue to be. All the research in the universe will take us far but not far enough. It's faith that will ultimately make the introduction between each of us and our mysterious destinies.

There are so many seesaws. The first, of course, must be the actual object. The seesaw was always my favorite. But, as an only child, I was constantly left to look for someone to ride it with me, and I very rarely found any takers. So, ever a realist, I took to the swing set instead and discovered that with just my own two legs, I could rise much higher on the swing than I ever could have on the seesaw. For a long time, I was pretty self-satisfied with that arrangement. My second-choice ride had become my first choice. Until I entered my thirties and realized that while I might be flying higher and seeing more of the sky, I was seeing it alone.

There's a Jim Croce song, "Walkin' Back to Georgia," that I love. For weeks after I returned home from New Orleans, I played that song incessantly. I had no idea why. M. didn't seem to mind. Probably because the song appears on Croce's album *You Don't Mess Around with Jim*, and that whole record is pretty perfect. I love the song from beginning to end, but more than anything it's three lines in the second verse that I waited to hear again and again: "She's the only one who knows, / How it feels when you lose a dream, / And how it feels when you dream alone."

No matter how hard I love, and I have loved hard—every man I have ever loved, I have loved him hard and fast and without regrets—I've still spent my whole life on the swing, pumping my legs as fast as they'll go, dreaming alone. I used to think that maybe someday I might meet someone, and I would know that I should stay, because we would dream together. Now I've met someone I want to be with, only we're still not dreaming together. But that might be okay. M. dreams these big, bold, beautiful dreams that would never occur to me, and they are part of why I love him. I continue dreaming mine, and they do not interfere. Maybe, dreaming alone, no matter whom we are with, is just how it goes for some of us. It's just what is. What "they is."

Because even what is seemingly grammatically incorrect, because even what might be considered less than ideal in the eyes of critics, still has a poetry I cannot ignore. As in Tobias Wolff's glorious short story "Bullet in the Brain," in which a man, Anders, a successful book critic, is shot in the head. And it is only then, in the moments after he has been shot, that he remembers when he first fell in love with language. It was not as a student in the library stacks but as a kid on the baseball diamond listening to another kid, who had come from someplace else, someplace Anders hadn't been, where the phrase *they is* isn't wrong; it's just communication in another form:

> He did remember heat and a baseball field and himself as a boy waiting for friends to gather for a game. One of the boys brought his cousin from Mississippi, who used the phrase "they is." As in "Short's the best position they is." Anders remembers being strangely roused, elated, by those final two words, their unexpectedness and their music. Now, just before death, Anders' mind chanted, They is, they is, they is.

CHAPTER SEVEN

First, I loved Holly Hunter, in every single thing she did, but most especially in *Home for the Holidays*, the darkly comedic Thanksgiving movie directed by Jodie Foster that remains the only film I rewatch. I saw it for the first time in November 1996 when I was eleven years old, and my father had been dead for eight months. Because I had never before seen a movie that depicted family so nakedly. Because it gave me more comfort in that year than anything or anyone else had. Because it made me laugh.

Next, I discovered Holly Hunter's Yale School of Drama roommate and very good friend Frances McDormand in the movie *Fargo*. Then I watched them be terrific together in *Raising Arizona*. A few years later, I saw Frances in *Wonder Boys*, which is the rare movie based on a wonderful novel that is wonderful in its own medium. By then I loved Frances fully. I loved her in the only way I could. That sheepish, pedestrian way we love celebrities we've never met.

Meaning I love the Frances McDormand she has chosen to present to the public; to me, she's the lady in your childhood neighborhood whose porch is overrun by potted plants and wind chimes, who scares the crap out of you when you're a kid but who later pretends not to notice when you and your first boyfriend make a habit of sneaking into her backyard and getting high.

Many years ago, I did, fleetingly, cross Fran's path. My friend Jill and I were having dinner at the restaurant above the Fairway Market on the Upper West Side of Manhattan—the one that's on Broadway and faces the Beacon Theatre. We had tickets to a Gillian Welch concert at the Beacon that night, and we were grabbing an early dinner before the show. It's no New York secret that Frances and her husband of thirty-some years, the writer and director Joel Coen, have an apartment on the Upper West Side. The Fairway restaurant, which may, technically, have its own name, but everyone calls it the Fairway restaurant, so that remains its truest name in my book (literally), is as quintessential Upper West Side Manhattan to me as Fran and Joel are.

I didn't know New York in the 1990s but walking up the worn flight of stairs to the restaurant and coming into its dining room always feels like getting a glimpse of what a certain well-read, no-nonsense sophistication must have looked like in the early nineties on this sliver of my favorite island. The food is straightforward and reasonably priced (for New York), and the lack of any sort of scene, coupled with the spacious dining room, means getting a table is usually not a complete nightmare. It's a sensible kind of establishment that has been around for decades and has never had anything to prove, its longevity speaking firmly for itself, thank you very much. Just the sort of place the Fran McDormand and Joel Coen of my imagination would choose to dine.

So you can imagine how delighted Jill and I were when we spotted the "McCoens" seated in the center of the dining room at a large round table with their friends that night. We speculated that their group was also on their way to see Gillian Welch at the Beacon, the lights of whose marquee streamed through the windows, alighting across our smug faces. Doesn't Gillian Welch seem like just the kind of musician Fran would appreciate? If Fran were a musician herself, she'd tour with Gillian, I'm sure, and they'd do sold-out shows at the Beacon together. Jill and I would go, I know. We did not, on this night, obviously, as proper New Yorkers, dare to even consider approaching Fran and Joel's table. Nor did we take a second glance when we, indeed, spotted them an hour later in the lobby of the theater. It was enough to know we all shared some modicum of sensibility, and it was more than enough to further entrench my affection for Fran.

Still, whenever I think of her, I remember a particular David Mamet quote, which I shall paraphrase as something to the effect of: the celebrities of whom we consider ourselves fans are just as likely to be people we would hate in day-to-day real life. *Hate* is a bit on the strong side, a bit too much of a Mamet-ish choice of words, but his point stands. The reality is that I cannot actually have any idea whether or not I love Frances McDormand any more than I can know if I would have loved Alexander Graham Bell.

It also could not matter less. I do not care what the truth may be. I love what I think I already know and will read any Fran interview I stumble upon and will almost undoubtedly finish it validated anew that my admiration is well-placed. In the last such interview, which conveniently came to my attention by way of the *New York Times Magazine* that landed on my welcome mat, the reporter opened the article by describing the actress: "She is 60 and sexy in the manner of women who have achieved total self-possession."

There are gem quotes and anecdotes throughout the piece that come right from Fran's mouth, but it is this opener that catches me and the one I have remembered and return to. The irony does not go unobserved—that what I remember best is not something Fran herself said or did but, rather, is the way the writer (whose photo appears at the front of the magazine and so who I am aware is significantly younger than Frances) is interpreting how the actress shows up in the presence of at least one journalist. It is only when I recall the lede and this specific sentence and fish the magazine out of the recycling bin to reread it that I stop to consider how Frances might have reacted when she read the same beginning: "sexy in the manner of women who have achieved total self-possession."

Sexy is the game we tap young women into: *You're up, girlie.* Old women are not permitted to play this game, because they have gone through the stark stripping of their sexuality: menopause. By calling the sixty-year-old actress sexy, especially right out the door in the first paragraph of her article, this reporter is defying our current cultural definition of sexy. I don't disagree with her. Frances McDormand is sexy as hell. But does Fran give a shit about being sexy? Does she care in the slightest about being sexy in the eyes of anyone other than herself and Joel?

As for the achievement of total self-possession, that might be impossible. It might just be yet another unicorn of the female narrative. Total self-possession may just be a myth the reporter and I would wishfully like to believe is attainable somewhere in what we hope will be our elegantly wrinkling futures; it sounds an awful lot like the fantasizing of youngish women, who continue to play the sexy game even though it has long since lost whatever appeal it may or may not have ever had for them. By far the most exciting Christmas present I got as a child was the Barbie Dreamhouse, that very sexy two-story pink house that came with an operable elevator and was built for one very sexy doll and her very sexy life. Manicured hands down, the most exciting Christmas present I've gotten as an adult is my Vitamix, even though I am fully aware that society expects me to operate it in ass-flattering leggings while preparing vegan protein smoothies.

I imagine Fran laughed when she opened the article and read that first paragraph about her sexy self-possession. I see her absolutely not wearing leggings but absolutely sitting in her kitchen. I hear her emitting a guffaw, a bark, at the oversized blond-oak kitchen table that surely she must have, the one whose red-wine rings tell you it's been put to good fun. I can almost see her shaking her head, rolling her eyes.

It occurs to me, rereading Fran's interview, that I might not completely understand what self-possession is. It must be awareness, but awareness, I am learning, doesn't always mean what I thought it did.

Hunter's definition is that awareness is, both simply and not at all simply, "to be without judgement." Which could be a definition shared with self-possession. Though I doubt anyone has ever accused Frances McDormand of being without judgement, and I am positive no one has ever thought that about me.

Self-possession might just be awareness of one's self without judgement, the learning to get over and beyond self-judgement. And self-ownership is wholly owning whatever it is you are, having outgrown the need to make excuses for it, to judge it, or to let it be judged. Or, as Fran puts it in the interview, "And what you gain after menopause is the power of invisibility. You become sexually invisible to both men and women. You gain the power of not giving a [expletive]." I sincerely hope the expletive here was a good old-fashioned *fuck*.

I quibble with her declaration that postmenopausal women are sexually invisible.

They frequently are, but I don't think they always are or that they have to be. Postmenopausal women are indeed sexually invisible to Harvey Weinstein and the forty-fifth president of the United States. Lucky them. But they're not sexually invisible to everyone. The people who find them sexy are just more discerning. Age weeds out the riffraff, which is part of the power of aging. You get to be invisible to the people whose attention you never wanted in the first place, and with the Harveys and the Orange Predators no longer blocking your view, you also have the opportunity to be wholly visible to yourself, sexually and otherwise.

What I'd like to know is if, for me, today, at half Fran's age, it is possible to speed up the process and skip directly to not giving an expletive right now. I think it is, and I think astrology might be able to help, and, yes, I do care if somebody thinks that's ridiculous. But I'm hoping it's the last time I give a damn about whether or not someone thinks I'm crazy.

Hunter may not have named his astrology course Self-Possession 101, but I remained undeterred. He calls it the Styles of Awakening

Training and describes it on his website in a single paragraph that made me think, *This is no kind of astrology I've ever heard of,* but, also, *Yes, please, where do I sign, how do I give you the money?*

"A kind of owner's manual for the human psyche, this in-depth training will empower you to not only better honor your own style of awakening, but to more accurately see, respect and support a full spectrum of body/minds—whether they be total strangers or those you claim to know and love. You will no longer merely 'like' or 'feel uncomfortable' around people; you will know which styles of awakening you are elevating or belittling in yourself."

He promises that over the course of three months, students will be given "direct experience of the positively-intended heart of each archetype." The class is twelve weeks, a week for each of the astrological archetypes or sun signs. The class I signed up for began in the fall, in the first week of October, and was conducted remotely through emailed packets of coursework and weekly calls with Hunter.

We decided to speak every Sunday night at 9:00 p.m., even though I knew immediately that it would be an inconvenience for M. Our apartment simply wasn't large enough for me to take these calls without disrupting him. He'd be forced to wear headphones for an hour, or he'd have to listen to my half of the conversation, or he'd have to leave the apartment altogether. I would have gone to a cafe myself, but I wanted to record the calls and take notes, and I didn't know any quiet coffee shops or restaurants where that was feasible and that were also open on Sundays at 9:00 p.m. But it was the only time Hunter and I could find that accommodated both of our time zones and our other commitments. So, I agreed to it, hoping that I was overthinking it and that the calls wouldn't be as intrusive for M. as I feared.

The first week was devoted to Aries, and the assignments for each day involved readings, questions to be answered, journaling, and activities like the one on the second day in which I was tasked with scheduling a one-hour massage for the following week. Most of the days were not so sybaritic. There were also tasks that yanked me out of my comfort zone, like some kind of hippie, team-building, trust-exercising hazing ritual: on the fourth day of Aries, Hunter's course material requested that I email six friends and family members (or, as I thought of them, the loved ones who drew the short straws) the following:

> Dear _____,
>
> I am enrolled in an interesting new online course. One of the assignments is to ask friends and family to name one risk that they think my soul wants to take, but that my self-image won't allow. I would be so honored if you would take the time to send me your brief emailed feedback as soon as possible.

The "as soon as possible" felt aggressive, so I altered that bit, but, otherwise, this is essentially the note I sent to my mother, one of my aunts, M., and three friends. Three of these six responded within minutes:

1. "This is a tough one, because I see you as being strong and confident and willing to take risks . . . I would say your hesitancy [sic] sometimes to show your vulnerability and your emotions. You have such high standards for yourself."
2. The second suggested that I have a baby. And, no, this was not my mother's response.
3. And then M.'s: "I don't know that self-image is a limiting factor for you. If you are held back in any way, which I haven't seen any evidence of, it's not [because] of your self-image."

I read his response once through and then read it again. I admitted to myself that I was disappointed and that I had been hoping for him to offer some kind of illumination of me I had not been able to discern. We shared a home and spent an inordinate amount of time together.

Surely then, M. should be able to offer me something of myself I couldn't see. Or, perhaps, that is one of the many heartbreaking ways we go wrong in relating—needing and assuming another person can explain us to ourselves. I was expecting M. to do something that wasn't his to do. It was mine. I was being unfair.

Still, I couldn't read his answer without questioning what it was we were saying to each other. Less than I thought. I am aware that I have a tendency, on occasion, to project an external confidence that does not always tell the whole internal story, but I had worked very hard not to do that with my ex B., and I had been sure that I wasn't doing it now with M. I had been so certain that I was laying bare my soul to this new man, with whom I was going to do things better, so certain that starting right from the night we met, I had been painstakingly showing him, *Here, here is who I am at the end of each day when I come home. See me. Please. Feel me. Please. Know that the only thing more terrifying to me than leaping before I look is standing still.* Either I was lying to myself about what I had been expressing or M. wasn't listening. Or I was overreacting and holding my boyfriend to a higher and more potentially damaging standard than the one I held others to. After all, he wasn't saying anything that everyone else didn't also seem to be suggesting.

The fourth response came a few days later.

4. "So, I think this would be to act or being in a life role where you do a lot of public speaking . . . I don't think you want to be famous in a superficial way, but I think well-known/respected is a more accurate idea. Anyway, I think pursu[ing] something in this space is of interest but

does not appeal to you because I don't think you like/can stand the bullshit that comes with it."

The fifth response arrived a couple of days after the fourth.

5. "If this specifically relates exclusively to self-image, it is harder. Because I feel as though you're not wedded to a self-image as much as most people I know, and also don't seem affected by the societal noise behind enforcement of projecting images as the rest of us."

I read these lines from a dear friend, and I liked them. Who wouldn't? But I was also tempted to look behind me, as in, *Is she talking to me? Really me?*

The sixth response did not come, and I was embarrassed. This sixth person was my high school English teacher, who has been a mentor to me since I was a teenager and has become, in the years since I graduated, a friend. She has long reminded me of Frances McDormand in both appearance (a little) and temperament (a lot), and now I was swiftly concluding that she thought my request was dumb and thought less of me for taking an astrology class and choosing to write a whole book of baloney. So much for that flawless self-image.

I recognized, too, that it was a lot to ask of my friends and family, especially because they had not signed up for an astrology course. These were not ideas they had already been thinking about. This was something I'd sprung on them, and their answers weren't the point. My asking was what mattered, precisely because it had made me feel uncomfortable. I had not wanted to do it, which I suspect is largely why Hunter created the assignment.

Temptation (and angst) got the better of me, and I eventually broke down and emailed my former teacher. I wrote just a single line and hit "Send": "I take it this email was just too 'woo-woo' for you to respond to?" Because, you know, of course I was going to be real chill about this whole thing. Her response appeared at the top of my in-box in less than an hour:

"No, no, no! I've been thinking about it a lot. The problem, Victoria, is that you are someone who DOES take risks . . . Okay, so two risks that I HAD taken by your age were marrying and having children. So I guess I could speculate that these are risks that your 'soul' wants to take but your 'self-image' won't allow. But ARE they? I'm becoming increasingly convinced that marriage isn't for everyone. It was the right choice for me . . . but . . . also, I read an article in the *NYT Magazine* about open marriage that thoroughly muddled the issue in my mind. So, you see, I have been thinking about your question but just haven't come up with an answer I believe in!"

I love so many things about this email.

1. That my insecurities about why I hadn't received a response were so totally unfounded.
2. That marrying and having children IS a risk.
3. That we are at a moment in American society when marrying and having kids, for some women, could conceivably conflict with their self-image—when for so many generations marriage and children ran the opposite risk of being the only available definition of a woman's self-image, though I don't think women are any better off with this approach, either.
4. That the reason I hadn't yet gotten a response was because she hadn't "come up with an answer I believe in!"

Belief. She wanted to send me an answer she believed in. This is not a person who considers herself religious. She may place herself somewhere on the spiritual spectrum but seeing as she put the word *soul* in quotes in her email, I'm guessing she considers spirituality an acquaintance, at best. And yet. She used the word *believe*. She could have written that she hadn't come up with an answer that she was confident in. We want to get the right answer. We want to feel good about the conclusions we draw, the assessments we give. But my former teacher did not use the word *confident*. This is a woman who has taught teenagers English grammar for the better part of four decades. I have never once known her to choose a word carelessly, and on this occasion, she had chosen *believe*. Even if she meant *believe* only in the sense of *confident*, these two words are not synonyms, though they are complementary, and they do interlock. Belief is the support beneath confidence and conviction, what holds them together and keeps them afloat.

Conviction is expressed verbally. We hear it. Conviction has the mic. Confidence rests just below and is what makes us pick up the microphone. We see confidence (or strong self-image), and we understand its necessity, but it's never the end of the story. Peel back the red herring of confidence to the layer below, and here is where we believe. Belief births confidence and conviction. We can't hear it. We can't see it. We *feel* it. And though we do not always choose to acknowledge what we feel, the feeling persists. If you woke up this morning and got out of bed, you believe in something. It may not be astrology or psychics or God or Allah or the Voodoo Queen. It may be immigration reform or E-flat or modernism or your sister's newborn baby or the phrase *they is*.

We believe in whatever we believe because of something innate to us. The crystalline beauty and desire to keep E-flat aloud in the world gets you out of bed in the morning, while I couldn't pick E-flat out of a lineup of one. It doesn't matter (at least not until E-flat picks my pocket). What does matter is that we own our beliefs and that they are worthy and true of us.

I don't know why anyone else takes Hunter's Styles of Awakening Training or, honestly, if anyone else ever has actually taken his course. But I had signed up and was subjecting myself to all manner of emotional and social discomfort at his discretion, because I really wanted that owner's manual to the human psyche he promised on his website. I wanted "to more accurately see, respect and support a full spectrum of body/minds." I had an inkling, as vague and embryonic as it was, that if I could just uncover and cultivate a belief system I could be proud of and rely on, I wouldn't have to wait another thirty years to achieve total self-possession. I could be "sexy [to *myself*] in the manner of women who have achieved total self-possession" today, not tomorrow. I could actually have the self-image and be the person who my friends and family thought I already was.

CHAPTER EIGHT

When I was four years old, my mother took me to see a touring production of *Peter Pan*. There is a pivotal moment in the show when the three Darling children lose their faith in Tinker Bell, and, consequently, her light goes out, and she dies. Peter Pan rallies the audience to clap, clap as hard as they can to bring Tink back to life, to turn her light back on. I clapped along, and I, too, cheered when her light returned. But, on the drive home from the theater, I asked my mother if Tinker Bell was real, if we had really clapped her back to life.

My mother was quiet for a moment, and then she said very softly, breaking it to me very gently, that my doubts were not unfounded. "No, Tinker Bell isn't real. That was just part of the show."

It was my turn to be quiet for a moment, during which I had another thought. "Is the tooth fairy real?" This was getting dark fast. No, again, my mother informed me. The thoughts kept coming. "What about the Easter Bunny?"

My mother took a deep breath and shook her head. "No, not the Easter Bunny, either."

By then my little mind had reached the North Pole, and I asked, "What about Santa Claus?" Another sad, sorry shake of my mom's head.

Years later, she would tell me that she had not wanted to lie to me but that she had felt terrible, popping so many fantastical childhood balloons of imagination in one fell swoop. But, by this point in the conversation, she had also assumed that we were mercifully done. There were no more balloons left to pop. But there were. I had one more question. "What about God?"

My mother sat straight up and replied forcefully, "Yes, God is real!"

My mother was born into a large Irish Catholic family, and her faith in and relationship with her God have always been incredibly important to her. For her, God's legitimacy is without question. Another parent might have struggled to answer my last question, might have had to wade through their own uncertainty. While my mother's resolve was unambiguous, it was not at all clear to me why or how Santa Claus was fake, but God was real. I had no more reason to believe in the reality of one or the other, beyond the insistence of some of the adults in my life. The issue was further muddled by the fact that my father and his family were not believers and were not shy about their lack of belief. Nor did it help that the nuns and priests at my Catholic elementary school and parish, the formal religious authorities in my life, on the periphery as they were, were intimidating and scary.

The thing about choosing not to believe in or worship anything that you cannot also hold in your hand and label and file and retrieve when you need the reassurance of proof is that everything becomes an accident, everything is random, nothing means anything. The solution lies neither in giving everything no meaning, nor in giving everything all meaning. The significant belief is believing in the *possibility* of meaning, of the existence of powers that cannot always be pinned down and categorized and neatly recorded in a ledger.

Nothing you experience is a happy or an unhappy accident but an opportunity to make a considered choice about your reaction. The boss who's dismissive of the report you worked all weekend to finish; the commuter who reaches the top of the subway station stairs and stops to get their bearings right in front of you and everyone else also trying to exit; the man who nearly pokes your eye out with his umbrella. Every time we experience one of these frustrating realities of life, it's an alarm clock going off: wake up, look around, make an observation, connect two previously disconnected, aimlessly floating dots, test a new hypothesis.

Dr. Lisa Miller has devoted her life to proving we are born in tune with that alarm clock. She is a professor of psychology and education and the director of the Clinical Psychology Program at Teachers College, Columbia University, as well as the director of the Spirituality Mind Body Institute and the author of *The Spiritual Child: The New Science on Parenting for Health and Lifelong Thriving*. She has spent decades researching and validating the hypothesis that we are all born spiritual—it is society that talks us out of these inherent beliefs.

The work of Dr. Miller, and others, has shown, along with the aid of new imaging technology, that "in the spiritually attuned person we see flourishing, healthy, thick portions of the brain right where, in the case of depression, for instance, we would have expected to see the thinner brain. Also, in the face of stressful events, a strong personal spirituality regulates our levels of cortisol, a stress hormone, which if deregulated or at sustained high levels, wears on brain and body and slows growth in children."

Multiple studies have looked at the brain-wave patterns of individuals who identify as spiritual and compared them with the brain-wave patterns of actual meditating monks. The results show "that the energy given off by the brains of spiritually engaged people when simply resting with closed eyes is the same wavelength as that of a monk during meditation."

That sounds like magic, like turning Tink's light on with the clap of a hand. Or, as Miller concludes, "It appears that their set point, or inner resting state of the brain, becomes a bright and peaceful state of transcendence."

Most significant to me is the science suggesting that spirituality is innate, not something taught or learned or imposed upon a child by parents or teachers or nuns. It can just as easily be fostered by the adults in a child's life as it can be stunted by those same shepherds. It is innate but not invulnerable.

In some ways, the science gets even more interesting when a little girl reaches adolescence and begins menstruating. Miller and her colleagues found that "once a girl has begun menstruating, a personal relationship with a higher power was even 50 percent more helpful in protecting against depression." *Are You There, God? It's Me, Margaret* was really onto something. Miller's work further determined that puberty is a time when girls become more open to perceptiveness, intuition, and empathy. Their sensitivity to themselves and the world around them increases, which includes an awareness of, or a depth for, spirituality that they did not previously have or possess at the same magnitude. Hence, some extra tears and extra drama.

As anyone who has spent time with a child knows, children are full of questions, constantly identifying tricky dilemmas for which conceivable solutions are contradictory from culture to culture, family to family, even from one parent to the other. They also do not hesitate to vocalize these discrepancies, often at impolite, socially inopportune moments. But this means that, as Miller argues, "children are our born leaders in the spiritual realm. Children converge immediately on the big questions." After the Tinker Bell incident, I stopped exploring faith in any genuine way. It didn't add up. It still doesn't. But now I know that I'd probably be better off if I believed in God and her alarm clock.

There were days when I'd wake before the sun and turn in bed to find that M. was also waking. We were each other's alarm clocks. We never had any good reason to be awake so early.

On these mornings, we'd pluck a mini adventure out of our imaginations and set off into the dark city to explore, to be out of doors alone with each other under a slowly brightening sky. Here is where I felt my closest to M., my closest to the life I wanted for us. These mornings were our church.

Sometimes, we'd take the subway up to Times Square and stand at the intersection of Broadway and Seventh Avenue beneath the lights and the screaming screens and the billboards and marvel at seeing no one else, at being the only two people in Times Square, as if the lights were on for us, as if the screens were speaking to us. We'd stay until someone else came up out of the subway station or a car drove by, and the spell broke. Then we'd buy coffees from the bakery Junior's, because it was always the only thing open, and we'd walk home along the Hudson River.

Other times, we'd leave our apartment and walk south and east over one of the bridges to watch the sun rise from halfway between Manhattan and Brooklyn, just us and the most dogged of the joggers. Once, M. and I were looking for coffee in a Brooklyn neighborhood we didn't know when we saw a bearded father walking with his son and carrying a couple of to-go cups. He pointed us in the direction of the nearest not-Starbucks, and we headed that way. I don't remember what exactly, but something about the man reminded M. of a friend of a friend, someone he knew from a handful of parties and a lot more Facebook posts. The most salient detail of this friend-once-removed, at least as far as M. knew, was that he was a young widower who had married his wife when she was terminally ill.

M. went on about how incredible that was, how moving, how romantic, that this man should have loved this woman so much that he was willing to marry her on her deathbed. I didn't know what he was talking about. I turned to him and said, "What kind of commitment is that? I'd marry almost anyone who was on their deathbed."

No one ever meets me and thinks, *Now, there's someone with a rich inner spiritual life.*

According to a 2010 survey conducted by the Fetzer Institute, 91 percent of Americans think the world is becoming more frightening and violent. Never mind that violent crime has actually fallen dramatically in American cities. There was a time in the latter half of the twentieth century when more than two thousand New Yorkers were killed every year. By 2014, however, there were only 328 murders in New York City, and in 2017 there were even fewer, meaning we can now cite one good thing from that year: slightly less violent death. Similar statistics can be found for cities across the country, from Portland to Portland. No matter all that. We live in a time when neither our facts nor our feelings are trustworthy, but feelings sometimes seem to have the upper hand because they are felt, are a part of us, belong to us. And the world feels scarier. That is a fact.

Today, we are much more likely to identify as having zero religion. Two-thirds of Americans, including both those who do continue to identify with and claim religion and those who do not, have come to the conclusion that religion doesn't impact their lives the way it did in generations past. That religion is no longer a trending influencer is not news. The Fetzer Institute, in the same 2010 survey, found that 60 percent of adults in America did feel, however, that they had grown increasingly spiritual in the last five years. Nearly 75 percent of Americans also believed spirituality helps solve "misunderstandings between cultures," and 90 percent of us prayed, not to "God," but to an "ultimate creator."

That Americans make a distinction between God and an ultimate creator says more about the political and social climate of our time than anything else. The difference between believing in and calling on guidance from an ultimate creator or god or beautiful mother lover of the divine is negligible. Many of us make a distinction between religion and spirituality, because religion has become loaded, calling forth connotations of power abused, greed, bloodshed, assault, sexism, racism, and homophobia. We have replaced religion with a vague notion of spirituality. In her book *The Spiritual Child*, Dr. Miller defines spirituality as "an inner sense of relationship to a higher power that is loving and guiding . . . the word we give to this higher power might be God, nature, Spirit, the universe, the creator, or other words that represent a divine presence. But the important point is that spirituality encompasses our relationship and dialogue with this higher presence."

Which is exactly how every psychic, astrologer, and shaman I interviewed described their work.

CHAPTER NINE

I had known about digital photographer and sculpturist Meghan Boody's grand and evocative work for years, but it wasn't until I learned that she had also created a series of oracle cards, which she named her PsycheSuperStar deck, that it occurred to me I could reach out to her and request an interview. She gamely agreed to meet, but, first, I had to figure out what oracle cards actually were. Take whatever vague knowledge I had of tarot cards and halve it—that's about what I knew of oracle cards when Meghan said, "Sure! Ask me anything."

A complete tarot deck has seventy-eight cards, twenty-two of which are the Major Arcana. These are the trump cards and include those you might have heard of, such as the Lovers, the Hanged Man, the Devil, the Sun, the Fool, and the Wheel of Fortune. The remaining fifty-six cards are the Minor Arcana. They are divided into four suits of fourteen cards: ten numbered cards and four court cards, the King, Queen, Knight, and Jack. Altogether, the deck is said to offer a sensate representation of the full human experience.

The tarot's system of suit cards is not unlike the deck of playing cards you used to be able to count on finding in most American households, usually, as it happens, in a drawer beneath the wall-mounted kitchen telephone, tucked in beside the rubber bands, half-peeled foil pack of mints, and dull pencils that rolled back and forth every time the drawer got opened. Finding a tarot deck therein would have been much less likely, but the similarities between the tarot and the boredom-avoidant deck of playing cards are not happenstance. The tarot originated as a simple deck used to play card games in the 1400s in Europe, most notably in Italy. It was only some four hundred years later that the tarot was introduced as a practice of the occult. Once upon a time, many would have likely considered our modern-day deck of playing cards as essentially interchangeable with tarot and oracle decks. Today, however, we play Solitaire with that deck and turn to tarot and oracle cards for connection and guidance.

Most of the tarot-card readers I spoke to talked about the decks (both tarot and oracle) as an opportunity for refuge, especially for people who don't feel a bond with the god figures to be found in the world's five most prominent religious traditions (Buddhism, Christianity, Hinduism, Islam, and Judaism). For some, discovering the tarot is a deep homecoming, with the cards serving as a resource for open reflection, allowing them to see both themselves and their communities more clearly.

Lindsay Mack, an intuitive tarot reader and holistic counselor certified by the American Association of Drugless Practitioners, believes that the tarot deck centers and guides her and provides an effective visual aid for her intuitive counseling work. She described a tarot reading to me as a dance she always looks forward to, a dance that is always unique. According to Mack, "[the cards] truly are different for everyone. There is never, ever an expectation of this card means this. Sometimes the Devil is awesome for people; sometimes the Sun is really hard."

In much the same way that individual cards can show up differently for different people, an oracle deck may look similar to a tarot deck, but it will always have its own space, its own philosophy. An oracle deck, unlike the tarot, can have any number of cards in it, which, most typically, ends up meaning fewer than seventy-eight. An oracle card might also feature a lengthy phrase or a quote, something that would be highly unusual on a tarot card. Then again, oracle cards can also be wordless, relying entirely on their imagery to convey their meaning, and, like the tarot, oracle cards aim to embrace and trace allegories of human experience. But the most important thing to know about oracle cards is that their only rule is that they don't have any rules. If the tarot is a guided language that helps some people communicate more directly with their own intuition or God or Spirit, a tangible aid to prayer not so dissimilar from rosary beads, then oracle cards may be more of a postlanguage that offers endlessly interpretative sparks of inspiration for unwritten, nonverbal clarity. Like lighting a match in the dark and tracing the resulting shadows.

However you choose to approach and use oracle cards, Meghan has designed her deck with the intention that they be useful for divination, and each card speaks to a different aspect of life, a different emotive experience. They have names like Revelry, Sitting Pretty, Hidden Knowledge, the Balancing Act, Sacred Rites, and Grace. The images on each card, the sceneries and the characters they depict, each painstakingly and elaborately staged and photographed by Meghan both on location and in her studio, are vivid and bold in color, forceful in nature, capturing seemingly everything that can be captured except anything beige, except neutrality. A million things are happening on every card and also nothing at all. The characters are frequently languishing, in repose, still, physically passive but suggestive of much overthinking and mental exertion. They are a reflection of the card's holder in that particular moment. There's nothing wishy-washy about any of Meghan's other sculptural and photographic work, some of which is enormous and some of which is tiny, literally the size of a thumbnail, but there's something about the cards, their physical lightness and manageability, that makes them both more powerful and more digestible.

A card serves a purpose. It can be a source of strategy, a game, or a tool, which makes it interactive in a way that a photograph on a wall is not. At some point in the early weeks of our relationship, M. and I had fallen into a recurring and age-old debate about the definition of art: he argued that if something had any kind of practical function, it could not be art. He claimed, for instance, that a vase could never be a piece of art. I disagreed. I see no value in filtering form and function in such a broad and indiscriminate way. I think we have to find and take art wherever we can, however we see it and make it. If a potter points to a bowl she's made and says to me, "This is my art," I will take her at her word. I will believe her, and I will never ladle soup into that bowl and not think that this piece of art has implanted itself into the smallest moments of my life, its very practicality enhancing its artfulness, not diminishing it.

Meghan's oracle cards represent the intersection point of art and a certain kind of free-form utility. That I can pick one up and hold it in my hand or wear it tucked privately into my bra against my bare skin and heart only enriches its artistic expression and worth to me. Meghan's cards vibrate with an aliveness and a sense of possibility that I don't feel in either her remarkable photographs, ultimately untouchable in their hugeness, in the way they tower over the viewer, or in her dioramas, exquisite in their minute and surprising details but ultimately too small to be handled in any way other than with supreme delicacy.

Her cards incorporate both sight and touch. And for all the power of sight, it, like hearing, can deceive in ways that touch cannot. Touch is the most Taurean of the senses. I didn't use to know this. Taurus, I have learned, is co-ruled by the earth. Taurus is grounded, at home in its skin. Our bodies are earthbound, and the Taurus's touch is bodily, animalistic, earthly. Hunter reminded me that "touch doesn't stop at the moment of parting" or the moment of putting down a card, because the energy of that touch reverberates. In his distillations on Taurus, Hunter writes, "You are not here to politely override your feelings and sensations but to incorporate them into your humble human offerings." This jolted me. All I am ever doing is trying (and failing) to override my feelings, to, through sheer force of will, dominate and subsume them, to succeed *in spite of* my feelings not because of them or in aid of them. But Meghan's cards have the power to pull me back into touch, my body, the earth, and my sensate reactions, whatever they may be in a given moment. I had spent so many years articulating and labeling and defining my sense of self in relation to what I did or didn't feel, but believed I should have, that I forgot feelings are just tools. My feelings are not who or what I am.

By the time I reached out to Meghan, I'd already interviewed numerous psychics, shamans, mediums, empaths, intuitives, and crystal gatherers. I was more than ready to interview someone who's also an outsider looking in, who is also trying to translate this work and these life choices and ideas into a more universal form of communication and connection. But whatever vision I had of Meghan being some kind of simpatico outsider in this world, which was new and so mysterious to me, vanished when she buzzed me up to her apartment. Not because she's tall and lissome, all legs and thick, shiny, stick-straight blonde hair—if you live south of Fourteenth Street in Manhattan long enough, you get used to seeing otherworldly supermodeling beauties completing the most mundane of human realities: carrying laundry, scooping dog shit, buying deodorant. Not that these activities dim their ethereality, no—if anything they only brighten them. Meghan is one of those, and sprites of her kind have long ceased to faze me.

What truly and immediately separates Meghan and me, what places us not on the same side of this spiritual investigation, is Meghan's home, a loft in New York City's Tribeca. It could have been designed by the Brothers Grimm, if they also wrote for *Architectural Digest* and were generally less downtrodden by their family's financial misfortune (true fact). Meghan's building started out a shoe factory (*There once was an artist woman who lived in a shoe . . .*) before evolving into a collection of crash pads in the 1970s for an overflowing mixed bag of occupants.

When Meghan took over one of the apartments in the midnineties, her loft came with a Japanese soak tub, curved walls, wooden columns, and three doors inexplicably set into the highest ceilings I have ever seen in a private home. To these architectural details, she added valances, balustrades, a secret room, dioramas, a trapdoor, and, in the middle of it all, a gigantic daybed, won from a Far Eastern importer by Meghan's ex-husband during a long-ago poker game.

It's not easy to compete with the ornate dragons carved into the posts of the daybed, but what struck me most about the home she had created were the shades of green. Not just the greens of the numerous potted plants but the pale green in the kitchen tile and the swirling darker greens in the leaves of the floral upholstery of the couch and the armchair beside it and the wooden frames of the dining room chairs and the smooth roof of a dollhouse and the raised pattern in a ceramic teapot. Together, in that spectacular loft light, they brought the apartment to life. Not just any life, but a specific state of aliveness: Ripe. Ready.

Meghan offered me a glass of ginger and turmeric tea, carefully straining out the knobs of fresh roots before she handed it to me. We sat across from one another, flanked by her cat and her dog, and I felt suddenly the least alive present. In this moment, before I opened my notebook, pushed "Play" on my tape recorder, and began to ask the questions I had prepared, I was helped by two thoughts.

The first was an artist's statement of Meghan's from a show of hers at the Brooklyn Museum that I had dutifully recorded in my notes:

"As I struggle to find my way in the world, I create phantom women and girls from another time who undergo parallel investigations of the self. As they embark on character-transforming quests in strange lands, I grapple with my own life, and our pitfalls and successes along the way guide and inform each other. My subjects often begin their wanderings lost and alone, Bambis blinded by headlights and babes in the woods. They stumble into predicaments and compromising situations as they explore the outer reaches of female territory. Body image, appropriate feminine behavior, youth and beauty preservation, power dynamics in male/female relations, desire of rescue and the search for true love, all these fraught issues and potential quagmires form an obstacle course where my urchins and heroines learn how to shape-shift and transform into more complete selves."

The second helpful thought was the sentence running through my head over and over again: *I'm the boss of you. I'm the boss of you.*

In my coursework for Hunter's class, I had been tasked with silently declaring *I'm the boss of you* to everyone with whom I crossed paths. Not because I'm an asshole but because "being present to *what is* means owning our true Aries impact." The Aries impact here applies to all of us, not just those of us born under the Aries sun sign, because we all have Aries in us, and we all impact the living creatures we come into contact with. We rarely miss the impact of others on us, but we tend to forget about our own impact. We forget about our impact on other people, on ourselves, on the planet, on the universe.

I looked out of a coffee shop window recently and watched a man open his car door and shove a magazine-subscription postcard, a receipt, and a coffee cup sleeve into the gutter. That action impacts the street and every single person who walks down it. It impacts the bugs and the rodents and the birds and the cats and the dogs. It impacts the street cleaner and the air above and the sewer below. It also impacts the man, because we are our actions; his decision to litter instead of choosing to find a trash can is part of how he has chosen to show up in the world; it impacts him, because it marks him as one thing and not another. In the same way, I am impacted by my decision to sit silently in the window, drinking my coffee from a ceramic mug, judging him, while I write on my laptop, which has its own long and devastating environmental impact, and choosing, too, not to walk outside and bend down and pick up his subscription postcard, his receipt, and his sleeve and carry them back inside to the cafe's recycling bin. The man never looked up; he and I never made eye contact, never spoke, but because we shared his action, he was, however briefly, the boss of me.

Hunter explained his bossy task this way: "We're all psychic, and we all unconsciously imitate each other. Your slumped or gently erect vertebrae is weighing down or buoying everyone you meet. The commitments you honor or cut corners on, the amount of time you spend distracted and entertained or rinsing away stories with meditative silence and/or creative absorption is wafting your aura, drifting from your lips, like an invisible contagion. Like it or not, you are a leader. Your presence is constantly inspiring others and leading them into the fullness of their being or subtly entraining them into craving, aversion, and indifference."

We don't hesitate to acknowledge someone else's presence or attitude or the vibe they're giving off. Somebody walks into a room, and, instantly, the energy of the room shifts—their energy, your energy, the fish in the fish tank's energy. Or it doesn't, which also tells you something of how that person or fish swims through life. If we ever stop to think about it, we also realize that if others' energy is doing that to us, then our energy is surely doing that to them as well.

I worked for years in a corporate environment where a string of differing job titles were bestowed upon me, each of which was defined only in so much as I understood that the work made me miserable and that I had no business doing it. During those years, my personal life was also unraveling. It was a long, winding period in which it became slowly apparent that the work I wanted to do might not be available to me and that the people I loved and had thought I could depend on, my boyfriend B., some of my extended family, weren't going to be a part of my future after all. My resulting fear and pain and bad attitude hurt my colleagues, and it made their jobs harder. I was, in that way, the boss of them. I was thoughtless with that power, and I will never not be ashamed of my behavior during those years. As punishment, I have banished myself from Corporate City and will spend the rest of my days toiling in Freelancers' Forest, where I must pay for my own coffee and health insurance.

And now, in this pocket of Freelancers' Forest, for however brief a period in time, I was the boss of Meghan. And, thank god, too, because I don't know how I would have fared in the presence of Meghan's expression of seamless self-possession without that bossiness to prop me up. It turns out that I was drawn to Meghan's oracle cards in part because, now having met her, they were so blatantly an extension of her, of her well-established sense of self. She was calm; she would not be rattled; she looked through me; she spoke with certainty; she asked more questions than she answered.

Sitting across from her, surrounded by her art, her ginormous photographs hanging high above us and her teeny dioramas on the tiny table below us, I saw self-possession under a microscope. I do not imagine that the foundation of my belief system will ever rely on the tarot or an oracle deck. But I think of something else Lindsay Mack told me: "The tarot is changing. It's evolving out of the old trappings of fortune-telling that it used to be and coming into this deep mirror for our soul expansion." Regardless of how the word *soul* makes you feel, I do know that Meghan's cards have attitude, have a "not giving a [expletive]" vibe, and I know that they make it easier for me to remember my Aries impact, to reject my bad attitudes, and to embrace my good bossiness.

We feel it all the time, and we say it all the time: *He had bad energy; I didn't like her vibe.* But if we take the word *energy* and push it further than that, if we try to apply it too liberally, crossing some ill-defined line, then all of a sudden we've gone from acceptable and wise and in tune with the people and the world around us to some kind of woo-woo la-la land, and our audience or our companion may shut off to us in some small but energetically felt way. But where is that line between the two? Between the acceptable *She's got bad energy* and the teetering on woo-woo, the, for example, *She's out of alignment with her soul.*

I put this question to astrologer Sandy Sitron, and she said something to me that, on its surface and to the ear of an astrology novice, would seem to have nothing to do with the stars: "It's all the patriarchy. Don't be confused about that."

Now, I happen to think about the patriarchy a lot, like really a lot, but until Sandy made this declaration to me in her friendly, noncombative way after more than two hours of astrological discussion, I had never considered it in relation to astrology.

She continued. "In the boardroom, people think nothing of saying 'trust your gut,' right?"

I picked up the thread. "Right. Everyone thinks that's real wisdom, a real smart way to do business. Trusting your gut is manly."

She nodded and finished the thought. "But trusting your intuition is suspect." Intuition is womanly, feminine, not to be trusted.

The gut's got science behind it.

Scientists Justin and Erica Sonnenburg, who conduct their research at the Stanford University School of Medicine's Department of Microbiology and Immunology, write in their book, *The Good Gut*, that the mind-gut connection is perhaps not only metaphorical: "Our brain and gut are connected by an extensive network of neurons and a highway of chemicals and hormones that constantly provide feedback about how hungry we are, whether or not we're experiencing stress, or if we've ingested a disease-causing microbe." They say that this highway is called "the brain-gut axis" and provides "constant updates on the state of affairs at your two ends. That sinking feeling in the pit of your stomach after looking at your postholiday credit card bill is a vivid example of the brain-gut connection at work. You're stressed and your gut knows it—immediately."

The enteric nervous system, which controls the gut, is often referred to as the body's second brain, and by *often referred to*, I mean by people like the Sonnenburgs who have made science their lives' work. The reason behind the nickname, and the wildest part of all, is that this second brain is capable of functioning *without* input from the central nervous system. So your gut can make decisions without your brain's help.

Apparently, your brain doesn't have to be invited to every party. (This is something I have started reminding myself of frequently. Unfortunately, my brain thinks crashing parties is hil-ar-ious.)

But what, then, is the difference between our gut and our intuition? The gut is real and intuition is fake, because we can point to our gastrointestinal system and we can't point to our "intuitintestinal" system? Because guts are masculine, and intuition and astrology and empathy are feminine?

I responded to Meghan's positive energy. You will never convince me otherwise. That was a real feeling, and it was in response to something equally real, even if her energy was not technically tangible, even if I could not pick it up, let alone point to it and say, *There, right there*. Of course, I like Meghan's work. It is an extension of her vibe. At the center of every one of her photographs, be they those hanging oversized on her living room wall or those printed undersized on her oracle cards, is a moment of intuition. They are mostly, though not entirely, of women and girls whose faces are turned enough toward the camera to capture their expressions, expressions that are contemplative, raw, determined. Her work honors intuition, heralds it.

Yes, it is intuition Meghan is working with, not gut. The word *intuition* has its roots in the Latin verb *intueri*, meaning "to consider." Intuition is nuanced. It is patient. It is perceiving many things at once and using those competing reactions to draw a conclusion, not necessarily to make a decision or to act, simply to conclude. Whether this happens consciously or subconsciously, rationally or irrationally, is subject to debate. It is this debate, this notion of inherent intuition, not gut, that has for centuries been given space and consideration in not only the philosophical writings of European philosophers, such as Plato, Aristotle, Descartes, Kant, and Hume, but also in religious texts, such as those of Islam, Hinduism, and Zen Buddhism. The modern study and practice of psychology has also not been shy on this topic.

Plato believed that intuition was part of our preexisting knowledge. He surmised that intuition exists in our "soul of eternity," lying dormant until such time as we are able to find a way to tap into it. This is, essentially, his theory of anamnesis, the idea of recollection, that we are the only ones who can answer whatever question we are asking. Descartes, on the other hand, wrote in his work *Rules for the Direction of the Mind* that intuition is "a conception, formed by unclouded mental attention, so easy and distinct as to leave no room for doubt in regard to the thing we are understanding . . . Anybody can see by mental intuition that he himself exists, that he thinks, that a triangle is bounded by just three lines." As a rationalist, he was arguing that we learn and acquire knowledge through the concept of rational intuition, which, in essence, is the very opposite of "just having a hunch."

Jung, of course, proposed that intuition is irrational. It is not based on our senses or even on our thoughts or feelings but operates unconsciously. And the fourteenth-century Sunni scholar and theologian Ibn Qayyim al-Jawziyyah, on the topic of spiritual insight, or *firasah*, said: "O you who are defenseless! Beware the spiritual insight of the godly one, for he sees your hidden deeds from behind a veil. Beware the spiritual insight of a believer, for he sees with the light of God." Intuition here is the blessing and defense, the protection, of the faithful.

These philosophical, psychological, and religious definitions of intuition conflict with one another more often than not, but they all agree that intuition is real, that it is worthy of attention and definition, and that it offers some kind of hopeful answer to the desire for connection, understanding, and meaning in this life. Meghan, by her art, agrees.

Maybe the search for meaning and even purpose is really the search for an intuitive connection with the rest of humanity. It's my search for you. For me. For us. Every time my feelings are hurt, intentionally or unintentionally, by family or friend, colleague or stranger, which, given my propensity for sensitivity, is frequent, I do something nice for somebody else. Usually not something nice for the person who hurt my feelings, because, I mean, come on. But something nice for someone else in my life, a friend I've neglected or been in some other way thoughtless toward. Or someone else who has not been in my life but will be now, alongside the periphery, a stranger at the grocery store or on the sidewalk, who has given me the opportunity to feel a little less strange, a little less outside. Is this kindness enough? No. But it doesn't hurt.

In *The Power of Meaning*, Emily Esfahani Smith cites a study that claims "four in ten Americans have not discovered a satisfying life purpose." Esfahani Smith uses this statistic as part of a larger argument proving the existence of a serious problem, that millions are emotionally adrift, that the extraordinary advances in science have drawn us away from our spiritual beliefs, our god(s), the traditions and rituals that we once relied on to give us meaning, to pull us through the harder days (and weeks and months and years). Science, for all its beauty and glory and, yes, comfort, too, has not proven a satisfactory or whole replacement for spirituality—for concern for the human, animal, and natural spirits, both those we cannot possibly see as well as those sitting beside us, whom we often choose not to see.

I asked Sandy another question about intuition, though I didn't realize it was a question of intuition when I put it to her: "Anyone can study astrology, but can anyone also be an astrologer?"

Her answer took twists and turns but, along the way, came to mirror Hunter's philosophy. "Anyone can be an astrologer for themselves. Anyone can use astrology as a tool for their self-worth and self-understanding."

But, of course, this opens another line of questioning: Can anyone, then, be a counselor? As Lindsay Mack put it to me, with clients, she has to be "spiritually hygienic. Whenever I do a reading I will always take a moment, and my prayer in silence is that I ask very directly to be of service to you, to pull from the energetic well of divine rather than my own energy."

Sandy, too, enters each astrological reading she does for another person with care. "Being an astrologer, you're holding a lot of responsibility. You're trying to talk about things in a way that aren't too leading and are a good balance of real, holistic, and hopeful. And you're also trying not to trigger anyone . . . People have ultimate potential. So if someone's interested in learning the tools of astrology and also in learning some counseling techniques and also in learning how their own appearance and being can impact another person and can be very self-aware . . ."

I'm the boss of you.

CHAPTER TEN

My mother is a diligent woman. She keeps a balanced checkbook and doesn't seem to realize that if you miss an annual physical, you don't immediately drop dead. Should you ever have the pleasure of traveling with her, I promise, you will not miss your flight. Her most indulgent predilection is for antiques, particularly side tables, lots of side tables, the more impractical the better, anything with a surface area too small for a meal to be eaten on or a letter to be signed. If a room has only one side table, what's even the point?

So, when I mentioned to my mother that a friend had gotten engaged and that her ring was an antique, it caught me by surprise that she responded with a shudder. "Oh, no. What if its previous owner had a bad marriage?"

What if. Given the reality of human nature generally and the disheartening historical record behind the institution of marriage specifically, there is a high probability the original ring wearer's marriage was indeed bad. Does that matter? For most of her long marriage to Joel Coen, Frances McDormand has worn the ring Joel gave his first wife. Reportedly, Fran saw no reason for a perfectly good ring to go to waste. If that's *not* self-possession, nothing is.

Given that the "McCoens" have been married since 1984, they seem to have been able to surmount whatever bad juju residue the used ring brought into their lives, and, at this point, the pedigree of Fran's ring only makes the story of their romance that much better.

Let's also get real here: Frances McDormand is not like most of us, and a lot of people would not be so blasé about wearing their predecessor's hand-me-down ring as a physical and public symbol of the supposedly unbreakable commitment they've made to their spouse. I suspect that most of us are more like my mom, side tables aside, and would prefer a "fresh" ring, a blank slate onto which the foibles of our marriage and ours alone can accumulate. Anything else gives us the willies.

There is zero scientific proof that the history of a physical object can negatively affect its current wearer or keeper. The proof is in those willies. In Japan, it is not unheard of for car salesmen to bless cars before their new owners drive them off the lot. In countries all around the world, athletes, professional and otherwise, routinely rely on visualization to enhance their practice and performance. The revered New York City–based acupuncturist and counselor Abdi Assadi says in his book, *Shadows on the Path*, that "the body cannot distinguish between thoughts and reality." If we think an antique engagement ring is bad luck, then you better believe that it is.

If we accept this, then we must also accept that a positive thought is just as real to the body as a negative thought. The astrologer Rob Brezsny, who was a musician and poet long before he ever considered a career in astrology, insists that his terrifically named Free Will Astrology column is not your average horoscope destination. To Rob, astrology—like any other belief system—is "something you shouldn't take 100 percent seriously." Rob thinks people should be interpreting horoscopes as metaphor, not fact, because astrology isn't a science but an art. "A work of magic, in the hermetic sense of the word, not as in stage magic, but beyond rational explanation."

It's as Nisargadatta Maharaj wrote: "Don't try to understand! It's enough if you do not misunderstand." It's what all of art does—opens us up to our imaginations and to the countless positive possibilities before us at every moment. It's also what Andrea and Reesha were trying to tell me when I first started down this path, when I thought Catharine River-Rain was handing me a fat, juicy future and not describing a possibility, one kind of life I could try on, imagine, and twirl in for a lifetime or, alternately, for just a little while. That, whatever ultimately happens, it will be up to me, not destiny.

This argument also reminds me of something Dr. Sarah Bamford Seidelmann, a fourth-generation physician, first-generation shaman, and lifelong Minnesotan, said to me about the subtle messages we receive when we give ourselves permission to imagine. "The imagination is not considered a false thing in shamanism, the way it is in our culture. In our culture, imagination is for little kids, storybooks and things like that. There is this implication that it is not real, just because it hasn't been experienced yet. But really, the greatest creations all come from our imagination, and that's why in shamanism we spend a lot of time working with our imagination. Because it's the way the doors fly open and we can go and do other things that haven't yet been created."

My apartment building in New York City sits on a corner and is across the street, south, from a public elementary school, and across the street, east, from a private elementary school. Every year on Halloween the students arrive dressed in their costumes and have a parade beneath my living room windows. I wake up to the delighted shrieks of tiny vampires and zombies, superheroes and race-car drivers. It is my favorite morning of the year.

Last October I introduced M. to my Halloween morning ritual. We sat on the fire escape and drank coffee and pointed out costumes we recognized and many more we were stumped by, old as we are, so far gone as we are from the age when we were up on our cartoon characters and popular heroes. The parents, who line the sidewalk straining for a view of their children as they parade by, are almost even more fun to watch. They know what their child is wearing; they helped them dress not an hour before and delivered them here, and still they are so excited. Their excitement, their enthusiasm, is purer, sweeter, than that of their children, who don't know it isn't always like this. These parents are not taking this for granted. They are holding on to this moment.

A week after Halloween, M. and I woke up to a different kind of gathering outside our living room windows. November 8, 2016. On that day, there were no costumes, and Halloween felt like another lifetime that had happened to different people, in a different country. We had gone to bed well after midnight the night before, numbingly sober, because though we had started the night drinking with friends in Brooklyn, we had lost our taste for everything when it became undeniable that Hillary would not be our next president of the United States. Bottles of champagne remained unpopped, pots and pans unbanged. M. and I had shared a somber, silent cab ride back into Manhattan with a couple of friends. Our stop was first, and we got out, barely mumbling goodbyes.

Our block was empty, both elementary schools looking desolate in the chilly dark, and it was not hard in my shocked, self-pitying state of mind to see how the world would look postapocalyptically, when everything was dead, education, all of what I had thought was knowledge, what I had thought were building blocks to something better. I fell asleep almost as soon as we walked in the door, the kind of hard sleep that comes when your body is heavy and your mind has spun to depletion. I fell asleep, because I was exhausted, but also because I needed to not be in the world for a while. M. stayed up, unable to look away from the car crash coming through his phone, clicking from one news article to another, from one tweet to the next. I do not know when he came to bed; I'm not sure he knows. But I know we woke up together, to the same sound.

On the street below, spread across the sidewalk in front of the public school, were about fifty parents and children facing a small handful of teachers. The group shared sheaves of paper, two or three to a sheet, as though the teachers had not expected quite this turnout. Together, they were singing the lyrics from "Imagine."

They sang a cappella and not precisely all together, so it was possible to hear the stronger, bigger voices first and then the younger, higher voices trailing, a rolling wave of music. I had been in such a deep, denial-full sleep that, at first, it was hard to know if I was still dreaming, just another one of Lennon's dreamers, or if this was real. The song and the voices were beautiful, but, more than anything, it was the sight of this community of people and the knowledge that they had gathered with so little notice and preparation. For if Hillary had been victorious, this would not be happening.

M. opened the windows, and we leaned out so far we could almost believe that we had joined them. My eyes filled with tears. It sounded like a brand-new song. I have never understood the merits of choosing to have a child to hold and to raise in this world as much as I did in the minutes it took for those children, parents, and teachers to "Imagine."

It was significant to me that this gathering was happening at a school, at our place of education, our twenty-first-century place of worship. Education has replaced religion as the foundation of our communities. Education, or the lack thereof, binds a community. It is our tie, our network for support, worth, work, and future viability. The question used to be *Where do you worship?* It has become *Where did you go to school?* Now, they are one and the same. We worship at the altar of facts, because we believe facts are proof.

I thought of the pediatric oncologist and professor of pediatrics and Christian philosophy at Duke University, the remarkable Dr. Ray Barfield. I first discovered Dr. Barfield's singular mind in the pages of the North Carolina–based magazine the *Sun*, which is one of my favorite publications and which strives with every issue to "honor the mystery at the heart of existence." In a long interview with the *Sun*, Dr. Barfield told writer Janice Lynch Schuster, "The best philosophers of science realize that if you form your theory of knowledge in a way that excludes the possibility of genuine religious experience, then you exclude a lot of the best science."

These public-school children, standing with their parents and their teachers at the entrance of their daily home of knowledge and science and philosophy, were singing a spiritual song, a folk song. The English antiquarian William Thoms wrote that folk music, folklore, is "the traditions, customs, and superstitions of the uncultured classes." That's spiritual talk. The word *folk* derives from the German *Volk*, for "people," whose meaning can be expanded to encompass the whole of a group or nation. That's community talk. Lennon may have been singing pointedly about a time beyond and outside religion, but his music is not beyond or outside the spiritual tradition of the uncultured classes' superstitions, the people as a whole.

Nestled between the public school and the private one, across my street, is a church. As the public-school children and their parents sang, I glanced over at the church, which was still and unmoving, not a light on. When they reached the end of the song, there was no clapping, no cheering, but hugs and hard squeezes and rubs on the back.

More than any fact of science, what we learn in school and in our childhood homes is how others expect us to be in the world. And what others expect us to be depends on who our parents are at the time that they raise us and who our teachers are at the time we enter their classrooms and in what part of the world we find ourselves starting our journey. So, sometimes, we end up being taught wrong, and that wrongness has dire consequences. But here was one morning, at one school, where the lesson was right.

This had been done, ostensibly, for the children, to give them something to hold on to, to give them some sense of immediate meaning as well as to create a memory they could return to and find comfort in through every one of the unsteady tomorrows to come. In the process, however, the adults had done something for themselves and for M. and me, too. After all, they could have chosen to sing inside, in the gymnasium, which I happen to know well, because it is my voting place, where, less than twenty-four hours before, I had walked in and placed my vote for Hillary. They didn't sing inside. They chose to sing outside where anyone who was lucky enough to be nearby could hear them. They were sharing this with their neighbors.

I went to work that day, at my big, corporate, adult company, and no one passed out the lyrics to "Imagine" and suggested we sing it together. Instead we moved through the office in mourning. Too often we find what we need only when we think of what a child might need, when we remember our responsibility not to ourselves but to the next generation. I wish we took as good care of ourselves as we do some of our children.

CHAPTER ELEVEN

"'I am my own muse,' wrote Frida Kahlo. 'I am the subject I know best. The subject I want to know better.' Would you consider trying out this perspective for a while, Aries? If so, you . . . may be led into mysterious areas of your psyche that had previously been off-limits. You could discover secrets you've been hiding from yourself."

This was my horoscope from Rob Brezsny on a day, October 17, 2017, when I really needed it to be. It was a week when I was realizing that my work was going to have to be personal, intimate, in a way I had been trying to avoid. It turns out that you can't really write about the future, about hope, about spirituality, without writing about yourself. Well, that's not true. People can and have. The Bible, for instance. But I can't. I'm not writing the Bible. I'm writing, on its surface, a "me text," but that's really just a self-conscious way of saying that I'm writing a "people text."

The British writer Philip Pullman said in a lecture called "The Republic of Heaven" that human beings demand meaning and joy; it is our nature. And that we have "to accept that this meaning and joy will involve a passionate love of the physical world." I do not want to be the kind of writer who can write impersonally about passionate love. Meaning and joy, by their very definition, are personal. Pullman, who has given us the trilogy His Dark Materials, says that he does not believe in God, but that he does believe in magic. He explained this contradiction as not naïve but "both believing and not believing. Skeptical about everything but credulous about everything, too."

Be open to everything until proven harmful. Not right versus wrong but harmful versus helpful. We need right and wrong, fact and fiction, but that's not all we need. If something helps you and doesn't hurt you (or any other living creatures), who cares if it can be proven? Pullman said, "I like the irrational, I like ghosts. They help me to write." He cannot prove that ghosts help him write; he also doesn't care. Neither should we.

How did Brezsny know that I needed that Frida Kahlo quote on just that day? That I needed the reminder that I could generate my own inspiration? He didn't. It's not about me, but his words helped me nonetheless. Very smart people have tried to establish proof that horoscopes can offer any tangible, specific prediction or assessment of a person based on their natal chart—literally anything at all that is irrefutable about that person or their life. And these very smart people have failed. They've also failed to not find proof. Maybe Frida was just a coincidence.

Great, what a fantastic coincidence. Maybe I read into my horoscope what I needed to hear. Great, I buoyed my own mood, my own "spirits." Good for me!

I embrace Pullman's insistence that we must accept meaning and joy and a passionate love for this physical world we occupy, including all of its people and all of their contradictions. I love people for their peculiarities and inscrutable insecurities. I love persons, what makes them personal, the complications they create, and the way all of us can feel one thing so completely one moment and then its opposite the next. I am captivated by the mysterious areas of our psyches and the things we hide from ourselves and each other. I love, much as they sting, the perceived slights and insults we are just as likely to dish out as we are to be served, because behind them are a million riddles made up of fidgeting convictions and borrowed confidences and newborn beliefs, every one helping me to write, helping me to live.

The poking and prodding at the irrational while simultaneously holding space and acceptance for it is empathy. Oh, empathy. Thanks, in large part, to the University of Houston professor and social worker Brené Brown—who has spent the better part of the last two decades researching courage, vulnerability, shame, and empathy and whose 2010 TED talk "The Power of Vulnerability" went viral—empathy has probably had the best decade of any of us. When even mindfulness has gotten the cultural side-eye, empathy stands apart in its consistent popularity and untarnished image. You could say a bad word about it, but I guarantee your humanity stock will take a hit and no one will care.

I didn't make the connection between empathy and fortune-tellers until I started interviewing psychics, many of whom have chosen to ditch the word *psychic* altogether for *empath*, preferring to think of themselves as highly empathetic individuals. In another time, they might instead have chosen to refer to themselves as healers. Or, if they were feeling spiritedly cheeky, as social workers. But they don't call themselves those things now. They have learned to distance themselves from those labels and to take up the seemingly faultless, the entirely innocent-sounding, descriptor *empath*. Psychiatrist Judith Orloff, who is a member of the UCLA psychiatric clinical faculty and the author of the book *The Empath's Survival Guide*, describes an empath as "an emotional sponge. [Empaths] absorb the emotions, physical symptoms, and energy of others into their own bodies."

No matter what they answer to, when you get right down to it, when you break down what it is they believe they are capable of and what service they believe they are providing, empaths, and their brethren "intuitives," are what you and I have always thought of as psychics. If being psychic is defined as being able to read and know the psyche of another, to have extra-ordinary perception of the people and energy around them, an empath is just someone who has those skills because they have an exceptional ability to empathize, to innately understand and embody the past or present feelings, thoughts, and experiences of other people. I've noticed that the psychics who prefer to be called empaths (or intuitives) tend to be harder to spot in the wild. They blend in better. They wear fewer caftans and more skinny jeans. They eat less tofu and more organic, grass-fed beef.

Through a series of interviews and research hopscotch, I tracked down one highly regarded empath-intuitive in Hawaii named Michelle Sinnette.

Michelle's work with her clients looks, on the surface, a lot like talk therapy. Clients have sessions with her, usually over the phone, because most of us do not live in Hawaii. During these sessions, Michelle and the client both work to help the client address whatever issues they are having, whatever is standing between them and their "highest and best." Unlike therapy, however, when a client starts talking, "their guides" start talking, too. These guides, as have been explained to me and as I have come to understand their definition, are beings who have never lived here among us but who are an integral part of the fabric of the universe and who exist specifically to help us. Such that, a client's personal guides provide Michelle with insights and information the client needs to hear. The information, though, is just a starting point.

During that first conversation, I somehow came to tell Michelle what another intuitive I interviewed told me, that I had to be careful with this book, not to go too far down the woo-woo rabbit hole, because it could discredit my reputation as a writer and kill my career. Her warning rattled me. As I confessed to Michelle, this other woman had given voice to my precise fear. I hadn't told anyone that this was something I was worried about (though it is a pretty obvious guess), but she had identified it within minutes of meeting me. By articulating it, she also made it all the more real. Suddenly it felt less like a warning or a fear and more like something that might be fated. Like I needed to run around the room and knock on all the wood.

I hadn't planned on sharing this incident with Michelle or anything personal with her, in fact. I had called her to ask her about how she approaches her work and her process with her clients, but somehow I found myself sharing—and almost not entirely of my own intuition, either. Michelle had set the tone for our conversation. Which is another thing I wasn't used to as the interviewer. She was the interviewee; I had expected her to follow my lead. We had been speaking for less than a minute, and I was just beginning my introductory spiel about my project and this work when she asked me, very politely, to pause. "Victoria, can you hang on a sec?"

I stopped. I thought maybe she had to let her cat outside (I assumed she had a cat).

Something about the way she asked made me think it had nothing to do with me but that the outside world was momentarily intruding. Only she was still on the line, silently. I could feel her there, the way you feel when someone enters a room behind you. It was not a creepy, psycho sensation but a still, meditative one. When she did speak again, she said, "Victoria, could you take three big breaths for me?" I did, and she listened, and then she said, "Okay, thank you. I wanted you to slow down, so you can be fully present for our call and get what you need." Everything shifted. All the tension, all the tightly wound focus I had brought to this professional interview, dissolved. I found what Hunter calls "silence growing on the tongue." My body fell very quiet.

This could have been a ploy. It could have also been an effective use case for that long body of research that science and medicine have given us about the power of taking deep breaths. Or, it could have been both. Regardless, it worked like a charm, and Michelle and I began again. Eventually I told her what this other intuitive in New York had told me, that I couldn't go too far out there, because it would make me look illegitimate when the book was published. I told Michelle that this warning hit a nerve, made me nervous, afraid even, and she responded by saying, "Beautiful." To which, with silence fully grown on my tongue, I thought to myself, *Wait, what?* She continued almost as if she had heard my internal question. "Well, it is beautiful she did that. She said it because it's inside you so well and because that's her thing. That's how people create dependency, by inviting you into some kind of fear . . . It did hit a point, so it was a fear, so it brought that fear right out into the light. And now, thanks to her, it reiterates to you that that's not the way to go. Here's where we were talking [earlier] about serving false gods, so to speak."

And here's where Michelle said something that hit me as hard as the fear of writing a book that will tarnish the career I want to have: "Were you born . . . were you literally born only to have a reputation with people who are all going to die soon? Is that the reason you were born? If you think about the millions of things that had to align for your soul to be . . . Did all the stars and all the powers of the universe align so that you can have a reputation in America as a writer?"

"You gain the power of not giving a [expletive]."

Michelle said later that people spend most of their time creating just to avoid pain. And I wrote it down, even though I was recording our conversation, because it struck me that when I started this book I thought I was writing a prescription, creating a piece of "helpful art," *art with a purpose*, all in order to help myself (and others) avoid pain. Do this, based on this research and this sociological study, and you'll feel better; life won't hurt so terribly, for so long. But now Michelle was suggesting that's not the "right" problem to solve. Pain isn't the problem. It's creating from fear of pain that is the problem.

I assume that creating without fear must involve a lot of meditation, a lot of recitation of poetry and philosophy, the imagery and ideas of Rumi and Attar, beguiling words, about rejecting the self, wisdom that goes back to the medieval Sufi saints and sages. A great deal of silence and contemplating of God or the Mother Spirit or whomever or whatever. Across traditions, for centuries, the self has been understood to be an impediment to God, to love, to embracing and accepting every living thing and being. I assume that self-denial and sacrifice are the only ways to finding and maintaining my "highest and best" as a being moving through the world alongside every other creature.

From Gilgamesh's story to the philosophy of Aristotle to Nietzsche, everyone is trying to figure out what the hell is going on. Historically, we've tried to answer that question with theology, philosophy, literature, and, now, positive psychology. Esfahani Smith writes in *The Power of Meaning* that meaning and the ancient Greek word *eudaemonic*, or human flourishing, are, together, the path to a life of satisfaction and fulfillment. "Leading a eudaemonic life, Aristotle argued, requires cultivating the best qualities within you both morally and intellectually and living up to your potential." I read this passage in Esfahani Smith's book weeks after my first conversation with Michelle, who has had former careers in social work and law enforcement and who culturally and circumstantially is about as far from the Greek philosophers as you and I are, but Aristotle and Michelle were twinning. She told me that she was not interested in whether or not she made a client feel good—like Aristotle not believing life is about the pursuit of happiness—but rather about doing good work with her clients.

"My desire is to work with people to open up their own intuition, to hear their own guides, to return back to their instinctual being so that they literally live their life in alignment with their soul rather than their fears, or their ego, or their brain chemistry, and all the 'shoulds.'"

Michelle asks herself and her clients to constantly ask the question: "Is it in the highest and best?" The *it* here being everything, every thought, every action, every person, every decision. The ancient Greek word *hedonic* can be translated as basically "feeling good," Esfahani Smith writes, whereas *eudaemonic* is doing good and "seeking to use and develop the best in oneself." Always moving in the direction of our highest and best without ego, without self, but almost certainly, at least sometimes, with pain. The more we attempt to dodge pain, the more pain we invite onto our path.

Those *highest and bests*, those *shoulds* come up constantly in life. When we go to psychics or even just when we contemplate a big decision on our own or with our closest friends, we default to should. We ask our psychics and ourselves: *Should I quit this job? Should I marry this person? Should I move to California or Timbuktu?* Michelle told me that when clients ask her these questions, they aren't asking what they really mean. What they're really trying to ask is *Will I be happy if I quit this job? Will I be happy if I marry this person? Will I be happy in California?* But since they don't ask those questions, she doesn't answer them. She answers the should question that is presented to her, even though the should and the happy aren't always one and the same.

Let's say you go to Michelle, and you ask her if you should buy this house you and your spouse like. And she says, Yes, you should. So you do. But six months later, a trio of burglars break in, tie you and your partner up, and take all of your most valuable possessions. After this trauma, your partner seems to bounce back but you have PTSD and aren't able to work for a year and eventually you and your partner divorce. Seems like maybe moving into that house wasn't such a great idea.

But, then, you get a job in another city and you move and your new job and new city are a much better fit for you, and you find a wonderful yoga studio whose classes really help with your PTSD and there you bond with the owner over your shared, and embarrassing, love of ordering pineapple on pizza, and she, in turn, introduces you to her neighbor, and the two of you fall in love and you get married, and it's so much better than your first marriage. And you live happily ever after. (Just kidding. Life is still hard, because that's life, but everything is richer and truer than it used to be.) So, yeah, you never spent a happy night in that house, but you absolutely *should* have moved into it.

Also, though. Respect. Way to cover your ass, Michelle.

CHAPTER TWELVE

In Hunter's course, the study of the archetypes associated with each sun sign begins with Aries in week one and ends with Pisces in week twelve. Hunter describes them as "impersonal archetypes that flow—in different proportions at different times—through everyone." Now *that* is a good rebuttal to the completely sound observation that there is no scientific evidence for astrology.

In his "Prayer for Liberation," the week of Gemini, day five, Hunter calls on his students to recognize that we are all "enslaved by these stressful me-stories." (This doesn't bode well for a memoirist.) The only freedom from these "me-stories," he says, is returning to "pure awareness" by "ventilating all stuffy, mental concepts about who I am with story-less presence and luminosity."

He goes on to ask that we earn the right to speak, which has, most immediately, an alienating, feather-ruffling connotation. *Excuse me, earn the right to speak? I have the right to speak, thank you very much, Mr. I-Have-the-Whitest-Man-Name-Ever. Who are you to hunt me down and try to prevent me from speaking?* My edge softens, however, when I learn the one rule of this game: "Shut up until you feel their suffering . . . If you can't feel someone's suffering, you're not qualified to speak, because you are not fully comprehending who it is you're speaking to."

Damn, that's good. It also seems hard to do if you're impurely aware, if your head is stuck up your own ass. The game Hunter is asking us to play is the empathy game, and the prize for getting your head in the game is meaning. There is no meaning without empathy.

But what if passing judgement, what if speaking *before* you feel someone else's suffering serves a valuable purpose, too? Every couple I know, including every couple I've ever been 50 percent of, talks to each other about other couples. You and your partner talk about your sister and her girlfriend, about your best friend and her partner, about your boyfriend's old roommate and his new wife. When you talk about these other couples, you discuss the apartment or the house they've chosen to make their home, about the kind of car they've bought, about the neighborhood and the city they've chosen to drive in or live in, about whether or not they have kids or will have kids, about where they go on vacation, about what she said at dinner and what he didn't say at the party. And you feel none of their suffering when you do.

Why do we do this? Because we're compassionless sociopaths? Unlikely. Because we're insecure and need to feel superior? Likely. Because we've recognized that other couples have made different choices, that they want different things from what we want and we seek to reaffirm that our partner is on our team, that the two of us want the same things and are a unit? Most likely. We figure out the kind of life we want to lead, the kind of person we want to be, by examining the choices the people around us have made.

Then again, maybe the whole exercise is futile. The vast majority of us end up in the same place regardless, and the gap between you and your friends, the gap you prided yourself on for so long, will close, if it was ever really there to begin with.

A colleague and I were once on a work trip together when we got stuck in traffic on the way to the airport. At five minutes before we had hoped to arrive at our terminal, we were still twenty minutes away. All of the worry that could be manifested was, shall we say, emanating from my person, and the driver and my coworker could both, without question, feel its weight. My colleague turned to me and said, "Relax, we're not late."

I gave her the look of death and replied, "What are you talking about?"

She, in turn, gave me the most pitiful glance and said, "We never planned to be at the airport yet. In six minutes, we'll be late, but we're still fine *right now*."

Don't worry until you have to. Even then, don't worry. Because once you reach the moment in which it might, just might, finally be appropriate to be legitimately concerned, you can act. You can begin to shift your next steps as necessary. And, for what it is worth, my coworker and I caught our flight.

Rebecca Solnit wrote that "to be lost is to be fully present, and to be fully present is to be capable of being in uncertainty and mystery."

Let's say you're twenty-nine or thirty-seven or forty-five, and you "arrive," whatever that means for you—a certain title or award, a certain salary, a certain kind of home, a certain number of kids, etc. Great. Good for you. You still have, hopefully, half a life left to live out. That's a whole lot of time to just kick it on arrival. Psychics, tarot-card readers, and astrologers tell me that the vast majority of the people who come to them ask the same questions. They are all questions that hinge on the idea of arriving and the fear that we won't: Will I get this promotion, should I look for a new job, am I ever going to find a partner, will we have a baby? Job. Mate. Baby. That's it.

When I was younger, I wanted excitement and distinction. Now I care about history. The history that's already happened, absolutely, but also the history I'm building with the people I love and the work I do, my history in the making, my future history. I used to so desperately want to be interesting, but I never asked myself why. Why do I need to be special? Why do I think I need some big me-story? The truth is that I don't. I'll tell you what's interesting. Commonality. It's interesting to have and to hold empathy with another human being. Empathy, when you look for it, is easy to find. You realize we are equally afraid.

Most of my friends, the women I spent a good deal of my twenties with, appear to have "arrived." I have spent the last several years going to their engagement parties and their bachelorette parties and their weddings and their baby showers and their BBQs in their new homes. And now they don't reach out the way they used to, not as often, and when they do, they send a half-hearted *Miss you* text and never respond when I reply suggesting coffee or a drink. I know it's because they're juggling careers and small children and long commutes and marriages and in-laws, but that doesn't take the sting out of it. I see now how tempting it is to just join them. To get married and have babies, so we're doing the same thing, going through the same challenges and rewards at nearly the same time, just as we did ten years ago when we were twenty-two years old and real nitwits.

This question of arriving, when I might and if I should and why am I so worried, formed and hardened throughout 2017, when the political climate, domestically and internationally, all darkened. This volatile, alarming year full of trauma that wasn't mine brought this highly personal question into high relief. It is also a large part of the reason the astrology content of Susan Miller, the AstroTwins, and *New York* magazine's The Cut all saw such spikes in traffic and engagement.

2017 has been a dark year, dark not as in evil but as in a year of shadow. When I interviewed Lindsay Mack, we talked about the many millennials who have come to her for tarot and intuitive readings this year, and she described our present reality as shadowed. "The shadow is a mirror to some aspect of ourselves that we really need to see or need to make peace with or understand before we can shift it. The shadow is important because without it, there is no light. Without it, there is no understanding."

This is not a new concept, of course, and it is one that is often understood in a deeply personal way. But it is equally applicable to our communities.

"Where we are really going as a collective," Lindsay went on, "is transcendence of the shadow, which doesn't mean acting perfectly. It means understanding that everything is equal. Everything is the light. Everything is an understanding. In our culture, there is so much shame about sexuality and mental illness and a lack of understanding about rights, race, religion, and beliefs—all of that is shadow work. A lot of people are asleep, and it's important to hold a space for people for when they are ready to wake up."

And what does it mean to wake up? It means to truly feel what you've done. It's the process of atonement.

My friend Mary and I went on a walk in Central Park, right before Thanksgiving, right before winter became a cruel, mirthless miser of the sun's warmth and the idea of walking around the reservoir still sounded pleasant and not like a human rights violation. On that walk, Mary said something wise, as she often does. This time it was about everyone being so eager to arrive, which, if I recall correctly, was "Everyone is so eager to arrive." Her implication being that maybe we shouldn't be so eager. Maybe that is in fact another backward goal.

Maybe the secret is to never arrive, is to pray hard and fierce to God or Spirit or whatever that I never get all the things—and as I recite this prayer, to remember what an extraordinary privilege such a prayer is.

And in place of all that worry and all that wondering if and when I'll arrive, I ask instead: Am I asleep or am I awake?

Claudia Rankine writes in her stunning book *Citizen* about the beating in 1991 of Rodney King, an unarmed black man in Los Angeles, and the shooting and death of Mark Duggan, an unarmed black man in North London, in 2011. She could have written about another who came between them: James Byrd Jr., an unarmed black man, who was beaten and urinated on and then dragged behind a truck for a mile and a half until his head was severed in June 1998 in Jasper, Texas. 1991. 1998. 2011. And she could have kept going, written about one for every decade past or published an updated edition about those who have come since, because in 2015 unarmed black people were five times more likely to be killed by police than unarmed whites. But Rankine didn't, because she had other topics to cover in her book, other atrocities, and because once you start down that path, where/when/how do you ever stop? Which is not the question Rankine asks, because she already knows that answer. No, she asks, "How difficult is it for one body to feel the injustice wheeled at another?"

Maybe so difficult that you shut up for life. Never earning the right to speak, never arriving, never tricking yourself into thinking you have earned anything. Or it is the opposite, not difficult at all, because our bodies have been side by side all along. How do you read the details of what happened to James Byrd Jr. and not feel your cheeks flush, your chest constrict, your throat close and want it not to have happened, want never to have heard of James Byrd Jr., because he lived out his life with his son beautifully, uneventfully? If the three young white supremacists who tortured and murdered James Byrd Jr. had not been able to feel James's suffering, would they have bothered to harm him? If they had not understood the pain they were inflicting, what would have been their point?

Some fifteen pages later, on a different topic, but not really, because it's all one, Rankine describes a crowded train ride with a single empty seat, only a black man sits in the seat beside it, so the white woman hovering above does not sit. But Rankine, a black woman, does. The white woman sits when another seat becomes available, a seat that does not make her uneasy. Rankine and the man beside her sit shoulder to shoulder but do not speak, do not acknowledge the world as it is, as it has always been. Rankine understands her part: "You sit next to the man on the train, bus, in the plane, waiting room, anywhere he could be forsaken. You put your body there in proximity to, adjacent to, alongside, within . . . You don't speak unless you are spoken to and your body speaks to the space you fill and you keep trying to fill it except the space belongs to the body of the man next to you, not to you."

The most powerful thing I can do is open my eyes, shut my mouth, and sit down.

CHAPTER THIRTEEN

I do not make a habit of paying attention to Lent, but its annual arrival is unmissable because Ash Wednesday is so savvy with its ashy-forehead advertising campaign. And I have enough relatives who do pay attention to it and adhere to it that I am also inevitably made aware of what each of them has chosen to give up for the season of Lent. The last time I personally thought seriously about Lent was when I was nine years old, and my least favorite teacher at my elementary school asked me, quite sternly as I recall, what I had given up. I said sex. At that age, giving up sex was a piece of cake. This year, I decided to partake in Lent again. I did not, however, give up sex. That would no longer be a piece of cake.

What I did decide to give up was no picnic, either. I decided to stop giving advice.

Unless, that is, someone asked me explicitly for my opinion, for what I might do in their shoes, then I could go nuts with guidance. Funny thing about that: people very rarely actually ask. Maybe that's because everyone else is always so eager to offer.

If people want something, anything, from you—advice, love, sex, friendship, time—they'll almost certainly find a way to let you know. So, I just stopped. I wasn't without my slips. There were a couple of occasions when I couldn't help myself, but, by and large, I didn't do it.

Here's what I learned.

It's hard not to give advice. It's hard to sit with a friend and listen to them recount a difficulty they are experiencing and to have no recourse beyond your listening ability. When you're not offering a solution or thinking about the solution you're about to offer, there is nothing to do but focus on what the person in front of you is saying, focus on the pain and confusion and fear they are expressing and know that you can't take it away, can't be the hero rushing in to fix everything. That it is not about you.

Anne Lamott writes in her book *Hallelujah Anyway* that "there is such depth to listening, and an exchange, like an echo from inside a canyon, when friends have listened to me at my most hopeless. They heard. Someone heard, heard what was happening, what was true and painful, when the center would not hold."

She is talking about bearing witness to someone else's experience, which may be the greatest gift we can give each other, to show up for another human being by acknowledging what they are going through. This is another way of holding space for people. It sounds simple. It is not. The impulse is to interrupt in the name of offering assistance, but in actuality this is only in the name of alleviating your own discomfort, in fulfilling your own desire to be needed and appreciated, and, in the process, taking away the other person's agency. This is not bearing witness. This is bearing a responsibility that is not yours to bear. This is making it about you.

Which is why it is also liberating not to give advice. Forget about yourself. You are not taking a test. You don't have to know the answer! I got a lot better at bearing witness, and I think I was a better friend. I became a safer friend. For at least a couple of people who told me so explicitly, I became a friend they could call knowing I would hear them out. In the silence, in the space I was holding but not filling, my friends could fill in their own gaps, find their own answers.

And if they didn't, I discovered that asking an extremely pointed question is a great way to offer advice on the sly. The deliberate inquiry was my Lenten loophole.

Writing is an exploration, and it is an exercise in humility, because when you write you eventually come face-to-face with all the things you do not know, which is most everything.

When this happens, a writer must abandon the solitude of their desk and pick up the phone or open the door, and find the people who do know the latest thing they've realized they do not. It's awesome.

Frequently, when I am interviewing someone and I ask them a question, I get an answer that has little to do with what I asked. But it is an answer to something, and that something often ends up being important to whatever it is I am trying to figure out. If I'm going to be a good writer, I have to be wide-open to listening, to really listening. This has long been my writing philosophy, but Lent, along with the people I interviewed for this book, helped teach me that it's also a good life philosophy.

One of the first things that Dr. Sarah Bamford Seidelmann told me was that "the best healers, no matter where they're working, whether they're a Reiki person or an acupuncturist or a doctor or a neurosurgeon or a therapist, they're listening. And I mean they're sensing, and that's really at its essence what shamanism is."

Every shaman, empath, and astrologer I have spoken to brings up listening, just that verb, that action, how vital, how sacred, the act of listening is. What they are trying to get me to understand is that they are not religious leaders or spiritual healers. They might not even be empaths so much as they are listeners. It's what my very first interviewees, Andrea and Reesha, in their way, were telling me. I just wasn't listening yet. I said this to Sarah, that I have underestimated the power of listening, and she responded by telling me a story:

"The first time that I ever saw a shaman working, I was in South Africa with a friend, and we had an opportunity to meet with the Sangoma [the diviner], which is kind of their traditional form of shaman there . . . So, we went and crawled into a little hut with these three women, and they threw bones for us. And we kind of told them what we were worried about in our lives. And then after they did the reading, we kind of crawled out of the hut, and they started to play these drums. There were like sixty people who had come from the area . . . And then they crawled out of the huts and danced and kind of merged with . . . they were like dancing spirits, basically. And I remember just sitting there with tears streaming down my face, going, *I don't know what this is, or what is going on here, but all I know is how incredible to go with a problem to somebody and to have them listen to you like that, and then to have them dance like that, and all these people to show up just to witness.* I couldn't even imagine. Even if nothing was happening in the spirit world, and that really wasn't real, this was real. This experience of really circling the wagons around somebody and showing them such attention and how much you care."

Every time I tell someone about this book, that I'm writing about psychics and shamans, there is about a 50 percent chance that their eyes will darken. It calls to mind a garage door rolling down and locking shut with a thud. What was an open, lively chat between two friends or colleagues shifts. Now the person I am talking to, who has asked about my work, my next project, is no longer open. They have closed up shop early and gone home for the day, despite their still standing beside me, our conversation halting to and fro.

They believe all psychics scam people. They think all shamans lead cults. They have no interest in these ideas or any book that is the end result of such an examination. They are judging me for choosing, of all the worthy topics in the world, one that is completely devoid of value. M. told me that when people ask him about my new book, and he gives them a brief summary, he finds himself also reassuring whomever he is speaking to. "No, no, Victoria's cool. She's not, like, weird."

For a time, I dreaded talking about this project. I could see the question, the exchange, coming, and I would try to steer the conversation in another direction, about their work, or maybe nobody's work, some completely separate topic as far from work or career as possible, like GMOs or Syria, anything important and serious and so consuming that the conversation would have a tough time winding back to what I do all day. It was painful otherwise, especially when the person I was talking to was someone I knew and respected and whose opinion mattered to me.

Being a wide-open listener as a writer or just as a "lifer" means being wide-open to criticism and doubt, not as things to internalize and hold me back but as facts of life. It's a bird, it's a plane, it's criticism!

An acquaintance of mine has a saying that I've adopted. One summer, she and her husband decided to spontaneously get out of New York City for a few days. Neither of them had ever been to Nantucket, so they went to Nantucket. All week, whenever they were deciding what to do or where to go next on their spur-of-the-moment vacation, they chose the option they knew the least about. They started calling such choices "Fuck it, Nantucket." Years later, it remains a shorthand between them whenever they're facing a tough decision or feeling overwhelmed. That's how I've come to view reactions to this book. *Fuck it, Nantucket.* For me, it's a shorthand for what I think Michelle was trying to get me to see, that living out of my alignment and in fear or with my ego is exhausting and unproductive and fails to serve a meaningful purpose.

That the secret is learning, somehow, to listen, remain open, and not give a [expletive] all at the same time.

CHAPTER FOURTEEN

Manifestation is the principle that energies attract like energies. It's part of the Law of Attraction, the belief that if your thoughts are positive, your experiences will be, too. It's the elevator pitch of the film and subsequent book *The Secret* that everyone, led by Oprah, lost their minds over in 2006. It's the idea that if you visualize what you want, if you write it down in exacting language, if you create a mood board of it and set your glorious intention out into the universe, your desire will be realized. It's a concept that has garnered enough buzz in recent years that entrepreneurs like Lacy Phillips, the so-called manifestation expert behind the lifestyle blog *Free and Native*, can build an entire career on it. Manifestation has manifested itself right into boundless popularity.

Lacy subscribes to the philosophy that manifesting is much more than just thinking about what you want and then hanging out until it materializes. She teaches the theory that authentic manifestation must begin first with what she calls unblocking, going "into the depths of your subconscious in order to unblock your limiting beliefs and expand your structure of beliefs to clear space for your manifested subjects to connect with you." Got that? If you want to attract strong, positive energies, you have to be strong, positive energy. Or, rather, you have to resolve your issues with your mom before you can manifest your dream apartment.

Should you decide to dip your toe in manifestation's bottomless internet presence, you will learn that you can manifest not only the roof over your head but also your soul mate, a better job, a fancy car, and even the Céline bag you've been eyeing. Let's suppose the internet knows what it's talking about and it is possible to manipulate the universe this way and you and I can get what we think we want. Then what?

Michelle, my favorite intuitive, both asked this question and answered it.

"Then you have to run on the rat wheel, constantly trying to keep whatever it is you manifested. Don't get it; go be who you came here to be. Be magnificently in alignment, and you won't even have to go get it."

While she gives credit to *The Secret* for reminding people to pay more attention to the spiritual, Michelle also makes the point that *The Secret* never stops to address the why or the should. "Just because you *can* manifest a mansion, should you? Is that really in integrity, in alignment, in the highest and best for all? Is it even what you came here to be or will it distract you?"

I haven't seen the movie or read the book *The Secret*, nor do I have any intention of doing so. Other than what I've gleaned from pop-culture headlines, I know very little about it. If someone thinks it was valuable for them, had some positive impact on their life, cool. Most things, especially those that are not indisputably cruel, have the potential to serve some means of purpose to someone, somewhere. I am interested in possibility, not grading different kinds of work or philosophies and saying this one is good and this one is bad. When I made this point to Michelle, she told me that she loved this idea, and then she broke it down in an even more straightforward way: "A real simple way to address it is there's nothing to fear. We don't need to fear fast food. We can choose fast food until we want to choose alive food. There's nothing to fear. That fast food is never going to be more powerful than alive food. The only thing that makes it powerful in your individual life is if you consume it all day. You give it you. You give it your attention. But we never have to fear it. It's silly."

When we go to a psychic or an empath, we go because we hope they will give us some kind of insight into our future selves, and we imagine the information they share to be the endgame. *Tell me she loves me; tell me I'm going to be successful; tell me I'll parent a healthy baby someday.* But whatever we do with the information remains entirely up to us and whatever tools we already have at our disposal, in our own personal arsenals, the ones we've been building all our lives in response to all the times they didn't love us and we weren't successful. That's Free Will Astrology.

Michelle is offering something else.

"I don't promise people anything but 100 percent integrity. I don't sugarcoat anything. I'm really blunt. If I see you're going to die on Tuesday morning, it's like, 'Okay, you're going to die Tuesday morning. Let's make a plan. Let's handle it. Let's get your paperwork in order.' Or if they're never going to have a partner or they're never going to have a child, then I'm just like, 'It's not going to happen.'"

If I knew I was going to die on Tuesday morning, I'm pretty sure paperwork is the last thing I'd be thinking about. But I get her point. Or do I?

Let's assume, for argument's sake, that psychic ability, that the ability to know if someone is going to meet and fall in love with and build a life with a wonderful partner in the next six months or in three years or never, is possible. What's the point in learning that? Most people don't go see a psychic the day they win the lottery. If we go see a psychic at all, we go when we're vulnerable, when we're scared, when we've been told that it's just not working out. We go when we feel our bleakest, because we hope we'll be told the future is going to be better. And why do we care whether or not our future is better?

Because believing our future is good makes us feel better *right now*. So going to see a psychic is not actually about the future at all. It's about the present. It's the quick, instant fix we're after.

Knowing we are going to die this Tuesday or that we're going to get divorced someday is not the kind of encouraging "your future is very bright" news most of us want to hear. What's the benefit? Is it better to be able to pencil in your death at 10:15 a.m. next Tuesday, or are we better off assuming that we'll be able to meet friends for drinks that night? Michelle said if you know you're going to die on Tuesday, you can make a plan, get your forms in order, but we all know we're going to die at some point. We're supposed to already have the plans in place, the living wills, the dotted *i*'s and crossed *t*'s, the signatures, the paperwork. Not to mention that people have been dying pretty successfully since before paper was even invented. I thought visiting a psychic was about hope, but Michelle is adamant that she isn't in the business of selling hope, only reality. It is news to me that this is marketable.

"If I don't know something, I just say, 'I don't know,'" Michelle told me. "I'm really blunt like that as well. I don't do any interpretive stuff, because everybody is their own expert. They know. When the soul hears the truth, it rings like a bell. You can feel it in your body when you're hearing something that is true. I work with [my clients] to really know their truth and to feel that. They're going to know more than I ever could what really is true for them."

This idea of finding what's true for you or me is really the idea of finding what Michelle would call our soul purpose and what many people I know would just call our purpose—as if the idea of having a defined, destined purpose were totally kosher and of the utmost rationality. Just don't put the word *soul* in front of said purpose. That's when you've gone too far.

Soul or no soul, why we are here as sentient beings, as individuals in this or that way, in this time, in this space, and not as someone else in another time or another space is the sole question. Everyone, every community institution, be it governmental or religious or the gang around the first fire or the last watercooler, has been trying to answer that since human beings were capable of thought. Michelle points out that we usually associate this question and its answer with what we're going to *do*.

Hunter argues that we underestimate the importance of spontaneously capturing, articulating, and acting "on our immediate experience free of outdated agendas and overly worshipped abstractions like 'purpose' and 'ultimate meaning.'" He is arguing in favor of the "moment-to-moment" truth, being fully present in a moment instead of trapped in a larger idea or philosophy.

Michelle believes that our moment-to-moment truth and our soul purpose are not about our jobs or what we "do" and are also not mutually exclusive. "People will seek their soul purpose, because they're uncomfortable, and they want to know what they're supposed to be doing." We want a road map; we want someone to tell us what to do. "But truly learning your soul purpose is actually fine-tuning what you channel, because that's actually who you are *being* on the planet."

It's so much easier to do something than to be something.

"We're constantly emitting a frequency out across the ripple of consciousness twenty-four hours a day. With every thought, with every breath, you are literally throwing a stone and sending ripples out all the time. When you get all the way down to the core, that's identifying the channel that you came here to be . . . It's really getting in alignment with that so that you are, as much as possible, sending out the frequency you came here to send out, the invitation you came here to be . . . Who did you come here to be? What do you stand for? Then how do you express that throughout, through whatever your thing is, for now?"

That *for now* strikes me as crucial. We act like our purpose is finite. Like it's a cut-and-dry answer we only need to learn once and then we will know forever. We get fixated on the instrument. This is where Michelle's philosophy intersects with Hunter's moment-to-moment truth: your soul purpose will evolve; it will take on different forms and virtues. Just because my soul purpose was to write this book or three books doesn't mean I will only ever write books. Finding your soul purpose isn't a onetime exercise. *Sweet, all set here, now I know my reason for being, let's wrap this up, ship it, and treat ourselves at that Nayarit-Sinaloan restaurant Jonathan Gold has been raving about.*

Nope. The work is ongoing and ever present. We can trust in this, at least, from Hal Boyle: "What makes a river so restful to people is that it doesn't have any doubt—it is sure to get where it is going, and it doesn't want to go anywhere else." You will get where you are going, and there is nowhere else you want to go than where your soul purpose and your moment-to-moment truth are taking you.

CHAPTER FIFTEEN

It makes complete and utter sense to me that psychics, shamans, and astrologers have been embraced and interwoven into the current wellness trend, that they have their own interviews and recommendations and tabs on Gwyneth Paltrow's Goop website, alongside the organic mascaras, the leaky-gut tinctures, and the restorative brunch recipes. Visiting a psychic or having an astrologer read your natal chart is just another form of so-called self-improvement, so-called self-care. Just another form of control, attempted.

On a late-fall afternoon in a downtown Manhattan neighborhood, the actor Fisher Stevens walked into the coffee shop where I had holed up to write and drink chamomile tea. When he entered, I looked up, my gaze lingering, because he had that famous-person energy; namely, he was wearing a cap pulled awkwardly low and sunglasses unnecessarily large, and he removed neither as he approached the counter. He had the build and the profile and the hair, what I could see of it anyway, to suggest he was Fisher. But it was not until he spoke that I knew it was him. "Are the vegan energy balls gluten-free?" According to the barista, they were not, and Fisher regrettably declined to purchase one.

It's never enough. I want vegan and gluten-free and sugar-free and healthy fats only, and even those in minimal quantities and with as little sodium as possible. And I know Fisher and I are not the only ones.

Some of us fixate on physical improvement and a so-called healthy lifestyle because eating a restrictive diet and maintaining a rigid exercise regimen are easier than addressing our anxieties and shortcomings or admitting our soul purpose continues to elude us. We hunger for control, and so we manifest that control.

I cannot talk about psychics without talking about orthorexia.

From the Greek *ortho*, which means "correct," and *orexia*, which means "appetite," orthorexia is the concept of a "correct diet" or of "perfect eating." (*Anorexia*, also from the Greek, translates as "without appetite.") Orthorexia is not a clinical diagnosis and is not currently recognized by the American Psychiatric Association, but the National Eating Disorders Association defines it as "an obsession with proper or 'healthful' eating" and elaborates that "while being aware of and concerned with the nutritional quality of the food you eat isn't a problem in and of itself, people with orthorexia become so fixated on so-called 'healthy eating' that they actually damage their own well-being." Paging irony!

My hyperawareness of nutritional health, physical well-being, and environmental protection (because, no, evidently, I could not pick just one obsession) began with wanting to lessen my carbon footprint by going vegetarian. It seemed innocuous at the time. For many people, vegetarianism is a healthful part of their lives.

But for me it was a gateway drug to the unwell side of the wellness industry, the social media–driven, highly lucrative complex that has exploded in the last decade and is catnip for anyone prone to perfectionism or anxiety or addiction or all three. It's a far-reaching industry that incorporates both proponents of banning all animal products from your plate and those who champion eating only grass-fed, organic beef straight from the farmer who pulled the calf from its mother only to slaughter it for dinner weeks later. It's an industry that warns against the dangers of gluten and sugar and advocates sprinkling fermented seeds on your micro greens and snacking on activated maca walnuts. It's a trend that will take you from an Instagram post suggesting you hydrate with "high-vibe" (and high-price) charcoal water to a post announcing a celebrity life coach's new line of manifestation crystals.

This wellness industry, at which Gwyneth Paltrow and her Goop empire and Amanda Chantal Bacon of the Moon Juice brand are perched, glowing and thin, at the helm, is a proponent of not just replacing your morning bagel with a nondairy turmeric smoothie but also of replacing your therapy sessions and evening nightcap with a shaman and a warm adaptogens tonic. Bonus that none of this is cheap or covered by insurance.

I have always been somewhat slender, but in the years since becoming an adult who could supposedly take care of herself, there have been times when it was difficult for people to look at me. I have, on occasion, been the kind of thin that results from adhering to a diet that makes ordering off of a restaurant menu virtually impossible and from following an exercise routine that permits barely a rest afternoon. The kind of thin where the only cheating you're doing is cheating yourself.

I got this kind of thin following, first, a vegetarian diet and then a vegan one; I no longer allowed myself to eat any animal products. No dairy. No eggs. No meat. No fish. Then I stopped drinking alcohol and caffeine. I gave up sugar. And gluten. All packaged, processed foods—if it came in a can or a bag or plastic of any kind, I wanted nothing to do with it. I was left to meet my caloric needs with legumes (but only if they had been soaked before being cooked); sprouted nuts; organic, seasonal vegetables; and specific, minimal locally grown fruits.

I ate an inordinate amount of massaged kale, soaked chickpeas, and sprouted almonds in order not to die.

I began my descent into orthorexia in the months after I finished and submitted my first book to my publisher. I had written a memoir about my relationship with my father that I was exhilarated to be having published and also completely, paralyzingly terrified to have given life to. It was 2013, and I suddenly had no more pressing deadlines but instead a pressing inclination for a new distraction and ideal timing: the wellness industry was picking up steam, and I had a well-scrolled Instagram account ripe for its message. I didn't know it, but I was also about to become even more susceptible, even more vulnerable, to its sales pitch.

When my book came out, some members of my family were upset by a particular passage I had written that delicately alluded to a decades-old truth we had chosen not to address. I included it because the reference made it easier to empathize with my father, and I wanted readers to understand him, to accept him in death in all the ways he never felt accepted in life. That passage, that entire book, was an invitation to my family to move with me out of our multi-generational grief and into self-acceptance. I know we cannot heal each other. I know we can only ever heal ourselves. I had hoped that my family and I could support each other in our individual healing. We could not. And in pain, I grew a new source of sorrow, becoming heavy with sadness for them and sadness for myself.

That was also the year when the fissures in my long relationship with B. became impossible to continue to ignore. He, several years my senior, was talking more and more about our future, about moving, about having children. Some part of me understood that he and I should not have children together. I could see that each of us was capable of being a good parent on our own, with other partners, but I could not see us as good coparents.

And though I badly wanted to be a writer and to think of myself as a writer, I could not find any words to say what I needed to say, to make anything right between B. and me or between my family and me. It didn't help that B. was emphatic that I was handling my family's rejection wrong, that I should force a relationship with them, whether they wanted one with me or not, that family was paramount no matter what they said or did or didn't say or didn't do.

I believe in family. I believe in integrity more.

For me, the loss of my father's family meant losing my dad all over again. For B., my willingness to let my family go made him anxious about our relationship. His disapproval of how I chose to handle the situation hit me like another rejection, like he was kicking me while I was down. That was not his intention, I know, but that is how it felt to me. He could feel me pulling away, and, because he does not like change, he panicked. He tried to talk me into staying with him not by asking me to but by telling me I had to hold on to a family that didn't want me.

I did not understand that then. I did not understand how I could have worked so hard, been so conscientious, so diligent about studying and writing and managing my life and my finances so responsibly for so many years, and still have failed everyone so spectacularly. I had tried to do everything right, but, all of a sudden, none of it seemed to count for anything. All this time, I'd been looking in the wrong direction, fixing the wrong problems, while creating other more disastrous ones. I hadn't corrected for any of the mistakes my father made; I'd just done him one better. *Hey, Dad, hold my beer.*

When words, words, which had always been everything to me, failed to save me both in my first book and in my relationships, I scrolled instead through unending Instagram photos of green vegan smoothies overflowing out of mason jars nestled in white sand at high tide, which, by the way, is not an exaggeration—those posts are very real. I examined countless selfies of deeply tanned, tiny-waisted women with defined biceps and abs wearing matching sports bras and leggings and touting the benefits of high-intensity interval training, sleek reusable water bottles, and manifestation mantras.

I became obsessed with both the pretty, brightly colored health and wellness industry and the environment and the devastating ways we treat our Mother Earth, the only mother I thought I might be able to understand. I tried to reduce my carbon footprint so much that I not only made my feet half a shoe size smaller, I no longer menstruated even intermittently, ensuring that the torch my father had lit and that I had picked up would extinguish with me, ensuring that I would leave no trace of my ever-shrinking self behind. My father killed himself with reckless sex, an HIV-positive diagnosis, and a bottle of sleeping pills, and for a time it seemed like maybe I was going to follow in his footsteps, not with sex or pills but simply by rejecting all forms of nourishment.

I am five feet, six inches tall, and, at my thinnest, I weighed 87.1 pounds. I have typed and deleted that number so many times, in so many drafts. It is extraordinarily hard to leave it be. When I was that kind of thin, people said nothing to my face and looked not at me but just beside me, just beyond my searing edges, because looking directly at my body made them cringe, and so they busied themselves searching for the rest of me.

A decade before I tried to make myself disappear, when I was still in high school, one of my aunts told me the story of alcohol in our family. It was very late at night on a Friday in early December, so late that it was almost certainly Saturday morning. The occasion had been my mother's annual holiday party. Everyone else had departed, and the horse-drawn carriage that had taken my mother's guests around the neighborhood to see the holiday decorations had been sent home, the clip of the horses' hooves long since receding down the street and out of earshot.

My mother and her boyfriend were inside, and my aunt and I were outside. Ostensibly, I was walking her to her car, but we had long since reached it, had already loaded her trunk with leftovers, and were now standing in the road, looking at the lights the block association had strung across the street, tree to tree.

I was a high school senior and did not yet know that this was the last time I would attend my mother's party for the foreseeable future: in the years ahead, I would be stuck on my college campus, studying for finals, and then later working numerous office jobs, my first foray into serious employment, where I was always far too junior to get the time off. But that night, I was still a teenager living at home, and all that was inconceivable to me.

My aunt may have already been anticipating it, which I imagine is why she said what she said. She told me that I needed to understand that women in our family have historically abused alcohol. We were not, she was clear, alcoholics. We simply had a propensity to abuse the spirits. At the time, in authentic seventeen-year-old form, I thought this sounded pretty lame. The distinction between being an abuser and being a full-blown alcoholic seemed to me exceedingly thin. To imbibe alcohol inappropriately sounded like an alcoholic's way of admitting a problem. I didn't yet know how to decipher the shade of gray she was coloring for me.

There is so much space in which to get lost between a healthy relationship with a substance and an unhealthy relationship with a substance. When I came to the conclusion that I had lost control of my life, that the choices I had made about my career and my loves were failing me, I concluded that everything I thought I knew and had learned, I didn't and hadn't. I responded by beginning to place severe restrictions on my intake of food. From those seductive Instagram posts, I pivoted to no shortage of studies and statistics and impassioned, eloquent op-ed articles that graphically and decisively supported my vegan diet as well as my eventual ban on alcohol, caffeine, sugar, gluten, and processed food sandwiched and sold between layers of plastic poison murder.

Here were the real weapons of mass destruction of our time.

I read hundreds of articles and more than a few books, and I watched very nearly every food-environment-diet-Mother-Earth documentary that's been filmed, edited, and streamed (there are *a lot*) detailing the industrial triangle of politics, power, and money that has hijacked our food systems and come to define farming in America. Don't worry, I also watched all of the movies that document the billions and billions of pounds of plastic debris polluting the planet's oceans and systematically killing its marine life and that describe the harmful chemicals in our convenience packaging that leak into our food, our bloodstream, our central nervous system, our every organ. I learned that most of the FDA-approved laundry detergents currently on the market leave behind a toxic film on our clothing. Toxins that our largest organ (our skin) absorbs as we go about our days.

When I read these articles and watched these films, I stopped thinking about the ways in which I was harmful, that I was bad, because there was a new bad guy in town. A new sheriff, too. I stopped using any cleaning products in my apartment and on my body that came in plastic or contained synthetic colors, fragrances, or preservatives. I looked for the shortest lists of ingredients with only recognizable and environmentally neutral chemicals. And if it wasn't unscented, forget it.

There was so little I could use and eat that there was almost no question, no debate, no thought necessary to determine what I would order or cook or buy. Having so few options meant having far fewer decisions to weigh. I knew exactly what I was going to eat and not eat. I had a food uniform. Eventually, I came to see that this also meant I could control exactly what I was going to weigh. There was a direct correlation between the nutrients I accepted and those I rejected and what my body looked like.

When I was a student, in high school, in college, in graduate school, I had been in control of my grades: take these notes, read these books, study these texts for this amount of time, write these papers, and, in return, get these good grades. But after, when I finally found myself in the postacademic professional world of corporations and murky office politics, I lost my blueprint. There was nothing comparable, at least, not as I understood it. I tried to navigate the media and publishing landscape of New York City, and I started to make my way but in rocky fits and starts. Now, with my body and the way I made my home, I was controlling my life again. I was self-soothing by cultivating an A+ environment, workout, and diet, the results of which were vitally consistent. It was so effective I didn't notice my body and mind were failing.

Almost all of the smart, accomplished millennial women I interviewed about the reasons they take the counsel of psychics, shamans, and astrologers seriously met with me over coffee or lunch. Most of them ordered herbal teas with a splash, *a mere suggestion really*, of nut milk, or they chose a vegan, gluten-free croissant that they tore into teeny pieces but did not consume. Most of them were also exceedingly thin.

I saw them. I recognized them. I knew them.

CHAPTER SIXTEEN

In her shamanic practice, Dr. Sarah Bamford Seidelmann has made championing what she calls "Core Beasties" a fundamental tenet of her own spiritual path as well as that of the work she does with her clients. She believes everyone can find their Core Beastie, an idea that has its roots in the pagan totemism of the New Age movement. You may be familiar with it as finding your spirit animal. The problem with the phrase *spirit animal*, however, is that it is flagrant cultural appropriation.

In its rampant use across pop culture, particularly as a slang term and meme on social media, it has become a humorously intended shorthand for something you like and identify with. As in, "the honey badger is my spirit animal." Or "New York City's pizza rat is my spirit animal." It doesn't have to be an animal, either. Maybe your spirit animal is Arya Stark from *Game of Thrones* or McKayla Maroney, the American gymnast and gold medalist with the infamous scowl. Or maybe your spirit animal isn't even McKayla. It's just her scowl.

Most of us don't mean anything negative or cruel when we use the phrase *spirit animal*, of course. We see someone else on the internet use it, and we find it charming and amusing, and we want to get in on the fun. But we're still being insensitive and oblivious and not taking the time to ask where or when or how or by and for whom such a phrase might have originated or been intended, which is usually what happens with cultural appropriation and part of the reason correcting for it can be infuriating and feel impossible. The term *pagan totemism* at least nods to a distinction between the cultural and ethnic traditions and history of spirit animals and the concept as it was spawned during the New Age movement of the last century. But I'm partial to Sarah's Core Beasties.

So I called Dr. Sarah. We did a video chat when it was very early morning in Minnesota and slightly less early in New York, and I asked her to explore the connection between shamanism and animals with me, which she did, smiling, despite the fact she hadn't had breakfast yet. I asked her why "Core Beasties," and she explained it to me in layman's terms and in such a gentle way that I could see what a wonderful bedside manner she must have had. "We've got so much going on, and it can be a little overwhelming to maybe start meditating or find some other way to go inside. [Finding your Core Beastie] just sets up a way for you to pay attention to one thing and kind of a fun thing. Animals are something that is kind of delightful to most people. So, you can start with anything, but I think the animals are fun, and often the messages we get from them are kind of absurd and sometimes silly, and sometimes that's the one thing that we are missing from our lives."

Intuition. Spirit. These so-called forms of guidance can be daunting, confusing, elusive. Even if you're comfortable admitting that you are interested in them, want to seek them out, how do you get from where you are to them exactly? Sarah was suggesting that animals can be that bridge from our fear to our preknowledge, our inherent silliness, our heart. I asked if this was what she meant, and she said that it was.

"That is a great way to think about it. Because when you are feeling really alone and not knowing where to turn . . . you can start to listen to those subtle messages [from your Core Beastie]. Sometimes they make so little sense, but they usually, whatever the message is, will help you do whatever it is you have to do or make you feel more peaceful and more calm or stronger. I always invite [my clients and my readers] to forge a relationship with a primary Core Beastie. Just inviting people to really play, because I think, too, that these can be mystical creatures, dragons, anything. Any creature . . . and to forge this relationship, you will never feel alone again. When you've maybe lost trust in all humans, the Core Beasties have this unending love and compassion."

But for all of the wonderful things that Sarah said, I still didn't understand what a Core Beastie was and what happened after you found yours. So I pushed her on it, and she explained further. "Our relationship with our Core Beasties is invaluable in helping us to maintain our own personal power and also to encourage us to be who we are."

There it was again, that idea of being as opposed to doing.

"Sometimes we've been trying to behave in a certain way, because we think that's what society wants for us, or that's what our mother wants us to do, or that's what our partner wants us to be. The spirits or guides [through your Core Beastie] will show you in an often humorous and funny way that the best way to be is the way that you are, who you are."

I like and respect Sarah a great deal, but when she said this, I couldn't help but feel like I was three years old and she was reading me a storybook. But maybe that's part of what she meant about receiving silly messages from our Core Beastie and how silliness is often the one thing missing from our lives. *Maybe I need to lighten up.* If you're palling around with a flamingo, it seems like it might be hard to take yourself too seriously. The more we talked, the more it sounded as though Sarah was describing the guides that Michelle and others, like Lindsay Mack, believe we all have. Our Core Beastie is a means of naming our primary guide, our number-one spirit, of giving it a recognizable, tangible form that feels more comfortable than letting it remain a nebulous concept of *guide*. Sarah was clear, too, that we have many beasties guiding us, whom we can pray to and ask guidance from. Apparently, once you identify your Core Beastie, the rest of the pack is never far behind.

But how precisely do you go about gathering your guide gang? I didn't get it. Sarah said I was overthinking it. (Surprise!) "Sometimes for people, it's as easy as just asking them if there's a wild animal they're drawn to.

Sometimes people know. When you start to ask them, they're like, 'At my house, I have multiple eagle sculptures and a carpet with an eagle on it.' Sometimes just looking around your house, you might get a clue of what's going on with you." As Sarah talked, I looked around my apartment. I got nothing. Oh, wait, there was some pigeon shit on my fire escape.

I asked her if there might be another way, and she said that on her website is a shamanic journey she has recorded, in which she walks listeners through the process of finding their Core Beastie. She told me that there is a third way, too. I can also ask to dream about it. Before I go to sleep, I can set an intention or I can pray to whomever it is I might pray that while I am sleeping, I'll be introduced to my Core Beastie.

That afternoon I downloaded Sarah's recording and followed her directions. The recording, I discovered, is a relatively straightforward guided meditation. There is deep breathing. There is the visualization of a place in nature. There is the drumming Sarah mentioned, and there are various sights and sounds to encourage your animal guides to show themselves. But no animal appeared for me. There was no Core Beastie. When it was over, I was relaxed. But I was still alone.

Late in the evening, as M. and I were getting ready for bed, I silently said a short prayer to the universe and set the intention to discover in my night's dream my Core Beastie. But I was not optimistic. I almost never remember my dreams. In the morning, however, I could recall one. I remembered a dream in which I was alone in a huge, beautiful stone house that belonged to a stranger. The ceilings had beams of rich, thick mahogany, and the floors were cool Spanish tiles. I wore a dress I didn't recognize. It was silk, and it was the color of wet emeralds, and, even now, as I type this many months later, I want that dress. I was barefoot. I was on the floor of the house's expansive kitchen, and I was cleaning out the sleek German-designed refrigerator. But the only beast in sight was myself, and though I sat on the floor, my legs spread wide, my head down, surrounded by food, by the contents of the now-empty refrigerator, I was not eating. I was ferociously scrubbing the crisper.

CHAPTER SEVENTEEN

In October 2017, the journalist Rebecca Traister wrote an essay in The Cut entitled "Why the Harvey Weinstein Sexual Harassment Allegations Didn't Come Out until Now." In it, she describes seeing Weinstein at an event for Planned Parenthood earlier that year.

"But I was also struck by his physical diminishment; he seemed small and frail, and, when I caught sight of him in May, he appeared to be walking with a cane. He has also lost power in the movie industry, is no longer the titan of independent film, the indie mogul who could make or break an actor's Oscar chances."

In a follow-up piece later that month for the same publication, "The Conversation We Should Be Having," Traister reminded readers that almost exactly a year prior, in October 2016, we had in fact been having a very similar conversation. Only not about Weinstein but about Trump and his locker-room talk, his "Grab 'em by the pussy. You can do anything" talk. I remember being so sure something real, something tangible would come of that discussion, and yet, as Traister and others have pointed out, we not only got nothing, we lost a tremendous amount when Trump was inaugurated. Harvey Weinstein and Kevin Spacey and Matt Lauer and Garrison Keillor and John Hockenberry and Charlie Rose and many more came to light in 2017, this story finally being told and so aggressively, because we were channeling our Trump outrage through these other men.

Harvey is obviously a most deserving scapegoat, but we are also well aware that there are other, many other, equally deserving scapegoats. So why did it begin with Harvey? We know that sexual assault is not about sex but about power, and Traister's point that Harvey had to be first rendered less powerful professionally, that he had to age and step aside for the new generation of Hollywood power, before all the horrifying things he has done and said and suggested over the last forty years could come fully and concretely out of the shadows, is important and revealing.

But, wait, no, that's not quite it, is it? In her memoir *Mean*, Myriam Gurba writes, "When his prey asks, 'What are you doing?' the molester answers, 'Oh, I didn't see you.' Which is true."

It's not that aging makes women unseen, because we've never been seen. Not really. Seen as in recognized, as in acknowledged, as in *known*. A friend of mine, who has two little girls, ages eight and ten, asked me rhetorically how she was supposed to prepare her daughters for a lifetime of being men's prey. It is a lifetime, too. Her girls are already prey. My friend and her daughters have already seen the looks and heard the comments just on their way to school, backpacks and lunch boxes in hand.

Speaking of children, let me make this plain. It is not only men. It is boys also. When I was twelve, my science teacher turned off the classroom lights and turned on a movie. I do not remember what the film was. I do not remember what we were supposed to learn. What I remember was what was beside me, my peer, one of the popular boys. He and I were not friends. We weren't not friends, either. I was simply not among the girls who reigned, who had hips and breasts and tans and sat together between classes swapping shimmery lip glosses and wearing Limited Too skirts too short. If he had female friends, they were them. I was not. But that day in the dark, I was tagged. I was it.

His long fingers and then his whole palm, which I had seen palm basketballs with never-faltering ease, applied pressure between my legs, enough to reach down to the bone. He leaned his face close to my ear, and his breath was surprisingly cool. It made me shudder. I smelled a reason. He was sucking on a mint. He said, "Mmmmm." It was perhaps the first word he had ever spoken to me directly, and it wasn't even a word. It was his pleasure. His pressure continued. His hand rocked back and forth with conviction, his fingers nimble and confident; he believed in what he was doing. I let him. It ended when the movie ended. I went to the girls' bathroom and sat in a stall and was ashamed of my wetness.

I told a friend. Years later, she and he would end up at the same college, and they would become more or less friends, galling me. After college, I would, for a time, remain more or less friends with one of her ex-boyfriends, the one who broke her heart. Too late, I would realize that galled her. So maybe we're even. I don't know.

A decade later, she was the only friend who said something to me when I weighed 87.1 pounds. She drunk-texted me, *Can we talk?* I called her the next morning and could hear the hangover in her voice when she said, "I'm so scared about your weight."

It will never not sadden me that these two boys, her ex and my peer, who were worthy of neither of us, became something painful between us, between our friendship, which should have had nothing to do with them. I hear, through the friend grapevine, that she is the mother of two little prey of her own now.

It may be that Trump's pivot to politics and Harvey's own long-rumored political ambitions are partly an unconscious response to Traister's point. That as men age on the studio lots in Hollywood and on the sets of their reality television shows, they start looking for another industry where age won't hinder their power. Politics has always been that industry. After all, in Washington, the older, the whiter the man, the more powerful he is. But here's something these men don't seem to understand: vulnerability and confidence can be complementary. They are not mutually exclusive. I am learning to be confidently vulnerable, learning to be a good example for all the little prey coming up behind me.

CHAPTER EIGHTEEN

The only bad thing about a young, still perfect relationship is knowing not if but when the first point of friction will emerge. You're waiting for the imperfection to show itself. Beneath all that early relish and giddiness is that underlying anxiety: When is our first argument going to happen, what will it be about, and will it be too much for us, for this new this, whatever it is or will be?

The first tension between M. and me really was just tension, not even an argument, because M. is so good at arguing. By which I mean, I cannot egg him on. He is calm and steady throughout disagreements. Or possibly that's not it at all, and when he sees disagreement coming, he checks out. Slips through the back door. Nobody home.

Our first tension mirrored the absurdly trendy tension that's been jet-setting back and forth between New York and Los Angeles for years at this point. Thirty years from now, maybe it'll be Cincinnati and Galveston having this debate. Our children will sit around discussing the finer points of Cincinnati as the city to party and Galveston as the town to chill. But, for now, the debate rages on between New York City and Los Angeles, between, as Paul Beatty describes them in his marvelous novel *The Sellout*, "the city that never sleeps and the city that never gets off the couch."

I have dabbled in other cities over the years, but I've mostly been a tax-paying resident of New York since I moved here for college in 2003, so by the time I met M. thirteen years later, my complicated feelings about the place had had plenty of time to settle in. It didn't mean I had stopped loving this city. I could spend hours talking about why New York City was cool, is cool, and will always be cool. But New York City, in its density, can be a lot, and it had begun to feel like too much.

Los Angeles, of course, is dense and is also a huge city. But its density doesn't slap you across the face by way of greeting. There's breathing room, and I had started to crave deeper breath in a place that did not feel claustrophobic the way my apartment and my street and my neighborhood had started to feel in New York. I had been here too long and taken too few breaks. My friend Amy's two-year-old son has been going through a phase lately in which, all day, he repeats, "Go away." He says it to everyone and everything. Not rudely. He's very polite about it. That's how I had started to feel every morning I woke up in New York City. *Go away.*

During one conversation with Dr. Sarah, New York came up unexpectedly. "And the Core Beasties can really help . . . one of their roles is to act as guardian and protector. And I also like to think of them almost like a spiritual bouncer. And I invite people to play with that. It sounds so crazy, but if you have a particular animal you're drawn to and so maybe you're in New York, and you turn a corner and you're like, 'Uh-oh. There's nobody around here except these guys coming toward me.' Just call in the spirit of that wild animal to be with you and protect you and see what happens."

There are bad guys in every city, but Sarah didn't choose any city for her example, and she certainly didn't choose Los Angeles. She chose New York. We could argue till the cabs come home that New York's reputation for being cold or scary or dangerous is outdated and absurd, but it doesn't matter. The reputation stands.

But M., after being in California for over a decade, had only just left Los Angeles for New York. The anonymity of New York City, especially because he knew so few people here, was liberating for him. In general, it is easier, too, I think, to move to New York City than it is to move to Los Angeles. Here, you do not need a car; it matters less where you live in proximity to your work; and you do not need to decide if you are an Eastside or a Westside person before you come.

There is a clear distinction between what is New York City and what is not. When you have left the city, you know. Los Angeles bleeds. You're in Los Angeles, and then suddenly you're in Burbank, and you're not sure when or how it happened. There are always interesting, unexpected events and opportunities in both places, but the cool things to do are glaringly obvious in New York and much harder to suss out in Los Angeles. In New York, you have a good chance of happening upon something worthwhile. In Los Angeles, stumbling upon value is harder. If no one has given you a date, a time, and an exact address, good luck with that.

It's not just M.; I find myself having this conversation about place with so many people I know well and so many I don't. We compare the benefits and drawbacks of individual cities and rural living to urban living as if we're discussing football team trades and the strengths and weaknesses of one coach to another. M. and his friends have their fantasy football league. My girlfriends and I have our fantasy address league.

Talking about where to live is another means of arriving, of literally finding your place in the world, especially now, when so much of the world feels so unrecognizable. Finding home is suddenly urgent.

Most of the discussions about different cities happen among people who know well only one or two of the destinations in question, if that. My friends and I sound like orthopedic surgeons discussing the finer points of biodynamic farming. We have no idea what we're talking about. Should I stay or should I go? It's the ultimate bourgeois nonproblem problem. It's self-created uncertainty. We keep at it because with the most uncertainty comes the most possibility, and we're not ready to close all the doors, to have all the forks in the road in the rearview mirror.

It has to do, as well, with something Gary B. Strauss, the founder and director of the Life Energy Institute and the Polarity Healing Arts of California, told me, "Problems arise when we're too habitual. We're primed for adaptation. We hurt ourselves when we stop adapting. We need diversity." There are countless ways we could go about incorporating more adaptation and diversity in our lives, but my generation, more often than not, figures the bigger the gesture, the better. We can't just take a new route to the office. No, we have to quit our jobs and move across the country.

Some part of us must have an inkling, too, that home is not just the Eastside of Los Angeles or the small section of Brooklyn that currently appears to be trying to speak for the entire much-larger borough. Some part of us must realize that our spiritual homes have also not yet been spoken for. We know anecdotally and because of the statistics tossed around online and in round-table discussions on the Sunday morning news programs that more and more young people are being drawn to live in cities overflowing with every kind of amenity imaginable except organized religion.

In cities, if religion is discussed at all, it is discussed in the context of culture and community, not doctrine or holy texts, and in the context of the importance of religious freedom—meaning both the freedom to practice a religion and the freedom not to practice any religion at all. But mostly religion is simply not discussed in any way that feels religious. Talking about where you're spending Passover or whom you're breaking the fast with during Ramadan isn't all that different from asking a coworker if they saw any good movies over the weekend. Religion is a social-etiquette time passer. That is not to say that city dwellers don't keep kosher or salah times, but those traditions and the meanings behind them, the *faith* that carries us to keep them, is not discussed. Urbanites have managed to make even religion feel secular.

Many of the biblical stories preached by Catholic nuns and priests demonstrate the value and necessity of community and magnanimity, but when I think back on the Catholicism I grew up with, I don't remember those stories. What I remember are the hard church pews, those wooden benches made from trees, the nature that was destroyed for the man-made church. Yes, a Catholic church is a beautiful structure: its architecture, its stained glass, its gold plaques, and its marble altar bring awe and solace to many people. But a church always feels, to me, entirely of this world. The marble and the gold remind me of the men, the power, the business behind the ornate façade. Never am I more aware of the limitations of human beings than when I am in a church. If you believe in God or Spirit or the Divine, you can find them anywhere, including, yes, in a church. But I would rather hang out with them someplace man didn't build.

When we hear *place*, we think a city, a town, a bench atop a hill we climbed once, the vineyards or stalks of corn we ran through as children, a spot where the sea meets the sand or the river meets the rock. But part of what shamanism encourages is the embracing of other kinds of places, additional realities. The boundaries are less rigid; this is an idea that archaeologically can be traced back tens of thousands of years, because shamanism is one of the oldest spiritual systems across ethnicities and cultures, and regardless of which cultures' shamanism you choose to study, you will find similar shamanic principles: that there are extraordinary transcendent realities, and the spirits, the guides, are real, existing independently of our awareness of them, and can be found whether or not you live on the West Coast or the East Coast or no coast.

Sarah told me that "when you go into shamanism, there are three worlds: this world that you and I are sitting in right now, which has a nonordinary aspect to it, too, that you can tap into, but it's not a place you usually go looking for helpful spirits, because it's sort of a mixed bag here." The second and third worlds are the lower world and the upper world, below and above us, and these are where we can find helping spirits. "And if you start to go and work in those realms, you'll start to realize that there's lots of different places you can go, and different places where different spirits dwell who can help you with different problems." Even in the spirit world, the idea that a new place can help solve our problems persists. "In shamanism, we say when you walk full of power—and that's not creepy power over other people, it's peaceful power that comes from being who you are and being full of the power of your own soul and full of the power of the Spirit—that we tend to be able to do what we came here to do, and we tend not to attract too many experiences that detract us from that work."

But sometimes a new place is exactly that, a distraction.

I liked that M. had just moved from Los Angeles. I liked that he knew the City of Angels so well and had so many friends there. I thought that I wanted to move there. I had lived in Los Angeles before but too briefly to befriend it, and I had been with someone who knew it even less than I did and who cared not to know it at all. I wanted to see M.'s LA, and, at first, he talked as though he agreed. There were more work opportunities for him there, he said. He had multiple places in Los Angeles where we could live, he said. It would be an easy transition. But he began to waver. Some days he was eager to move back, so much so that we'd pick a move date. But the date kept getting pushed back. The uncertainty, I think, more than whether we were in New York or Los Angeles, became the tension between us. I know, I know, certainty is a figment of our imaginations, but if M. had sat me down and said, "Look, I prefer New York. I want to stay," I would have said, "Okay, cool." Because clarity always helps.

Instead, it was frustrating when he would say he thought maybe he wanted to stay in New York and then the very next day email me links to the kinds of cars he thought I should consider buying for the move. I've dated a number of lost souls. It's a type I've long been attracted to, but attraction to someone is not the same as feeling good when you're with them. I started to feel as though maybe M. was toying with me, but that's not fair. I was just too caught up in the wrong people, the wrong places, the wrong animals, the wrong kind of power.

Time. Space. Place. These were sacred things that M. and I—in our rush to validate and solidify the intensity of our attraction to one another and the instant connection we felt—had not given each other or ourselves. In so many ways, big and small, my ex B. and I had never been able to quite reach each other. Being with someone like M., who stood so enthusiastically before me, so conscious of his and my being physically and mentally close, was a salve. But for six and a half years, B. and I had lived together in the very same apartment that M. and I now shared, and for however much B. had felt unreachable, he was still all over my apartment. I don't know that I wanted Los Angeles so much as I wanted M. and I to have the chance to forge our own time, our own space, our own place.

Occasionally, always on a weeknight, usually after dinner, either M. or I would turn to the other and say, "Wanna get a hotel room tonight?" So we would. We'd pick a hotel somewhere in the city and just go. We'd take nothing save our toothbrushes, hop in an Uber, and spend the night on some high floor in some new neighborhood. In the mornings, we almost always woke too soon, something about being in a different room, under different sheets, and we'd linger, looking out the windows at a view we didn't have memorized. I loved our hotel nights the same way I loved our sunrise walks. Those nights fell outside of time and space and place, because hotel rooms look the same most everywhere. When you wake up in one, you could be waking up anywhere in the world, and that is both the most exciting thing about them and the most depressing.

CHAPTER NINETEEN

Each week, Hunter's class challenged me to adjust anew the way thought I about power and perspective, archetypes, and dynamics. His course materials could be obtuse and academic, but they were also piercing and intimate. I looked forward to our hour-long calls every Sunday evening when he and I would dissect that week's lessons.

Unfortunately, M. did not. He hated these calls. My apartment was small, and taking Hunter's calls at home meant that M. would be forced to leave, wear headphones, or contend with listening in. He could have left, but that's a lot to ask, and I never did. So M. was there for every conversation I had with Hunter, and right from the start he was clear that the calls made him uncomfortable. He didn't understand what Hunter and I were talking about. He thought all this talk about dichotomies and the push and pull of how we present ourselves to the world and to ourselves was creepy and a weirdly intimate discussion to have with anyone, let alone some guy on the other side of the world I had never met.

I began to dread Sundays. Every week, without fail, as soon as Hunter and I got off the phone, M. would drill me about some aspect of the call, something he had heard me say, and he would want an explanation of how that related to my book. I told him he was only hearing one side of the call, to which he replied, "Yeah, no kidding. Who knows what Hunter is saying to you? The whole thing is weird." I told him I didn't always know how or if something was going to be a part of the book immediately, that it took patience and trust.

Hunter brought forth a deep, irrational fear in M., and M. was starting to bring forth a kind of fear in me, as well, although I didn't yet know if my fear was shallow or deep, rational or irrational.

The last time I talked to Sarah, she brought up the Bible and said, "You hear these quotes in the Bible where they say, 'Be afraid,' or 'Be very afraid,' when they talk about the fear of God. I've never understood that, because I was like, 'God is benevolent. Why would you fear it?'"

It's a fair point, but what I said in reply was that "it seems to me like it's *be in awe* of this power, be overwhelmed by this," not afraid of it.

And Sarah responded, "Yes, yes!" And then she told me about Peru.

"I am so glad you mentioned that. I went to Peru this summer. One of the things that I was working on was getting rid of my fear, just getting rid of any excess fear, which is a whole area. I will probably never get rid of all of it, but it was like, 'Let's get rid of some of it.' We did a medicine ceremony with a shaman there with San Pedro, which is a plant medicine. San Pedro is Saint Peter; it's thought to open the gates of heaven so you can have a connection and get messages from the Divine. It's a way of altering your consciousness, again, to connect with the Divine and learn more to help ourselves, to help our communities. At the end of the day, I was sitting and staring at this incredible mountain. Through the medicine, the mountain was showing me these faces of serpents and dragons. This mountain was just becoming everything . . . The medicine basically said to me, 'Hey, Sarah, instead of being afraid'—because you can imagine sitting in front of a mountain that's morphing into all of these things, it's a little like, 'Wow,' it's overwhelming—'instead of being afraid, why don't you just be in awe?' It's that get-down-on-your-knees-and-just-be-like, 'I have no idea what this great mystery is, but show me how to be, what to do, how to work with this, with what I've got' [moment], which is very small, but it's a small part of that vastness; you, we, have a role to play. That's such a great exchange from when you're scared, what would it look like to be in awe?"

I adore this. I told Sarah, "There are so many things, helpful tips and calming ideas, that I read about, concepts I come across when I'm in a peaceful place, where I think, 'Oh, that makes so much sense. I just need to remember this the next time that I'm frustrated or over-whelmed.' Of course, I never do. But I think I could maybe hold on to the idea of just being in awe. That seems almost small enough."

Sarah replied, "Somebody said we are the great forgetters. I think that's so true. That's why we're here, is to continue to try to remember."

It was not small enough. I still forget to be in awe constantly. Every once in a while, though, I do remember.

My friend Mary has, of late, also been struggling with living in Manhattan. She longs for snowy mountains and vast vegetable gardens and swimming holes with mossy floors. So she and I created a WhatsApp chat entitled "Reclaiming New York," and we send each other photos and brief anecdotes of charming moments and interactions we have in the city. Anything to remind us about all the things to love and marvel about this place where we are.

When she or I find ourselves feeling especially dispirited, we send out an SOS and get together ASAP. One afternoon, after M. and I had had yet another series of will-we-or-won't-we LA-or-New York conversations, Mary and I met up at Lincoln Center. Sitting beside the huge wall of glass at Alice Tully Hall, we drank from tiny green bottles of San Pellegrino and told ourselves to pull it together, for Christ's sake. Mary and her boyfriend had plans that night, and I was supposed to meet M. at the grocery store, so she and I didn't have time to wallow in our self-pity for quite as long as we would have liked. Too soon, we said our goodbyes, and I headed to meet M. As I hurried down the subway station steps to the downtown platform, I got lost in worry about being late and about all the things we needed from the store. The reassurance and promise of Lincoln Center had already evaporated.

In front of me, a man who looked to be of Middle Eastern descent and who wore sufi pants was rushing to catch a departing train when the slim briefcase he held popped open, spilling poker chips down the stairs and onto the platform below. It was the last thing anyone would want to have happen, in the worst possible place. All around us, impatient commuters rushed to get aboveground or onto a train below. It was the kind of incident that just makes your heart sink or, if you are me, makes you think, *Goddamnit, fucking hell.*

Without a word, the man knelt down and began to slowly and steadily collect his chips. He was crouched over, head down, resigned to his predicament, and so he did not see us: a young Asian man, a middle-aged white woman, a black teenage boy, me, and a fiftysomething black woman on the platform below who passed chips to me through the metal bars of the staircase railing. The five of us collected handfuls and sorted them by color. (Okay, fine, it's true, only I was sorting them by color.) Two downtown trains and one headed uptown came and went as we worked, but none of us stopped until we were nearly done and the poker player stood and turned around and realized he was not alone. He might have said more, but all I heard was "Oh." It was not an *oh* of disappointment or resignation but of awe.

A third downtown train had hurled into the station, and I handed him the last of the chips before running to slip between its closing doors. I sat, trying not to touch a thing, least of all myself, because my fingers had just been all over the floor of a subway station, and, my god, let us not linger on that reality. I held my hands out awkwardly in front of me and thought about working in tandem with those strangers, whose lives and concerns seemed, superficially and presumptuously, so different from my own. How satisfying it had felt to work alongside them and to hear the wonder in the voice of the man we helped.

Maybe it really is as simple as that. I wanted to tell Mary about it, wanted to remind us both that New York provides the opportunity to reach out to people, lots of people, who look and think so differently, all the time, spontaneously, when it's the last thing on your mind. You can't get that so readily on a snowy mountain. It's that Frank O'Hara poem M. and I walked to on our first night together: "I can't even enjoy a blade of grass unless I know there's a subway handy, or a record store or some other sign that people do not totally regret life." It might be why I keep coming back to New York. Escaping someplace beautiful and rural and serene, or at least as serene as Mother Nature and all her brutality get, is wonderful and valuable but comes at a price. A price I'm not sure I'll ever be ready to pay permanently.

CHAPTER TWENTY

In an interview he gave in 2016, Harvard professor of psychology Matthew Nock said, "Around the world, more people die by suicide than by wars, homicide, and violence combined. We are each more likely to die by our own hands than by someone else's." There are many valid responses to such a depressing fact, but when I read it, I chose to consider the rest of us. Those of us who have not and will not take our own lives.

It is meaning and purpose that keep us here. Either having found them or still believing we will. There is a famous children's book called *Are You My Mother?*, which is about a baby bird trying to find its mother by asking the animate (and inanimate) beings it comes across if in fact they are, at last, his mother. Sometimes, I feel a bit like that baby bird. Are you my meaning?

Not long ago, a generous friend gifted me a certificate for a facial. My facialist, apparently, was also trained in Reiki, the technique in which a healer supposedly channels a patient's energy to help the body return to (or find) its emotional and physical center. In the middle of what had so far been a routine facial, she asked if she could perform some impromptu Reiki on me. I was lying faceup on the table under a thin sheet, naked save for my underwear. My face was thick with goop, and there was a warm towel over my goop, so that when I opened my eyes, I could see only the dark color of the terry cloth backlit by the light overhead. I was at her Reiki mercy.

She reached her hands and arms beneath me, down my bare back, until her fingers grazed the sides of my abdomen and my hips. I could feel her face hovering above mine and her chest pressing into the crown of my head. She cocooned me like this, breathing deeply and slowly, for what felt like was going to be the rest of my life. When she finally slid her arms up my back and out from under me, she said she had felt a deep well of sadness inside of me and that it was urgent I address it. Then she left the room, and I blinked under the towel, wondering if there was anyone for whom such an observation would not resonate. Maybe, if I found my purpose, I'd lose my sadness.

The ancient Greek poet Pindar wrote, "Oh my soul, do not aspire to immortal life but exhaust the limits of the possible." I have never aspired to immortality (that sounds truly terrible), but what are the limits of what's possible? Some of the things, many of the things, we deem impossible today will be possible tomorrow. They could already be possible—we just don't realize it, having prematurely and erroneously decided they are fictitious. I do not know what the limits of possibility are, but I know we have not exhausted them.

When I was about nine years old, a year or so before my father died, he bought me a paperback copy of *A Wrinkle in Time* by Madeleine L'Engle. We read it together, a little every day. I read aloud to him, and when I stumbled, he would ask me to start from the beginning of the sentence, until he didn't even have to ask, and I'd begin again at the first hint of mispronunciation. I loved that book more than any other book I had ever read, but I have never read it again, never read it on my own. The only quote I remember from its pages is "Believing takes practice."

I am afraid if I read it again, it will disappoint me, that what it meant to me to read it with my father when I was nine is not a meaning that can be recaptured. But I have always liked L'Engle and have sought out her interviews, the quotes she has dropped like bread crumbs along the path. She once told *Life* magazine, "The only certainty is that we are here, in this moment, in this now. It is up to us: to live fully, experiencing each moment, aware, alert and attentive."

According to Rob Brezsny and his Free Will Astrology column, the sculptor Henry Moore once told the poet Donald Hall (bear with me) that "the secret of life is to have a task, something you devote your entire life to, something you bring everything to, every minute of the day for your whole life. And the most important thing is—it must be something you cannot possibly do." A task that keeps you from ever arriving, that is your present but also your past and certainly your future.

And then there is empath-intuitive Maureen Bright Healer, who tells me that "the past doesn't exist; the future doesn't exist; only the present exists." It sounds good, and if you can believe that, it probably makes L'Engle's advice easier to follow. But I don't think it's true. I think the past and the present and the future all exist right now in this moment. And to be stuck in any one without the support of the others is the real fallacy.

When you fall in love with someone and are in those electrifying months at the start of the relationship, your delight is partly for the very person standing in front of you in the present, but it's also for the past—the times before when you worried you'd never have this with someone again and the other times when you did feel this kind of love and support, and here it is again, and your appreciation for it now is precisely because this isn't your first rodeo.

Your ability to love this new person and be good both to them and for them and to yourself and for yourself is based in part on what has come before, what you've learned, and how you've grown. It's also for the future—for whatever this person and you aspire to build.

Maureen would tell me lots of things, but before she told me anything, my friend Maz went to see her. She told Maz to eat more root vegetables and to stop eating ice cream, because both the sugar and the coldness were not good for her body and mind. (As it happens, Maz has a deeper appreciation for ice cream than most people.) Maz asked

Maureen when she would be able to eat ice cream again, and Maureen said, "When you resolve your issues with your mother."

So, assuming Maz and her mom are anything like the rest of us, probably never.

Let the record also show that the last time Maz and I discussed this incident, we did so over cones of ice cream. During that conversation, I asked Maz what she liked about her *180-minute-long* reading with Maureen. "She told me things I think I needed to hear. She was very definitive. That clarity was really helpful."

When it was my turn, I met Maureen at her house, the only geodesic dome on the block. Maureen's home looks the part inside and out. Her office is also her crystal shop. She has amethyst clusters, citrine points, lapis lazuli spheres, pyrite clusters, rose quartz points, and hundreds of others I could never hope to identify. There are also Merlin statues and dragon figurines that I don't believe are for sale. "Merlin's kind of my guy," she said.

If you entered Grand Central Terminal in the middle of rush hour, and I told you to find Maureen, you would have no problem.

She is tall and strong with long hair dyed pitch black. She has a snake tattoo on one arm and a snake ring on the other hand. When I met her, she was wearing a huge crystal around her neck, a long, flowing black dress, and black ballet flats studded with silver beads. Her nails were painted purple, and her eyes, ringed darkly with liner, were faded, like dusty turquoise. Her pupils were dramatically dilated, which can occur when we:

- focus;
- think about something stimulating;
- are attracted to someone;
- are interested in what's going on around us;
- feel confident in our actions and beliefs;
- have ingested marijuana, cocaine, heroin, barbiturates, hallucinogens, or aerosols.

Because the past and the future do not exist for her, Maureen's readings are about the present. They are a mirror held up to the recipient for them to parse through. Only I did not go to Maureen for a reading. I went to interview her about her life's work.

Within minutes of my arrival, she explained that "psychotherapy is New Age therapy. Spiritual therapy is old-age therapy." She said there is physical therapy, mental therapy, and spiritual therapy—and spiritual therapy is a critical part of wellness and taking care of ourselves. She asked how I had heard about her, and I said a friend had come to see her and had had a "revelatory experience" (my words, not hers). Maureen did not ask who my friend was. Instead, she told me a story.

In the late 1970s when Maureen was twenty-seven years old, she had a dream about a statue. At the time, she was still married to her ex-husband, who was a collector of antiques. A few weeks after her dream, her husband received a call from a dealer about some new pieces he might be interested in, and so they drove out to the man's warehouse to look at the contents of an estate he had purchased. Maureen's husband and the dealer were only interested in the estate's many clocks, but a stipulation of the sale had been that the dealer had to buy the entire estate if he wanted the clocks. So there were a lot of items to see that her husband and the dealer didn't care about, one of which was a statue. Exactly like the statue in her dream. Maureen convinced her husband that they should buy it. Ten years later, when they were divorcing, her husband refused to let her take the statue.

In the late summer of 2016, Maureen had another dream. She dreamt of a fifty-page manuscript written in Chinese, a language she does not know. A few weeks later, in September, her ex-husband died, and Maureen's stepdaughter offered to let her have the statue. Maureen and her new husband retrieved the statue without incident, but when they got it home, her husband noticed there were papers tucked inside the statue's base. It was the fifty-page manuscript Maureen had dreamt of.

Her husband placed the statue in their entryway next to the door to Maureen's office, where she sees her clients and where we sat while she told me this story. When she was finished, she led me to the statue. At least five hundred years old, it is from the Ming dynasty. Around its base, she has wrapped garlands of purple cloth roses. There are also, if fire safety is a concern of yours, an alarming number of lit candles. Candles above the statue, on the wall beside it, on an altar nearby. Maureen positioned me directly in front of the statue, gripping my arms. Though it stands on a raised platform, the statue itself is no bigger than a small child, maybe one who is five or six years old and not in the highest or lowest percentile of any physical development chart. Its eyes were closed, but if they had been open, they would have stared at my neck.

Maureen told me to close my own eyes and to talk to the statue. To ask the statue to help me, whatever I might need, because I am, according to Maureen, an empath, and so I might need to ask for help letting go of other people's stuff, whatever I have picked up inadvertently and am carrying for others. She told me to take as long as I needed. She said she would wait in her office. Then she said not to fall forward into the statue. She let go of my arms, and I heard her walk away.

The statue and I were alone. I started to take a deep breath, to center myself, to come into this moment. But I stopped. Because I was swaying. First to the right and then to the left and then forward, not enough to fall, but enough to see how that could happen. It didn't feel like a push or a pull. It felt like a dance. Like we were partners and it was leading. I was struck by how well, for once, I was following. Like the statue had sprinkled glitter over me, and it was floating in my hair and atop my eyelashes with its own flow of electric current. I did not feel as if I couldn't move away, more like why on earth would I ever want to?

I spoke to the statue, prayed to it, I suppose. Silently but clearly and without hesitation. I asked it to help me live with integrity and to help me be in service to others and to the planet. To help me let go of the energy and pain I was carrying for certain people in my life. People I have known my whole life. My grandmother. More than one of my aunts (I have a lot of aunts). People I have known for just a sliver of my life. M. I told the statue that a Canadian psychic may have thrown off my judgement and that I couldn't tell if M. and I were on a short walk or a long one.

When I opened my eyes, I felt not myself. Everything was sharp and made my skin tingle. I was speechless, because the feeling was beyond speech, and every attempt to speak lessened it, weakened this sensation I didn't want to let go of. If that was true, then I never wanted to speak again. My heart felt closer to the surface of my body than it had ever felt before. But it wasn't pressing through my chest, exploding or expanding. It had simply stepped out from hiding. It was announcing itself fully, and the first coherent thought I had was *Oh, so this is my heart.* It didn't pulse. It moved as lake water. A big, deep lake that stirred of its own accord, sometimes imperceptibly, always to its own singular rhythm.

When Maureen walked me to the door to leave, I asked her if I could see the fifty-page manuscript. She said she had given it to someone for safer keeping. I was disappointed. Her no, this convenient absence of the manuscript, was a shadow across my experience with the statue.

CHAPTER
TWENTY-ONE

Rob Brezsny gives all kinds of advice in his weekly astrology column. Some of it goes, "Brag about what you can't do and don't have. Confess profound secrets to people who aren't particularly interested. Pray for the success of your enemies while you're making love. Change your name every day for a thousand days." Some of his advice I appreciate more than others. I'm never going to think about my enemies while I'm having sex. Let alone pray for them. But I'm a writer and a memoirist, so I'm always ready to brag about my shortcomings and confess secrets no one wants to hear.

I cannot even remotely begin to carry a tune. And even though English is both my native language and my livelihood, I tend to bungle the pronunciation of its most random words with more frequency than is charming and use obscure words in circumstances that are just a beat off from their intended usage. I can only hear out of one of my ears, and so I mishear things constantly. This is not my fault, of course, but it has led me to develop the unfortunate habit of rushing to answer in the affirmative even when I don't agree, know the answer, or get the reference. I'm trying to cover for what I haven't heard or understood, hoping I'll catch up before anyone notices the lag. I do this without thinking. I almost always regret it.

What else? Oh, yes, you've never seen anyone take as long as I do to make a salad or try on clothing. At the drop of a hat, I can tell you every coworker I have ever had who thought I was lazy and dumb. I can judge people too harshly. I have tried, with varying degrees of success, to apologize to most (but definitely not all) of those individuals. I am also convinced I remember every one of those instances; I am wrong.

No, I haven't heard of that band.

I can be entitled and indignant and lose sight of all the ways the world rolled a red carpet out for me when I was born. I emotionally vomit indiscriminately. My friend Mary once tried to teach me and two of our friends to knit, and I was the worst, learning the least, my stitches somehow both too tight and too loopy. I still have yarn in my closet that will never be anything other than the softest, bluest-greenest, most expensive ball of unspun potential.

As for what I don't have, I don't have a tan or any chill or diamonds or a television or a high alcohol tolerance or a father or a green thumb or a nightstand or a baby.

I really want a nightstand. I could have had a baby.

That's a profound, to me, secret you're probably not particularly interested in.

I learned I was unequivocally pregnant on October 19, 2016. M. and I had been dating for three and a half months. I was thirty-one years old and three and a half weeks pregnant. The zygote had just become an embryo. I found out because I suspected I might be pregnant, and I suspected it because, sure, my period was late, but my period has a reputation for showing up whenever she damn well pleases or not at all. So, mostly, I suspected it because my body was shouting at me that it was.

My breasts were hot. They felt hot on my chest and against the back of my hand like fever. All of a sudden my entire body had become dead-weight. I was a paperweight, capable of nothing beyond trapping shit under me. I was exhausted. I did not know it was possible to be so tired. I slept deeply and excessively, but every morning I woke up feeling like I hadn't slept at all, and my arms, every time my alarm went off, remained asleep. They were numb, useless, and only slowly became thick with that heavy, awful, tingling sensation of coming back to life. It would take full minutes before they were fully operational for the day. When I did Pilates, I suddenly found that shoulder-tapping push-ups took every ounce of effort I had to give and that after class I needed to sit down to gather the energy necessary to change out of my workout clothes and walk downstairs and out into New York's energy and density.

I thought about taking an at-home pregnancy test from the drug store, of the one- or two-line variety. But do you know how expensive those things are? I did not. I stood under the fluorescent lights of Rite Aid and decided those tests were too rich for my urine. Besides, I knew that if the test was positive, I was obviously going to go to the doctor, and if it was negative, I wouldn't trust it and would go to the doctor anyway. So I walked out of Rite Aid empty-handed and called my doctor's office.

At my appointment, I peed in a cup, and not five minutes later the nurse practitioner walked back into the little room where I was waiting and said, "Yeah, you're pregnant," all in less time than it took for her to walk from the door to her desk. When she did reach her chair and sit down, she asked if I was okay.

"More or less."

She said she would email me some brochures about my options and that I should think about what I wanted to do and come back when I had an answer.

On the street, I called M., who knew I was going to the doctor, who knew there was a chance that our "baby-making" had produced an actual embryo.

"I'm pregnant."

"Are you kidding?"

Kid. Kid. Kidding. Kid.

"No."

There was a pause.

"I didn't think you'd *really* . . ."

His voice trailed off, or I cut him off. I don't remember which. "I have a work call, like, right now, but can you meet me after?"

"Yeah, okay, text me when you're done," he said.

We hung up, and I walked three blocks to Madison Square Park. I found an empty bench next to the park's popular fast-food joint Shake Shack, which reeked of fried meat and potatoes. I sat, ignoring my stomach, which was performing somersaults of revulsion, and called a candidate in Australia, whom I was interviewing for a job opening in my company's Sydney office. She and I spoke for thirty minutes, and I asked her all the appropriate questions. I only know this because I wrote down each question in my little work notebook as I asked it. I stared at the blue ink and the white paper, and every time she used a verb, I wrote it down below the question she was answering. When I had no more questions to ask her, and she had no more questions to ask me, I walked another three blocks to Twenty-Seventh Street and sat on another bench, this time outside an office complex and a fast-food Indian sandwich spot that smelled strongly of curry and onions, and my stomach was like, *Seriously?*

I texted M. where I was, and he wrote back that he was in a meeting and would come downstairs when he could. While I waited for him, I thought about the fact that I, of all women, was pregnant. I thought about the women I knew—straight, lesbian, transgender—who weren't pregnant but very much wanted to be. I felt guilty for tripping into something they were working so hard to get. I thought about how useless my guilt was to them.

I had never been pregnant before. For most of my adult life, I didn't even menstruate. This pregnancy had happened largely because I had long ago assumed I couldn't have children and so had grown cavalier about my birth control methods. I made this assumption not because any doctor told me this was the case but because it fit with who I had come to believe I was and what I thought I deserved.

Years ago, barely out of college, a friend and I were walking down the street when we passed a baby in a stroller, and she said, "When you see a baby, don't your arms just ache to hold it?" I had no idea what she was talking about.

Much later, when my friends did start having their own babies, I went to a party. It was a new kind of party. This party started in the early afternoon, at an hour we once would have called brunch, and there were babies there. No, I don't mean the man-babies who litter New York; I mean actual babies. Someone handed me one. Not a newborn but one who, as I recall, was closing in on his first year here. Like, he could hold his own head up and crawl and stuff.

In my nonaching arms, he started to cry, which I understood to be him communicating that he did not want to be held by me. I appreciated his self-advocacy and set him down on the rug, where he immediately toppled over. He was upright and then he was not. I realize I should have handed him to one of his parents, but, in my defense, not only was he fine, he stopped crying as soon as he was out of my embrace. He fell over, sure, but he didn't cry.

Apparently, face-planting was preferable to being in my arms.

I thought about that incident, now, freshly pregnant, and I reminded myself that I didn't grow up around babies. I didn't have any younger siblings, and the two younger cousins I did have had lived hundreds of miles away. Most of my childhood friends had been the youngest in their families, so when I had playdates at their homes, we were the babies. It was not, I told myself, that I couldn't be good with children; it was just that I hadn't had any practice.

M. came, and he hugged me. We didn't say much. There were some *whoa*s and *wow*s and an *Okay, we're gonna figure this out*. I wasn't upset or scared or even anxious. For someone who complains often about never having any chill, about all of her anxiety, I was calm and relaxed. I have always been good in a crisis. Except this wasn't even a crisis; when you live in America, are insured, and have money, an unplanned pregnancy is the furthest thing from a crisis.

What surprised me most was realizing that I was pleased. Pleased to know that I was capable of pregnancy. If I could have, I would have given my uterus a high five. The pleasure I took in this knowledge, in this ability of mine to participate in the survival of the human species, was unexpected. My body had exceeded the extremely low expectations I had set for it. It had overcome the limitations of my brain, the fear of my mind. I had not been a good caregiver to my body, but it was stronger than I was. I was grateful.

I didn't say any of this to M. He got out his phone and asked a woman walking by to take a photo of us. He told her it was a momentous day for us. Her eyebrows shot up, and she grinned and said, "Oh yeah?"

She clearly thought that we had just gotten engaged and was waiting for one of us to say so, but M. just smiled in return and replied only, "Yeah! Real big day!" Her face clouded for the briefest of moments, but she didn't push it. She took the picture.

In the resulting photo, M. has his arm around me, I'm leaning into him, and, technically, yes, we are both smiling. Incidentally, it is a terrific photo of M., but I look weary and sick. I am most certainly not glowing. I didn't know why he wanted to take the photo. I didn't ask. It caught me off guard when he jumped up from the bench and invited this stranger into our moment. I didn't know what was happening. It never occurred to me this was a photo op. Documenting it then, there, felt invasive. Documenting it now, here, feels inclusive.

I spent a lot of time on public benches that week, which feels very New York to me. Like, somehow, naturally, living in Manhattan, my pregnancy and my course to a decision about it would obviously include numerous public spaces. Life in New York City is lived more publicly than not. The way I hear my neighbors arguing when I wait for the elevator in our building. They're at home, but even then, home is partially public. Or the way once, after a particularly epic fight with my ex B., another neighbor, a single woman, suggested to me that it must be hard living in a small apartment with my boyfriend. I appreciated her tact, but I got the message.

In New York, you can be more alone, with more privacy, in the middle of a city block than you are on your own couch.

The day after I found out I was pregnant, I called my therapist, who was based in San Francisco, and I spoke to her after work from a bench in Washington Square Park. I knew M. was already home, and I wanted to have this conversation in private. So, I stayed out. She was unfailingly supportive and repeatedly said whatever I decided to do would be fine. I couldn't help but get the distinct impression that she wanted me to hold on to this embryo and to nourish it into a life. Not because she was antichoice, not because she did not believe fervently in women's rights and the freedom of women's bodies. I mean, she was a lesbian therapist living in San Francisco. But, rather, because she seemed to think that it would be good for me personally to have this child. Or, more precisely, for me to have a child in general, and, hey, this one was already in the making, why not just roll with it?

I thought about it very much. And, I think, that M. did, too. I was thirty-one, he was in his early forties, and we were more than old enough; hell, we were practically bordering on too-old, last-opportunity territory. We were fortunate enough to earn the kind of living that could provide shelter and organic vegetables and even a college education for a child. We were not sixteen years old. But we had only known each other for a handful of months, had only been dating for a hot second, and neither of us was sure. Having a baby had not been top of mind for either of us until it was forced to be.

It was under this forced reckoning that I came to realize something else, which was that if we made this baby, whether we survived as a couple or not, I would raise the shit out of our child. That was a new feeling. But I felt it wholly and adamantly, and it was my own private recognition. I did not share it with M. It was mine alone. It soothed me. I repeated it to myself as a lullaby. I knew that if I said it out loud to M., his reaction to it would rub away its reassuring sheen, its potency, and I needed it too much to risk its tarnishing. For the first time in my life, I acknowledged that I was capable of bringing another person, *an entire human being*, into this world, who would only exist because I decided they would, and that I could bring them here and give them a beginning and the tools to tell their own story. Without question, I would fail them in countless different ways over and over, because that is what parents do. But I would also give them something to hold on to, something they could steady themselves on, that would make it possible for them to discover whoever it is they were and however it is they wished to be in the world.

In the process, I would give myself one of the very few slivers of certainty that is conceivable, the certainty that being a mother is endless. Under no circumstances does it stop—once you are a mother, and you feel like a mother, you will always be a mom, you will always feel like a mom. To become a mother (by however means, and there are many) is to become puissant. The past and the present and the future may intermingle and exist all together all at once, but there is before motherhood and there is after. If that is not weight, I do not know what is.

I did not keep it. I went to another doctor, who performed an abortion I was privileged to have access to and to have covered by insurance. Where I was privileged to come to under a blanket on a gurney tucked into the corner of a large, clean, well-lit room. Privileged to be babied by a young, freckled nurse who brought me plastic cups of water and pulpy orange juice and a basket of snacks, the likes of which I hadn't seen since childhood: Nature Valley granola bars, Nabisco Ritz peanut butter cracker sandwiches, and those cheery little red boxes of Sun-Maid raisins. She told me not to get up until I had finished the orange juice and eaten at least one of the snacks, and then she left me alone. I pulled myself up to sitting, sipped the water, and found myself thinking about my neighbor in California.

Loretta had lived across the hall from the apartment my ex B. and I shared in San Francisco. She was in her seventies, long divorced, childless, and not to be messed with. Unless you were B., whom she utterly adored. As much as she liked him, she disliked me just as much.

When I baked a batch of vegan granola sweetened only with organic, no-sugar-added applesauce (I swear it was delicious) and knocked on her door to gift her a bag, she told me she had just started a diet that precluded all sugar and carbohydrates, apples most especially, and shut the door. Not a week later, when B. made Magnolia Bakery's famous Nilla wafers banana pudding and shared a bowl with her, she liked it so much she wrote him a thank-you note.

Near the end of our time in California, B. left our apartment one evening to return something of Loretta's that he had borrowed. I do not remember what it was. It certainly wasn't kindness. While he was gone, I changed out of my work clothes, sorted the mail, and started reading the latest issue of the *New Yorker*, managing to read most of the longest article—the little black diamond was in sight!—before he finally returned. He had been gone nearly an hour, but when he walked through the door, he went straight into the kitchen where he grabbed the bottle of our nicest scotch and came into the living room. "Loretta's cat died. She's pretty upset. You should come over." Then he was gone again. I remained on the couch, staring at the doorway he had just vacated. I could think of so many reasons I should not go over and only one that I should: B. hated cats, and I did not.

Loretta's door was open. B. had known I would follow. I closed it behind me. I found the pair of them seated across from one another at her kitchen table. An empty bottle of scotch stood on the table between them, alongside the second bottle B. had just brought over, seal broken, two glasses already filled. It was a bottle we had purchased at a distillery on the Isle of Skye the winter before. I had thought we were saving it for a special occasion. Though this was, I was beginning to realize, a special occasion of a kind.

When he saw me, B. stood, crossed the room, and opened a cabinet to retrieve a third glass, as if he had known this kitchen his whole life. I sat down in the chair between them and looked into Loretta's face. Tears streamed down her cheeks, and her palms were cupped as if to catch the teardrops, but her hands were shaking too much. I covered them with my own hands, and they instantly stilled. I said to her, "I am so sorry." She opened her mouth, and a deep, guttural sob emerged. B. placed a glass of scotch before me, and I picked it up and clinked his glass and then Loretta's before taking my first sip.

The three of us had emptied the second bottle before B. and I realized that Loretta was not a drinker and that we had gotten a seventy-something woman drunk on an empty stomach.

Apparently, the last time she had had anything harder than an Arnold Palmer, her last cat had died. She revealed this fact to us in the middle of a long speech about how wonderful B. was. When she was done raving about the scotch and how she really oughtn't to have neglected liquor for so many years and listing all of the ways B. was, like the scotch, excellent, she turned to me, her head wobbling, and said, "But you."

I stiffened.

"He has all the warmth." She jerked her head back in B.'s direction and did not take her eyes from mine. "You're hard. Cold." And I swear to god she shuddered like a gust of wind had just blown through the kitchen.

She clapped her hands in my face as if to wake me up to my own cruelty. I looked at B., and he shrugged. I looked back at her and felt my eyes well. I had been getting my feelings hurt by Loretta since the day we moved into the building, but now my feelings were getting hurt while I was also drunk. I stood and walked to the sink. I filled a fresh glass with water and placed it on the table in front of her.

"I don't want that," she said.

B., of course, was able to convince her otherwise. While he coaxed her into emptying the glass, I opened all of the cupboards until I finally found one with food in it—row after row of Annie's macaroni and cheese. I stared at all those boxes of organic pasta, and they broke my heart almost more than her dead cat did. And then I picked one off the shelf and began to prepare it on the stove top.

Loretta cried into her bowl of macaroni while she talked about her cat, his favorite places to hide around the apartment and the way he had always known when she needed him, leaping up into her lap at just the right moment. How she needed him now. How the only one who could possibly comfort her now was him. But she did eat, and when most of her noodles were gone, she did not protest when I gave her another glass of water. B. and I walked her to her bedroom, her between us, an arm around each of our necks, and we sat her on the bed. B. went back to the kitchen to clean up, and I helped Loretta unzip her Patagonia vest and slide it off her shoulders and down each arm. I knelt before her and removed her socks while she got her turtleneck stuck on her head, so that by the time I got her socks off and looked up, her face was gone. I unwrapped the shirt and slipped it off her head, and she immediately began to yank at her jeans.

By the way she was moving her limbs, as if they didn't belong to her, as if she did not like them one bit, and by the way her increasingly argumentative syllables collided into one another, Loretta was even drunker than I had thought. And I had thought she was quite drunk. There was some comfort in knowing that tomorrow, she, at least, would not remember aggressively stripping down to her bra and panties in front of me. I tucked her into bed and placed another glass of water on the nightstand. She looked so tiny and alone in her big bed. I wondered if her cat had slept beside her. And before I had even turned out the light, Loretta was out cold.

It was Loretta I thought of in the first moments coming to, out of my abortion, because the night Loretta's cat died was the last time I could remember mothering somebody, however poorly I may have gone about the task, and because I now wondered if that was to be my future, too— long single, childless, judging younger women a bit more harshly than necessary, surviving on macaroni coated in powdered cheese, mourning dead cats. It wasn't the future Catharine River-Rain had predicted for me, but it also wasn't not the future she had predicted for me. She never said M. and I were going to marry or have children. Nor did she say we'd have an abortion. Of course, I hadn't asked these questions of her, though part of me now almost wished that I had. That I'd spent my session with Catharine asking just those sorts of questions: *Is a horrible, painful illness ever going to befall someone I love? How many times will I hurt someone beyond what I can repair? Am I going to have an abortion someday?*

I opened a box of Sun-Maid raisins, and the smell that popped out took me straight back to the cafeteria of my elementary school, to the shrieks of my classmates, to the whistle of the lunchroom monitor, to the cardboard milk carton's wet, sour lip. I didn't eat the raisins, but by smell alone I tasted all of the raisins I had eaten as a child. I put the little red box and my little cup of water down on the little table beside my gurney and felt like a big baby. I never thought I would feel quite so young, raw, and unfinished this side of thirty.

When I pushed back the blanket and edged myself gingerly off the side of the gurney and onto my own two feet, I knew at once that I was no longer pregnant, because I was no longer heavy and hot. I was weightless and cold.

If I had not gone to that second doctor, that embryo would have become a baby, and that baby would have been born at the end of June 2017 (astrological sign: nurturing Cancer) and would be only a week or so older than my best friend Jane's baby girl.

There was a single moment—when I held Jane's wondrous newborn for the very first time—that I did think about the one M. and I chose not to have. It seemed to me, it will always seem to me, though I understand this is completely irrational, that our baby would have also been, *could only have been*, a baby girl. I know it was a girl.

We would have given her the name that M. has loved for decades, the name he has long wanted to give his daughter someday. The name isn't mine to share, but the first name is not only extremely uncommon but also, on the rare occasion it is bestowed, considered exclusively a boy's name. The middle name would have been M.'s mom's maiden name. Neither is a name that, on my own, would ever have occurred to me to give my child.

But, in this alternate reality and birth, I would not be on my own, and the decision to have this baby would have come from what we thought was love but what was mostly rational, careful consideration. Deduction. I have no doubt that I would have agreed to the name, even though it meant that our daughter's first, middle, and last name would all have been of M.'s choosing, all of M.'s family, representing nothing of me, let alone anything of hers alone.

But, in this fantasy, I would also never call her by this name. From the moment she is born, I would call her by the only remotely reasonable nickname that could be devised from the letters of her given name: Elvie. Eventually, I would realize that I have essentially renamed her L. V., as though she is some kind of inversion of my initials, of myself, proving I am no better than her father.

I would think of that wonderful line in that wonderful Evan S. Connell novel *Mrs. Bridge*, in which Mrs. Bridge herself, first name India, observes, "It seemed to her that her parents must have been thinking of someone else when they named her." I would think of this line again and again, knowing it's true for our daughter and knowing that the someone else we were thinking of when we named her was ourselves.

We would be thinking of ourselves, too, when we separated. We would have never married, so the separation, which would happen

Victoria Loustalot

before Elvie is old enough to create memories of us together, would be easy, as easy as it could ever be to part.

Elvie would grow to be very tall like her dad and have his shimmery blue eyes and his thick, dark curls, unruly in every single childhood photo, because I, with my straight, straight hair, would never learn to rule them, would never want to learn, would secretly adore their rowdiness. She would have my eyebrows, my neck, and she would have a strong, athletic build that is uniquely hers, unplaceable in any family album, as though her first act of assertion was calling dibs on her strength, on how she would move through this world.

She would be raised a vegetarian and, except for a few months in her sixteenth year, would embrace vegetarianism her entire life. She would eschew college, infuriating her father, who was not afforded the luxury of going away to school, who feels the wound of that missed experience still, and who thought he would finally heal it when he moved his daughter into her dormitory, when he gave her a standing ovation as she walked across the stage to accept her diploma. But that is too much to ask of your child. The purpose of her life is not to provide her parents the fulfillment we failed to find in ourselves.

When she is grown, she would fall in love with a Canadian woman, and they would buy land in Ontario and become dairy farmers and each other's wives. Elvie and her father, in their mutually placid way, would each, independent of the other, make the silent, conscious vow to overcome their rift about diplomas and make amends. Elvie would tell her dad it doesn't matter what degrees they have or don't have, and he would come to believe her. Elvie would adore her stepmom, a costume designer from Rhode Island who is also an accomplished potter and who somehow manages to bake an endless variety of vegetarian casscroles that taste deliciously impractical and sophisticated but never seem to have more than five ingredients.

Elvie and her wife would have children of their own, and I would visit them, my family, on their farm for a long weekend at the end of

June, near, but not on, Elvie's birthday, having long ago assumed she would rather spend the actual day of her birth first with her friends and now with her wife and their children. She, of course, would have no memory of the day she was born. Every year, her birthday, for her, is about taking stock of the present and about what she wants the next year to bring. Every year, for me, her birthday is about the day we met, the day she became a daughter and I became a mother. It is about our past. I would mark the occasion the way I felt when I gave birth to her: alone.

In the car on the way home from dropping me at the airport, my daughter-in-law would remark, not for the first or the last time, that she has never known a mother and a daughter with a quieter relationship, and Elvie, in a signature move she perfected in the high chair of her toddlerhood, would shake her head, smile, and shrug all at once in a single, perfect gesture. She would know I love her. I was always conscious that my own desires should never be a barrier to helping my child. I would only ever make one request of her, that she be anything she wants to be except a victim.

Elvie would be decent and good, no better or worse than most people. She would not be a rocket scientist or find the cure for cancer. She would have a mystifying love of puns. She would have inherited my moods, but she would be better at managing them. When she feels one coming on, she would know to go out to the fields, to stroke the long, lean back of one of the cows or rub the ear of a goat. She would be tender with everyone she loves and even most of those she does not, but there would be a certain depth of compassion that only comes when she's among the animals, eyes on them, corralling them, feeding them, bathing them, their hearts beating beneath her listening palms.

I would be proud of her, proud of the love and authenticity she brings to the world, but I would never like her mom. I would never like the woman I become, or maybe I mean remain, as her mother. The cold, hard woman Loretta saw and whom I also saw on that October morning I woke up and realized that another something had happened to my body, that I was very likely pregnant. I sacrificed Elvie's chance at existence for my own future, for my potential as a woman, and, maybe, someday, as a mother I will like, will be proud to be.

I held Jane's beautiful, perfect baby girl, and I thought of Elvie. For only the briefest of moments, I thought of that light M. and I had decided not to turn on. I know we made the right decision, because I know the real reason I didn't choose to remain pregnant. It wasn't because my relationship with M. was too new or because he and I weren't sure if we wanted children together.

I knew if I had had Elvie, I would have loved her completely. I would have loved her far more than I can comprehend not having had her. I never doubted that. But I also knew that I would have needed her love in return. That terrified me. It is your job to love your child, but it is never your child's job to love you. I know that intellectually, but until I know it emotionally, I will not bring a baby into this world, will not allow any baby of mine to have a beginning that I mistake for my own second chance—no matter how much my arms may start to ache. That is the promise I make to myself, to the man, M. or otherwise, who could one day make me a mother, and to our child.

That is the story of my abortion. I have written it down, because I am not ashamed of the choice I made and because it was a privilege to have had that choice. There were things that were not easy about getting pregnant unexpectedly, but having an abortion was not one of them. This is more of my good fortune. It is, in and of itself, a tremendous gift of place and circumstance given to me by women who are older than I am, who willed that gift into first their and now my reality. My abortion was entirely routine, as it should be for every woman who finds herself in a position of making the choice to have one.

My abortion was the right choice for me, in that relationship, in that moment of my life. I share it with you, because if I am not willing to say that I had an abortion, to admit it on the page and in life, then I had no business having one in the first place.

CHAPTER
TWENTY-TWO

Spirituality and religion have both, independently and in conjunction with one another, gotten a bad rep over the centuries. Religion because of abuses of power and money and control, like all large enterprises in which profit margins matter. And spirituality, sometimes for very similar reasons, but also for becoming a punch line, for being a weasely way out of committing to anything at all, for choosing to identify with something that has been so poorly defined, for everyone who claims it is free to invent their own definition of the term. Your spirituality may be taking a daily walk in the forest; someone else's may be meditating in front of an altar of candles and crystals; another's may be chanting and dancing in a drum circle. If you choose to identify as religious, if you choose to identify as religiously Jewish or Muslim or Christian, each means something concrete and is an identification you can point to and say, *This is my faith, religious text, ritual, history, people*. If you choose to identify as spiritual, who the hell knows what you're talking about.

During my first conversation with Michelle, the Hawaiian empath, I asked her about spirituality and religion and the difference between them, and she replied, without missing a beat, "I would love for you to actually create a different word than *spirituality* . . . Maybe we should start calling it *instinctual practice*. It's just returning to our being, which is a soul in a human form with access to all the answers. Because, to me, spirituality has become identical to religion almost . . . You can sit in church every day, but that doesn't give you a relationship with yourself or God. You can sit and meditate every day, but that doesn't give you a relationship with yourself or God. [Spiritual and religious leaders] are emphasizing the actions more than the point, but that's because most of the people leading have only memorized that stuff, they haven't embodied it."

These actions and disciplines are appealing, because they give us a sense of control. But that's our first mistake, wanting control, thinking control is anything other than a soothing fairy tale. As Michelle put it to me, "When you are truly in alignment with your soul, you don't feel in control. You feel peacefully loved and supported in the total unknowing at all times."

There are meditation and yoga practices with long, storied histories that are particularly popular right now that encourage their disciples to do things like wear all white and meditate and chant for hours at a time. There is nothing wrong with this in theory, and for many people, I am sure, these practices are life changing. But all together, they might for others be a way to trick themselves into thinking they're successfully working toward becoming better people, when, really, they're just using the ritual to avoid the work of real growth.

I think of one of my graduate school classmates, whom I quite liked but who every week seemed to have a new scheme, a new best idea ever. She was always taking up a new project that, first and foremost, necessitated an expensive trip to Home Depot or the Container Store. One semester, she decided she was spending too much money on flowers, so she bought and potted several plants instead. In theory, over time, the plants were going to cost her less than buying a fifteen-dollar bouquet of flowers at the bodega every week, but by the time she would have made up the cost of the plants, pots, rocks, and soil, the plants were long dead, because she vacillated between over- and underwatering, never fully committing to either murder method.

I have long been leery of any "solution" that involves a lot of up-front costs or an elaborate and complicated learning curve, but it had never occurred to me to include the most-basic-just-five-minutes-a-day-what-have-you meditation in that handwoven basket. Meditation has always seemed to me, as the pure product of my generation that I am, like a most innocuous practice with a most extraordinary amount of potential benefit and benevolence. But Michelle described it as run-ning the risk of just being another distraction: "The word *meditation* is so misunderstood, and the perceptions of it are so misunderstood. It's used as an excuse, big-time, for people who are not ready to say yes, because they're like, 'I'm trying.' It's like, 'No.' Like I said, you can sit in a church pew all day long, but that doesn't make you a good person. It doesn't do anything. It's what's your attention, what's your intention."

That attention and intention can be meditation, and for some people it is, and Michelle isn't against that. She just doesn't believe meditation is the universal cure-all popular Western media has turned it into. She doesn't see it as one size fits all, any more than Christianity or Islam fit everyone. A few years ago the *New York Times* published a story on the health risks of yoga, and a certain demographic of upper-middle-class America lost its damn mind over it.

The idea that we could get hurt doing yoga was shocking and com-pletely unacceptable to people. Yoga was supposed to be safe. It was sup-posed to be physical therapy—the thing you do to heal your body, not harm it. The article didn't say the rate of injury in yoga is higher than in any other physical pursuit, just that it is on par with most popular sports. The thing is, when we move and contort and ask our bodies to stretch and strengthen, we're taking a certain amount of risk that we'll push or pull too hard. Land funny. Twist something. We know this.

Yoga is safe the way tennis is safe. The article's findings were only jarring because we'd placed yoga on a pedestal.

On a neighboring pedestal is meditation, whose benefits have been touted in much the same way yoga's benefits have been nearly universally heralded. Even if we all have the potential to benefit from meditation and yoga, setting aside the vagueness of the very words themselves, what they actually mean, and what their cultural and historical connotations and traditions actually are, we won't necessarily all benefit in the same way or to the same degree. There are also other ways to achieve meditation's physical and mental benefits that don't involve meditating strictly in the way that most of us in the West have come to view the practice.

What guides Michelle's work with her clients are not mandates to think, act, move, or silence the mind in a specific, narrow way. It's making sure that anyone she agrees to work with is ready to step up and to say, "I want to say yes to my soul, and I'm going to let go of getting what I want."

I love the idea of hiring someone to help you not get what you want. Pretty much everything we do around here is in support of seeking out our whims. (Raise your hand if you don't want things. Put your hand down, Pema Chodron, you don't count.)

When Michelle told me she only works with clients who are ready to let go of their wants, I was thrown. I did not know this was an option. *Tired of not getting what you want? Just stop wanting!* I realize this is Buddhism and Philosophy 101, but I'm a lapsed Catholic who's long been in the habit of praying only at the altar of literature, where it is literary law that all characters must have wants. So, forgive me this, what may feel, only to me, like an earth-shattering concept. I replied to Michelle with the first thing that popped into my mind: "Nothing in the world sounds better to me than divorcing myself from what I want." It sounds like freedom. I used to think that money was freedom, because it gave you the gift of choices. But if you can just stop wanting, choice becomes beautifully irrelevant. (It also backs up my distrust of restaurants with lengthy menus; it is my experience that the shorter the menu, the better the food.)

Isabel (Isa) Unanue is a doctoral student in clinical psychology in Palo Alto, California, whose focus is on liberation psychology and helping disenfranchised individuals and communities heal by tapping into the cultural practices of their ancestors and history, strengthening their intuition, and making space and value for traditions that have been routinely dismissed by centuries of colonialism.

As Isa put it to me when we spoke, "We have to embrace and nurture the ten-year-old kid who's hearing voices." And not automatically assume a child who's hearing voices needs to be medicated or institutionalized. I thought of Andrea in New Jersey. She was lucky. Her parents might have been scared, but they listened to her.

I still don't know if Andrea has the skills she says that she does. But I did track down her seventh-grade math teacher, Jennifer Corforte, who remembered Andrea as "an A student, a hard worker, never a student I had any reason to be skeptical of." She told me, too, that she'd known nothing about psychics or mediums, that what happened with Kyle's spirit had been an unprecedented experience. Nearly a decade later, however, she said it remained a vivid memory. "Everything checked out. Andrea told me that Kyle had been the 'alpha' in his friend group and that there was a baby coming." Just a few days before the incident with Andrea, Jennifer's friend had visited Kyle's grave, had told him that he and his wife were expecting a baby, had reminisced about Kyle having been their leader, their group's "alpha."

After Andrea told her that Kyle was always in their class, Jennifer had found herself alone in her classroom and had waved and spoken to Kyle. The next day, Andrea came up to her and said, "Kyle says that you acknowledged him yesterday."

As Jennifer put it, "I'm a math person, and [Andrea] hit way too many variables for me . . . It made me feel kind of safe. It's nice to know that there's life after. But I did tell my principal, 'If he does the penny trick up the door [from the movie *Ghost*], I'm outta here!'"

Jennifer believes Andrea. She embraced her student just the way Isa says that we should. I want to believe and embrace Andrea, too. But I still have questions. I couldn't get any of the police officers Andrea connected me with to speak on the record, and all of the cases she worked on with the cold cases department remain cold.

I didn't mention Andrea to Isa, but, if I had, I think Isa would have said it doesn't matter. I think she's right.

In different places, in different conversations, and by different sets of people, both the Andreas of the world, the ten-year-olds hearing voices, and the palm readers sitting in strip malls across America might be called *psychic*, which is evidence that we don't have a clear and consistent understanding of what the word means. When we use the words *psychic* or *spiritual* in conversation, we can have little hope that the person we're speaking to has the same definition or even a remotely similar one to our own.

For Isa, spirituality is having a relationship with an outside reality and embracing what she sees as this truer nature of reality in order to open a new realm of tradition that taps into an individual's own interior. Religion she understands as a practice that takes the place of that interior work. Spirituality is a process. Religion is a discipline. Religion is memorizing your multiplication tables; spirituality is learning why the multiplication tables work—knowing not just that seven times seven is forty-nine but knowing why.

When I interviewed Isa, she was about to leave her home in California and travel to Puerto Rico. Hurricane Maria had made landfall on the island eleven days prior, and Isabel was going to help her many relatives whose lives and homes had been destroyed. She spoke to me with an urgency and a conviction that I imagined might have felt all the more critical to her now in the jarring reality of Mother Nature and our government's abysmal lack of response. Isa was emphatic that *psychic* is a single word trying to encapsulate the work of someone who can help you undo yourself from your mind, who can help you embrace the unconditioning of the brain and allow your free will to augment as you release more and more conditioning. Michelle in Hawaii would agree with her.

But Abdi Assadi, the revered acupuncturist in New York City, emailed me a slightly different point of view:

> The reason psychic phenomena are so weird/frighten-ing/exciting is that they lie outside the realm of the thinking mind. You cannot understand it in your head, you can only experience it. That is infuriating for the thinking mind, which wants to be in control by understanding. But that function has limitations. And it runs into a brick wall with these kind[s] of things. I have no interest in proving or disproving such phenomena. I can say this to you, such things do not make us special or give us any leg over anyone else. Years ago I came across, as well as studied with, people who had profound psychic abilities. Some told me things decades ago that are still coming to pass. Fascinating? Absolutely. Did it make any differ-ence in my own life? Absolutely not, I still had to go through what I had to go through. Were any of these people any better off than you or me? Almost always the opposite. They were mostly ungrounded to an extreme, which brought much hardship to their lives. What I would offer you is this: sit with yourself with some kind of daily practice where you can step out of your chattering mind. Learn to tolerate that

space, and much of what you are grappling with will be revealed. I leave you with my favorite quote of the Third Zen Patriarch Seng-ts'an, [from] *The Mind of Absolute Trust*, written in the last sixth century:

"The more you think about these matters the farther you are from the truth.

Step aside from all thinking,

and there is nowhere you can't go."

Which brings me back to Michelle's idea of rebranding spirituality, of calling it *instinctual practice*. That phrase isn't bad, and I think even Isa would approve. But it feels bulky to me, a little cottony on the mouth. *Instinctual practice.* I like the notion of being responsible for my soul and living in a desireless state, open to every possibility, and I know I'm overthinking it, but the phrase *instinctual practice* still sounds vague, no more solid than its mother root, *spirituality*.

CHAPTER TWENTY-THREE

Sometimes we are able to let go of what we want, and sometimes it gets taken from us.

Debbie Saalfield agreed to talk to me because she believed it was important that people know what happened to her.

She was a single mom living in Florida. Only she was also commuting part-time to New York City, both for her marketing job at a dance company and to rehearse with her ballroom-dance partner, who was based in New York. Her boyfriend was also in New York, a handsome man with a good job and a great apartment. After a few tough years, it had felt to Debbie like things were finally turning around for her.

Until all of a sudden, they weren't. In the span of a single brutal day, she lost the marketing job and her dance partner, and then, that night, her handsome boyfriend broke up with her. Suddenly, she had no income (and she had already refinanced her house in Florida); she had no way of continuing to pursue ballroom dancing and the dance competitions she adored; and she no longer had the emotional support of her boyfriend, who might have helped her through the other losses.

Most of us can only handle a certain number of setbacks simultaneously. There is a threshold. Debbie lost too much all at once. She became, in a matter of hours, exceedingly vulnerable, and it is when we have that scarlet letter *V* written large across our chests that we are most susceptible to being taken advantage of and are most likely to seek out a psychic or an astrologer.

The last thing Debbie had to do before she left New York City that terrible day was pack up her belongings at her boyfriend's—ex-boyfriend's—apartment, but when she was done, it was still too early to leave for the airport. So she found herself on the street with a dangerous combination: tears in her eyes and too much time on her hands.

There are many things that can feel like quintessential New York City experiences. Drinking a beer on the Staten Island Ferry and toasting Lady Liberty as she glides on by; watching the sun begin its descent from the rooftop exhibit of the Met on a summer evening; or, the most quintessential rite of passage of them all, walking down a New York City block in broad daylight sobbing and assiduously avoiding eye contact with every single being you pass, as if everyone is holding a clipboard, trying to get you to donate money to every worthy cause you can possibly imagine except the one you need right in that crying, self-pitying moment: the worthy cause of yourself. Because I don't care if you've lived in New York City for ten years or fifty; you're not a New Yorker until you've been humiliated in public, until you've fought with a significant other on a street corner or cried so hard a homeless guy asks if *you* need anything.

So, in a way, it was on what she thought was her last day in the city that Debbie took a big step closer to becoming a full-fledged New Yorker—she did the walk of the ugly cry.

I have no idea what Debbie looks like. I don't know how old she is. But when she described that day over the phone to me, about her tears and her pain, I could not help but think of a woman I saw once on Hudson Street in the West Village. She was much older than I am, and older, I think, than Debbie. She was tall and slender, with nearly shoulder-length blonde hair in what I believe we're to call, this season anyway, a *lob*, that long bob that gives terrific hair swing. I suspect she was somewhat north of sixty years old, and she had that oh so casual elegance that announces, *I've had money since before you were born.* Her blouse and slacks were exquisitely tailored, and her jewelry was minimal, understated, but real. It was a weekday, near noon; she was carrying a bottle of champagne, and for a split second an image of Anjelica Huston in Woody Allen's *Crimes and Misdemeanors* flashed in my mind. It's the moment in the film when Anjelica is walking home to her New York City apartment. She's purchased flowers or wine or a baguette or all three, I forget, and she's crossing the street in a long, deceptively simple-looking coat in that sophisticated, dramatic Anjelica Huston way; she's carrying whatever it is she's purchased, and she takes the viewer's breath away, right before, in the next scene, her own breath is taken, and she's murdered.

This woman on Hudson was just that kind of perfectly polished, except that she was crying. Hard. I found myself sheepishly surprised. Because, for all the many people I have seen crying in public in this city, they have never been this. Never this nicely dressed, never twice my age. They're always a bit of a mess or young (ish) or both. They always remind me of myself.

This woman, yes, I felt bad for her, for whatever was making her cry, but I also thought, *Christ, does it really never end? Could I be eighty-three years old, dragging my oxygen tank down Ninth Avenue, tears rolling down my oxygen tube?*

So even though I knew she wasn't Debbie, it was this elegantly crying woman I pictured as Debbie told me her story. It was this woman I pictured when Debbie described seeing the psychic sign in neon-red cursive on a triangle-shaped two-story brick structure that came to a point right on the corner where Bleecker Street and Seventh Avenue South meet in the West Village. It had a dramatic picture window on the Seventh Avenue side of the building, the busier side, with red curtains that looked like velvet (but who knows what they were really made of) and gold-colored tassels holding the curtains aloft to reveal a chandelier and a small table flanked by two upholstered dining chairs and the richly patterned Oriental-like rug beneath. Even if you aren't sad, even if you aren't crying, the building is hard to miss, hard not to wonder about, be intrigued by. The building itself and its location—this was prime Manhattan real estate, after all—lent a strong air of legitimacy rarely associated with the storefront psychic trade. As Debbie was describing this building to me, I had no trouble picturing it, because, as it happens, I know it well. I have been walking by this building for years, and too many times to count, I have wondered how any psychic could afford the rent. Debbie was about to answer just that question. She told me that she carried her luggage up to the door and rang the bell, wiping away her tears, asking herself, *What the hell else do I have to lose?*

When we, like Debbie, follow that blinking neon sign of the psychic, we think it is because we are worried about the future. We're not. We are wrapped up entirely in the present. We only want the palm reader to tell us that the future is going to be good, because that reassurance will make us feel better now. The only time we can count on being truly present, truly in the moment, is when we are suffering: *Make this pain that I feel stop.* In that present moment, Debbie was in enough pain that she forgot there is almost always more to lose.

An attractive, polished woman in her midthirties answered Debbie's ring. She was dressed in a suit and kitten heels, something a judge might wear beneath her black robes. She ushered Debbie and her baggage into the front room, to the little table beneath the chandelier, and even before she drew those thick curtains closed and introduced herself, she knew what she would do. She handed Debbie a menu (it was suspiciously long), a selection of readings, escalating, naturally, in price. Debbie, naturally, chose the one you and I would probably choose: the cheapest one (or perhaps the second from the cheapest, just to seem even a tad couth). The psychic told Debbie her name was Zena, and then began. Only, much to her overt dismay, she quickly discovered that the reading Debbie had selected was simply not going to be anywhere near enough for her needs. Because Zena had spotted a curse.

There is always a curse, and no one ever seems to catch a cheap curse.

According to Zena, Debbie was cursed financially, and this dark curse of money woes was bleeding into the rest of her life: her career, her dancing, her romance. She told Debbie that she must address this money curse if she was to have any hope of improving anything ever.

Fortunately, Zena could help. She could lift the curse. The fine print was that in order to do so, she would need $30,000. Immediately. But only temporarily, just for twenty-four hours: the essential key to dispelling the curse was Debbie trusting Zena. Debbie needed to unburden herself of her tight and unhealthy grip on money. By relinquishing the money, she would prove that she was not attached to it, and only then would she be liberated from this dark place in which she had let herself fall.

Any accountant, any friend, even Debbie herself in a less vulnerable moment, would have known that she could not afford to part with $30,000. She wouldn't even have had it to give, except that she had recently refinanced her home in Florida, and so she did, unfortunately and purely in the technical sense, have ready access to that sum. Debbie knew the difference between having an amount of money at her disposal and being able to afford to spend that money, but she also felt drawn to Zena, who, in her beautiful suit and piercing gaze, exuded the only reassurance Debbie had been able to find all day. It was far more than she had gotten from the company that let her go, the dance partner who didn't want to dance with her anymore, and the boyfriend who left.

It was time to try something, someone, else. Nothing made sense anymore anyway. None of the stability she had counted on had been stable after all. So she decided to trust this beautiful woman in her beautiful shop, who was the very image of picture-book success—everything Debbie wanted but which felt impossibly elusive. And Zena had promised she could come back tomorrow for all of her money. So, Debbie left Zena's shop and walked across the street to the nearest bank, because banks are on every corner in New York City these days. Banks, mobile phone carriers, and psychics, three businesses of the most dubious reputation and ethics, are the only institutions left that can afford Manhattan rent. Oh, and Debbie's ex-boyfriend, too, of course, who had warned her about this very shop on late-night, hand-in-hand walks home to his apartment. But Debbie didn't need him. She could do whatever she wanted now.

She got the money. When she walked back out onto the street, however, she saw Zena standing in the doorway of her shop, and Debbie realized that this psychic she didn't know at all had followed her outside, stood, and watched her go into the bank. There was something about seeing Zena in the sharpness of New York City daylight, outside that ornate little room, waiting expectantly, intensely, that did not feel right to Debbie. She had the envelope in her hand. She was not crying anymore. The bank was behind her but only just. She could turn around and go right back in. She had a small, distant flicker of doubt. But then she thought of everything she didn't have anymore, all the instincts she had followed in the past, and the boyfriend, who had said, "Don't trust that shop, trust me." She crossed the street, followed Zena back inside, and handed her the envelope, and then, having been reassured and reassured again that she could come back tomorrow for every last penny, Debbie left. She canceled her flight and got a hotel room. She wasn't done with New York City, and the city was not done with her.

Debbie and I were speaking by phone. She was at home in Florida, and I was at home in Manhattan. The two of us have never met. We were connected by a retired New York City police detective I had already interviewed. This was the first time Debbie and I had ever spoken, but the whole time I was listening to her story, I couldn't help but feel I was right there with her at every step. This was partly because Debbie described what happened to her, even years later, with clarity and focus; she is on a mission to warn others, to make people understand how this not only happens but happens often. But I also felt as though I had been beside her, because the psychic parlor Debbie found herself in, that impossible-to-miss corner building, is barely two blocks from my own apartment. I knew the sign and the curtains and the chandelier and even the bank across the street. It was a coincidence, certainly, but when she mentioned the street her ex-boyfriend lived on and how close it was to the psychic, I had to stop her. I had to ask just where exactly he lived. The answer was my very street, my very block.

I am not saying this means anything at all.

According to the mathematician Joseph Mazur, the odds of any one person winning the lottery four times, as Joan Ginther did when she won $5.4 million in 1993; $2 million in 2006; another $3 million in 2008; and $10 million in 2010, aren't nearly as impossible as you and I would imagine. He calculates the odds at five million to one, which is a lot, but not so much that you can't wrap your head around it. Mazur claims, too, that a "magical" coincidence, like meeting someone abroad who's from the same small American town you are and, what's more, who lives in the exact house you grew up in, is not magic or crazy or impossible, either. "People think that their address book is essentially the people they know, and it turns out any address book is about one percent of the people they know in some way," Mazur explains.

Okay, fine. Our coincidence doesn't mean anything. Debbie and I are in each other's extended address books. Still. I'm not going to not mention it. Especially because it is undeniable that it lent a force to, a certain feeling of connection between, Debbie and me. Her voice audibly shifted as we discussed neighborhood restaurants. She relaxed. It's exactly the kind of coincidence you hope to stumble upon as an interviewer, because you know it'll put your interviewee at ease.

When Debbie returned the next day for every penny of her $30,000, Zena was nowhere to be found. Debbie did, eventually, manage to get her on the phone a couple of times, but each time Zena said simply that the money was unavailable. Of course, when Debbie called the bank to stop the transfer, it was too late. The money was gone. With the help of a private investigator, Debbie eventually found another victim of Zena's, and charges were brought against her. She was found guilty and sent to prison.

But none of this is what surprised me about Debbie's story. That there are fraudulent psychics is not news. What surprised me is what Debbie told me when I asked her if she still believed in psychics. Not only did she still believe in them, but she knew one who was real. Or had been. This psychic had recently passed away, but she had lived in Florida, and after Zena had gone to prison and Debbie was back in Florida, she had gone to see this woman many times. Like Zena before her, this psychic requested money from Debbie, but unlike Zena, she only asked for the nominal, flat fee she advertised as her standard rate. There was nothing in Debbie's aura or her future that ever required additional funds. She was not cursed. For Debbie, this psychic proved to be a wonderful source of genuine insight and comfort.

Wait. What?

It was hard for me to imagine going through what Debbie had gone through, and over a period of *years*—the scam, the expense, the investigation, the trial—and not being forever soured on psychics. I would be keeping my palms to myself for the rest of my life. But Debbie didn't seem to understand my surprise. To her, what made Zena's actions truly awful was that she gave real psychics a bad name, casting long shadows of doubt and ill will across anyone, from any culture, who has this ability or believes that they do and, regardless, wants to honor the spiritual tradition of their heritage and of themselves.

It is often exactly our spiritual traditions, our heritage, that make us vulnerable and can be used against us. In 2010, over the course of eight months, Orlando resident Priti Mahalanobis was successfully scammed out of $136,000 by a woman claiming to be psychic. Priti and her family are Hindu, and she told me that part of the reason the fraud worked was because the woman knew Priti's religion. "She used a lot of Hindu beliefs, like the past lives and reincarnation. Like, 'I'll look into your past lives to see if there's any bad karma.' . . . She homed in on my faith and used those beliefs to manipulate me." The economy in 2010 was also particularly bleak, and not only was Priti's father's business struggling, but she was in the process of launching a new business herself. There were many reasons to feel especially anxious and vulnerable and susceptible to someone promising help and good fortune.

Unlike Zena, Priti's psychic didn't ask for a large sum of money right away. "At the end [of the first visit], she said, 'Okay, I feel there is something here but to look into it more, to do a deeper meditation and see what is the root of the problem, I'll have to do some more work. To do that, it will cost two hundred dollars.' So I agreed to it. I figured it's only a couple of hundred dollars," she told me.

I asked Priti how she felt when she left that first appointment, and she said, "I felt like there was a possibility." I thought of that Emily Dickinson line, "I dwell in Possibility—A fairer House than Prose," and wondered if ol' Em was wrong.

That hope carried Priti through the next eight months. The psychic became her confidant. Priti shared the fears she didn't want to burden her family with, and the psychic, in turn, told her the things she wanted to hear. "She was always like, 'Don't worry. I'm going to help you. Just trust me.'" The psychic told Priti that her business was going to be successful, and Priti came to believe that this woman genuinely cared about her. She went back for the assurance and support, and each time, it cost her a little more.

It was only when her business was unsuccessful that Priti began to have doubts. "Things weren't going so well in the business, and then what happened was she started to turn it around and blame it on me, saying it was because I was being negative . . . I had to have faith and trust her, and not be so negative."

Eventually, Priti was forced to close her business. "At that point, I think I had hit rock bottom, not just financially, but emotionally as well, because of all her emotional blackmail. So I just prayed a lot for an answer." She finally told her family what was going on. The scam artist might have used Priti's religious beliefs to lure her in, but it was also her religion that helped pull her out.

Even psychics whose intentions are not discernibly malicious have the power to potentially cause harm. One of the psychics I interviewed offered to give me a reading at the end of our conversation. But it immediately deviated from the readings I had grown accustomed to. The very first thing she said to me was not about any work I was doing or any man I was dating. It was not about me at all. What she said was, "Oh boy, I feel one of your girlfriends is going through a lot of distress."

Without thinking, I replied, "Yeah, take your pick." Because it was true. At the time, a number of my good friends were facing challenges that had made us realize we weren't so young anymore: these were adult problems with consequences that would have implications for not only my friends but also for their partners, for their children, for the rest of each of their lives. And these distresses that had befallen so many of my friends had arrived in quick succession. More than once, right in the middle of worrying about one friend, I had gotten a text from another detailing some horrible thing that had just happened to her. It was a pileup.

Which was how, over the course of the proceeding hour, this psychic came to describe the predicaments that two of my good friends were currently struggling with—as well as exactly what each of them needed to do to extricate themselves. Her instructions were specific, and she gave them to me under the obvious assumption that I would pass them on to my friends.

But I wasn't so sure that I should.

In the years that I had known them and long before I ever set eyes on Catharine River-Rain, these two particular friends had both been compelled to visit psychics. I knew that they believed in the possibility of guidance from something bigger than us, something universal, something unexplainable. They were open to the numinous. Too open maybe.

If someone we loved and trusted came to any one of us and said, "I saw a psychic, and she told me some big things about you and your life," it would rattle us, even those of us convinced that psychic abilities are hogwash. But these two friends, more than most, I believe, would be deeply rattled. Without question, the information I had been given would cause my friends more pain in the immediate future. It was possible, yes, that this information could help them avoid additional pain later. Possible, but far from guaranteed. Because what this psychic told me was nothing they wanted to hear. She confirmed to me what I knew they both feared, what, right now, they both felt was the worst imaginable outcome.

Each of them had said to me that they didn't know what to do. But they did know. They just weren't ready to do it. It's rare that we truly don't know what to do. Most of the time we know exactly what to do; it's just not the choice we want to make. So we stall and toss and turn. No one can make the choice for us. This psychic didn't tell me anything my friends didn't, on some level, already know. And hearing it from me wasn't going to magically make their predicaments any easier to face. I kept my mouth shut.

This psychic never suggested that she needed any large sum of money, never said my friends were cursed. I believed then and still that she genuinely thought she was helping. But if I had shared her predictions, her warnings, with my friends, I would have contributed to their confusion, to their pain. I would have caused them harm.

CHAPTER
TWENTY-FOUR

I initially predicted that I would devote a substantial portion of the research for this book to the work of proof and fact, but that has turned out to be both an elusive and unrewarding effort. Right around the time I was old enough to make my own money and buy my own books, the phenomena of pop psychology and self-help books exploded. They were and continue to be everywhere. You know them. The titles are almost always short, often just one word, colon, lengthy subtitle. The covers are frequently white; the titles, one of the primary colors; and the words on the many (but not that many) pages inside follow a certain trajectory: cite a study—> share an engaging/charming/moving/relevant anecdote—> throw in a few surprising statistics, the rates of this and that—> quote an expert with advice about how the reader can avoid/ improve some component of the dilemma the book is suggesting it can definitively resolve—> repeat until you reach seventy thousand words.

These books cover every topic of literally any pertinence to our lives: how we relate to our parents or our children or our partners; how we age; how we exercise; how we sleep; how we eat; how we breathe; how we talk; how we make decisions; how we spend or save or lose money; how we fail; how we succeed; how we make friends; how we hate; how we love.

Do these books sell solutions or hope or both or nothing at all? Is the science cited in these books irrefutable? We treat the studies and the statistics researched and rolled out in these books as if they are. If a scientist at a respectable institution we've heard of says it is so and a writer who has written for reputable publications we've also heard of writes about it, then the brains agree: it is so. The MIT astrophysicist Sara Seager, speaking to the *New York Times* about the possibility of extraterrestrial life and mysterious objects and incidents, said, "What people sometimes don't get about science is that we often have phenomena that remain unexplained." Seager was arguing neither in favor of nor against the existence of aliens but only pointing out that science continues to have far more questions than answers.

Another thing people sometimes don't get about science is that it's a field of work and exploration conducted by human beings, human beings with careers and reputations they are invested in, human beings who, like everyone else, have insecurities and ambitions and blind spots. We have an unfortunate habit of putting unrealistic expectations on certain professions: scientists, doctors, religious leaders. We expect them to be somehow outside failure, beyond the shortcomings that routinely trip up the rest of us.

Social psychologists have felt this dichotomy acutely in recent years with the rise of the replication movement, which has taken to task a number of social psychology studies that have received impressive publications and wide acclaim in the scientific community as well as crossover renown in popular media (and the aforementioned self-help genre) but whose results cannot seem to be satisfactorily replicated by other social psychologists. While social psychology may have spearheaded this debate, dubious results and findings are widely understood to be rampant across chemistry, biology, and the rest of scientific inquiry; the replication movement, which pertains to all of the scientific and medical communities, raises valid arguments and will undoubtedly push research and the conclusions drawn toward more consistent and transparent methods and standards as well as help create better scientists and better science. That is all true, but we can't forget that the scientists behind the replication movement also happen to be human. They are calling the work of their colleagues into very public question, and they have something to gain in doing so: the taking down of someone else's research and, in some cases, an entire career, benefits their own work and opportunities for future success.

There is bias on every side, as the reporters and scientists who are following, discussing, and writing about this situation have all pointed out. It's more than just bias, or it is exactly bias, so long as we realize that the term *bias* is just an emotionless way of describing an extremely emotional situation.

The replication movement is rife with feelings: fear and anxiety and shame and the kind of psychological pain you feel physically—in your chest, stomach, shoulders, any place in the body that the mind can think of to hold its overflowing suffering.

The revelation that, as Susan Dominus wrote in October 2017 in a *New York Times Magazine* article, "the enemy of science—subjectivity— had burrowed its way into the field's methodology more deeply than had been recognized," speaks to a part of the research process that had not been sufficiently scrutinized previously: every time a scientist decides to exclude or include a subject or a finding with an unusual result, the conclusion of the entire study has the potential to shift dramatically.

The replication movement can be traced back to a paper published in 2011, entitled "False-Positive Psychology," which was written by Joseph Simmons, Leif Nelson, and Uri Simonsohn and which, according to them, was partially inspired by Daryl Bem, professor of psychology emeritus at Cornell, and a study he conducted supposedly demonstrating evidence of the reality of extrasensory perception. It would have been easy for me to cite Bem's study without ever acknowledging Simmons, Nelson, and Simonsohn's paper and the doubts it raised, especially because, to date, Bem's work has not been explicitly delegitimized.

Even in our courts of law, with our trials and defense using the facts of a case as they are presented, none of the lawyers, the judges, the witnesses, or the jurors come into the courtroom week after week for proof. No, they are there to make decisions—huge decisions in which a person's life may hang in the balance—that are based not on proof but on doubt. It is a question of reasonable doubt, not proof.

And, yet, we remain obsessed with proof.

I know women who feel they did not become real adults until they became mothers.

These are not women who became mothers at seventeen or even thirty-one but at thirty-five and thirty-eight and forty-two. Women with careers and bills, employees, broken hearts, and debts. But it all felt like child's play until they were responsible for a helpless infant. I have had moments in which I have stepped up to or in the direction of adulthood, but I finally became a "mostly adult" this year.

Because this is the year I gave up on the fantasy of proof. I have reasonable doubt about all psychics, empaths, astrologers, and shamans. One of the reasons I am more mature than I was a year ago is the realization that neither Virgo's discerning proof nor Pisces's blind faith is the answer. It is not either-or. I do not have to pick a lane.

I take solace, too, in words from Dr. Miller, who reminds us that "at the very heart of science and innovation is the passion to expand knowledge, explore the unknown, and draw from all possible sources of insight and information—to think outside the box. Chance, intuitive hunches, and serendipity have always played a role in scientific discovery."

My friend Lila came over to my apartment for dinner, and while we were eating, she asked about this book, how the research was going. And I answered by talking about what a tricky subject this was when it came to proof, because so much of the material I was reviewing is impossible to prove definitively. And the people I was interviewing (the self-professed psychics and palm readers and shamans) had been incredibly generous with their time and willingness to talk at length with me, but emphatically uninterested in the exploration of proof or certainty. They tell me I'm asking the wrong question. They ask me why proof matters, what my point is anyway. I tell them that the people who read this book are likely to be varying degrees of skeptical and that I want more people to be open to the possibility of wonder and the power of the unexplainable, but I need to give them some reason to reconsider their skepticism. The psychics are unmoved. They do not care if you or I believe them or even if the things they see, the things they say, are right or wrong. I find myself throwing up my hands, going round and round, listening to them but having their miraculous stories slip through my fingers like fog, relentlessly shrouded.

The night Lila came over, I had been having a particularly frustrating week and was feeling exasperated and insecure about the validity of my project. So I vented, and when I was done, she replied, "Yeah, you gotta prove it, because otherwise it's just like *Eat Pray Love* or whatever and like, *Here's some stuff that happened to me*." I think I nodded, she said something else, and then we moved on, but the comment embedded itself into the anxiety loop already playing on repeat in my head. I knew it had gotten to me, because I had interpreted Lila's tone as disparaging and because she had inadvertently tapped into a sensitive topic I was already self-conscious about. Namely, the questionable legitimacy of my work, the legitimacy of the way I had chosen to spend the vast majority of my time, my life.

A couple of days later, I found myself on the phone with a relative of mine who also asked about the book. I started to explain what I was working on and where my research had taken me so far when she interrupted and asked, "This isn't going to be one of those dry, dense books that are hard to read, is it?" She mentioned a nonfiction book she knew

I had read and continued, "I tried to read that book, but I couldn't get through it." My relative seemed to be asking for a different book from the one Lila seemed to want. Assuming, of course, that either of them *wanted* this book at all.

It's our insecurities and our self-doubt that lead us to seek out psychics in the first place, but it's not only about reassurance. It's also about making a connection, because that was part of the discomfort of the conversations with Lila and my relative—feeling disconnected from them, feeling not unseen but too seen and judged for what was seen, and, consequently, feeling unsupported. When you sit down with a psychic, the hope, in fact the promise, is that you'll connect to something bigger than yourself, some sense that you are part of, are connected to, some meaningful larger whole. That it's not all on you, that you're being supported by a vast universe whose very nature is supportive, whether or not you're aware of it or believe in it.

In Hunter's astrology course, one of his exercises was to write down on a piece of paper the question: "Is this really how you want to spend your shrinking birth/death interval?" And then hand this piece of paper to fifteen different people as you go about your day and ask them if they'll read the question to you and listen to your answer. Moving past the social torture of making this request to fifteen people and mostly to strangers at that, I found my answer was always the same: yes.

But I was disappointed that the exercise was set up so that *I* was answering this question repeatedly. I was much more interested in how the people to whom I was handing this question might answer for themselves. I suspect they were also much more interested in their own answers than in mine. Long after I had handed the question to my fifteenth person, it occurred to me that perhaps the real point of the exercise was not whether any of us are ever doing the work we want to be doing but the realization that there is no birth/death interval, and it is not shrinking. It's all (or just) the one single whole. In the same way, the question of whether or not psychics are real is maybe not the right frame of thought. How's this for an answer:

Yes, emphatically, yes, psychics are real, because all *psychic* really means is the ability to embody, experience, and express extreme empathy. Telling the future is a myth, because we always have self-determination. There's a reason Rob Brezsny calls his horoscopes Free Will Astrology. And it's not only because such a name is his get-out-of-jail-free card. It's also because we do have choices. Maybe things really do spontaneously dawn for all of us, but do we notice? It's the difference between thinking of heart pain as heartbreaking or heart opening. Same event, same pain, wildly different perspective. Which is right? Trick question.

CHAPTER
TWENTY-FIVE

When I signed up to take Hunter's astrology course, I thought I was signing up to learn more about astrology. I still don't understand astrology. Hunter, someone who sells and teaches an astrology course, maintains that astrology is not to be understood. The goal is to learn more about yourself.

The daily assignments that Hunter emailed asked me to address rather elaborate questions. On day three of the week of the course devoted to the sun sign Cancer, I was asked: "Can you express urgent watery feelings and needs according to a mutually agreed-upon language and in a mutually supportive setting such that others do not feel the need to defend themselves against emotional manipulation? Or, do you lose your objectivity, confuse authenticity with catharsis, and play hurt victim to others' resistance and insensitivity?" *What the hell, Hunter. Can't you just tell me if today's going to be a good day and which other sun signs make the best romantic partners for my sign?*

But, also, okay, yes, perhaps, certainly in M.'s opinion, I do have an extremely irritating habit of disagreeing such that he can only commend me for my debating skills while throwing up his hands, exasperated that

I can't just talk like a human being, because I'm too busy making points and crafting zingers. *Is that what you might mean, Hunter?*

This behavior of mine, as M. describes it, is not conscious, is not meant to be intentionally difficult. I'm always under the impression that I'm talking like a human being. I certainly feel human during our disagreements, excessively so, as a matter of fact. But I suppose I must be abandoning the mutually agreed-upon language if M. feels so immediately alienated and threatened. I cannot remember the last time we had an argument in a mutually supportive setting or even a mutually unsupportive setting, unless that corner of Bleecker in front of that one bar counts . . .

When I argue, how quickly it seems no one is supported. My objectivity evaporates at the first hint of criticism. I know there are people for whom this is not true, but in my estimation they are superhuman, and I don't understand how they function any more than I can remember what the Higgs boson is no matter how many times I google it.

How do I change my behavior? Awareness doesn't seem like enough, especially now as I calmly write, with no external criticism looming on any periphery. It is something else entirely to retain this awareness, this rationality, in the face of a perceived slight or difference of opinion. Hunter suggests that astrology can help, but somehow that feels way bigger, way harder, than expecting astrology to know if M. and I will live happily ever after.

On day four of the week of Cancer, Hunter wrote, "Cancer knows that we're putting down and pulling up roots many times every day—and that being present means becoming emotionally honest enough to uproot consciously and make peace with the 'homes' we leave behind . . . Every interaction is a miniature lifetime."

Out of the blue, a former professor of mine emailed me a quote from the review of a new memoir that had recently appeared in the *New York Times Book Review*. The critic opened her review by pointing out that memoirists often do something other writers don't—they lead with their vulnerabilities, their worst selves forward. I am slightly embarrassed to admit (but not enough, clearly) how grateful I was to my teacher for passing this quote on to me. I quietly collect these kernels of reassurance, of justification, for my work.

On one of my weekly calls with Hunter, we wound our way around to my work, to writing, and to what it is I am trying to do. And he said to me, "You are here to be the articulate face of subtle energies that you sense and see and feel, that break your heart. You relieve suffering by naming energies. This is the truth people don't talk about. It's not a mental avoidance to name something. If you name it in ways that help people feel it, then it's not a concept anymore, it's a catalyst. It's a healing . . . You've just lobbed a healing bomb into their space just by these words and the way you said it. It's a spiritual induction. Which is what I think your words want to do. Spiritual meaning, sensitivity to subtle energies, that we all feel but that we don't always know we're feeling. So we're walking around reacting to things we don't understand. 'I don't like this person, but why don't I like them?' Layers and layers and layers. How can we walk around actually lucid, current with what's happening with the undercurrent of our senses, name it, work with it, learn from it, awaken by naming it, go behind the concept to the direct experience?"

He said this right out in one single stream of thought. Maybe he tells all the girls that. If he doesn't, maybe he should, because it worked on me. It was a stream of validation I had not known that I needed and yet I did, and here it was. When Hunter and I got off the phone, I looked up the quote my former professor had shared with me. I wanted to read it just as the reviewer, Daphne Merkin, had written it, not as the poorly paraphrased version I had managed to tuck away in my memory.

Memoir writers, not unlike Blanche DuBois, depend upon the kindness of strangers . . .

Really not a great sign that it begins by comparing me and my kind to Blanche DuBois. I had conveniently forgotten that detail.

> Although such writers are often saddled with accusations of narcissism and self-indulgence, what commonly gets overlooked is the tremendous vulnerability that inheres in exposing oneself to the world's scrutiny. The wish to tell one's story may be stronger than the anxiety of exposure, but not by much; there's always the chance that your story will meet with a different response than the one you're hoping for. Indeed, the violation of privacy that memoirs specialize in is as often reviled as praised. As social media has made clear, most of us go public by putting our best face forward, sharing our triumphs and achievements rather than our sorrows or failures. Memoirists, especially good ones, tend to reveal the hidden anxieties and conflicts underlying their lives, and in doing so, take the risk of being judged not only on the quality of their prose but on the content of their character. In a self-promoting culture, they dare to lead with their worst side.

Renate Aller is a German photographer long based in New York City who has done multiple series set in dramatic, natural landscapes—*Oceanscapes*, *Ocean and Desert*, and, most recently, *Mountain Interval*, a series of mountain vistas in which each finished piece is two separate photographs, two different mountains or ranges from disparate parts of the world, one overlying the other to create a single image that appears to be one unified mountain; only this final image does not exist anywhere in nature. Although all three of these series are grand in scale and examine challenging landscapes, they did, initially, feel very separate to me, very different. Which is what I said to Renate the first time I visited her at her Soho home and studio. With a shake of her ash-blonde hair and swaying linen sleeves, she swiftly corrected me: "No, no, my work is all one, each series leads to the next and even replies in some way back to the one that came before."

Just as Hunter said, layers and layers and layers. Years ago, I read an interview with a film director, though I no longer have any idea who it was, and she said that every director only has one story to tell, that a career can be made, a good career, out of finding new ways to tell the same tale. Documentarian Susan Lacy's 2017 HBO documentary, *Spielberg*, makes the case that every single one of Steven Spielberg's movies is, on some level, a coming-of-age story, a boy finding his way in the face of disappointments, of realizing adults, other people, are not who or what he thought or believed they were. Her film, which was made with Spielberg's full support and participation, argues that he has never gotten over his parents' divorce when he was seventeen years old.

I thought that when I finished my first book, I had resolved my tension and conflict with my dad, my childhood, and myself. In the months after that book was published, a lot of people wanted to talk to me about that story, about him, about us, and I mostly spent that time grateful people were interested and simultaneously thinking, *Can't we just talk about something else? It's done. I have made my peace. He is free. I am free.* The thing is, that book wasn't really about that. It was about heart opening and the gaps we feel in ourselves. That is the story I am beginning to suspect I am not done with, that I will never be done with. We can fill many of these gaps, and we can build bridges across others, but we can never close them all, not completely.

I think of people I have known who live for those gaps and, in fact, rely on the knowledge they will not close. These are mostly men, though not exclusively, and they are the same ones who are under the impression that fifty-two is the new thirty-five.

It is not. What it's actually like is the television series that stays on the air a season (or several) too long. After they do go, these men sometimes think, *Oh, I could have gotten another year or two out of that scene,* but if they had stayed, they would have stayed another five, not another two. These are men who have stopped starting over, if they ever began in the first place. They have their interactions and their lifetimes, but they live the exact same ones over and over again, looking not to fill or bridge the gaps but to jump down into them. Then there is the man I know who married his first serious, postcollege girlfriend. A woman who, when he proposed, said thank you instead of yes. He told me this in the same conversation in which he told me that he was just so glad he didn't have to date anymore. They're divorced now.

Where do you want to go? And by what means will you travel?

If you drive, you are quite literally responsible for other people's lives. In New York, a city with many cars but few drivers, you are responsible not for people's lives but for their personal space. Walking is the most intimate communal space we have with strangers. More so than sharing a train car or even an airplane row. In those means of transportation, we are sedentary. We are moved. When we walk, *we* move. If you are in a pedestrian city like New York, you travel by navigating in relation to everyone around you, and you do it within inches of these strangers, whom you will never be so close to again. It's just this one moment when you and this particular stranger are as close as a couple in bed.

When you drive, the hulking tons of metal and glass between you and other drivers make it easy to forget the human beings around you. When you walk, any slight, any perceived deviation from polite public etiquette, feels personal, because it's right in your face. I used to think of walking as a solitary ritual of independence. Now I think of it as a group activity, practically a team sport.

Hunter suggests a walking meditation that calls for chanting to yourself, "From person, to presence, to witness of even that." To be a good player is to take responsibility for the respect of others as well as yourself, to move from being a presence to being present to witnessing to making space for your fellow witnesses.

It is Aries who cling to our "separate somebody status" and Pisces who embrace "a psyche of cosmic dimensions." Pisces are our feet, "constantly hovering and landing, hovering and landing, each footfall reincarnates our lofty Aries head into a new line of sight, a new vantage point or worldview," Hunter writes. We need both our Pisces feet and our Aries head, and neither is bad. Both are less without the other. M. is a Pisces, and I am an Aries, and I used to think how nice that was, a Pisces and an Aries. But we can all embody both Pisces feet and an Aries head. We don't need someone else to complete the equation. As any true Aries will tell you, *I can do it by myself.*

When I asked Hunter if astrology is genuine and if reincarnation is real, he gave me answers like the ones he writes. The truth about reincarnation can be found, he explained, in walking. "During your next meditative stroll, ask yourself: One, what is this hovering and landing, hovering and landing, all about, if not to help us weave earth and sky back together and finally know them as two halves of the same sentient thing? Two, does not every Pisces footfall incarnate our Aries head into a new worldview? Three, is not every step forward the release of a temporally expired past life and the embrace of a yet-to-be-embodied future life? Four, is there anything but reincarnation?"

My god, what a fabulous answer. Wholly dissatisfying. But still wildly fabulous.

Asking the questions, looking for proof of some kind, reveals itself to be repeatedly disappointing. "The Pisces feet are the only part of the human body that is constantly pressed against—merged—with something else. In this sense, they symbolize our unbroken connection to the divine ground of Being . . . so long as personality and will [Aries] are pausing for permission to proceed from the signs and symbols of the unified field [Pisces], our life flows in harmony with the Tao."

Sure, Hunter, sure. Astrology for Hunter is about prostration or positive disintegration, which is exactly the kind of what-the-fuck phrase I'm drawn to. What is the point of prostration?

In the documentary *Joan Didion: The Center Will Not Hold*, the English playwright and director David Hare describes the significance of Didion's memoir *A Year of Magical Thinking* as the first handbook for grief by a person and for people without a religious or spiritual faith. Didion is a stunning writer, thinker, and observer, and she and I were both born and raised in Sacramento, California. So, obviously, I think she is the cat's pajamas. I read *A Year of Magical Thinking* and her follow-up *Blue Nights* and had my breath taken away and my eyes filled with tears, and I thought, *Yes, this human being has captured grief in its pure, raw form on the page as it was happening to her.* It is a remarkable feat.

But I did not read those books and think, *Aw, finally, a secular instructional manual on grieving.* I do not believe grief is secular. Grief is not earthly or temporal. Grief is about being left behind.

Late in the documentary, Didion herself says the fear of death is about the people who will survive you, how will they take care of themselves—have you indeed left them with everything they need to be all right without you? Then she says that with both her daughter and her husband gone, she is not leaving anyone behind. The moment is captured with a camera close to her face, only a small portion of white wall visible behind her, but she is in profile, so we cannot completely see her or her expression. From this truncated perspective, she appears not detached but depleted. The phrase *leaving anyone behind* implies that someone gets to go somewhere, gets to move on, and that someone else doesn't. Whether she intended this implication or not, Didion's choice of phrase suggests that she believes there is in fact somewhere else to move on to. Not even Joan Didion's grief is secular.

The documentary concludes that Didion does have faith, but that she has placed all of her faith in human achievement, in accomplishment.

I'm not entirely convinced that is Didion's whole truth, but I do know that such a belief system is insufficient for me. I will prostrate myself. I will try. With Hunter's help: "The power of physical prostration is that it exposes this burdensome devotion to me-ness that assigns godlike importance to our feelings of enough and not enoughness and is, therefore, humiliated and flooded with feelings of inauthenticity when-ever we place our head at the feet of anyone or anything else. Prostration helps us pass swiftly through this fire of egoic humiliation into a state of positive disintegration—the great unburdening that transplants our orphaned ego into the soil of true nature: awareness itself."

If you are going to try prostration, to whom or to what do you direct your prostration? David Foster Wallace said, "Everybody worships. The only choice we get is *what* to worship. And an outstanding reason for choosing some sort of god or spiritual-type thing to worship—be it JC or Allah, be it Yahweh or the Wiccan Mother Goddess or the Four Noble Truths or some infrangible set of ethical principles—is that pretty much anything else you worship will eat you alive."

I wonder if Didion is familiar with that David Foster Wallace quote. If Didion represents Aries (all personality and "I am"), and David Foster Wallace represents Pisces (all surrender and present), then the unity of them might be Ramana Maharshi ("The I removes the I, yet remains the I").

Put another way, Hunter's way, "What passes for sovereign Aries self-assertion is often fear of the disorienting identity death that empa-thetic Pisces merging might suck them into . . . What looks like gentle Pisces selflessness is often fear of showing up enough to wisely navigate their own and others' emotionally manipulative egos."

Bringing Aries and Pisces into unified harmony and collaboration demands that something else must die. "What must die is our fantasy that there is any place in time where rape [as a stand-in for Aries] and suicide [as a stand-in for Pisces] isn't happening."

Why choose rape and suicide to illustrate his argument? For Hunter, "these are positive, motivating, Zen stick words that describe how Buddhist 'craving and aversion' actually play out down here in the dirt." Which is maybe just another way of describing the usefulness of Hunter's version of astrology: how the philosophy of the stars and the planets and our minds and hearts play out on earth, day to day.

I never told Hunter that he reminded me of the Puerto Rican poet Marigloria Palma. But I should have. The way he described Aries and Pisces made me think of her poem "Este Momento Mío," which Carina del Valle Schorske translated as "This Moment of Mine," and its opening lines as "I drink down my aspirins and watch the stars shiver. / This is my time, time of jet planes and plastic bombs. / Atomic era of the calculator. Ecological time, biochemical time, transplant time, cancer time."

CHAPTER TWENTY-SIX

Astrology, at its most readily available, most superficial, is a me-centric activity: What is my horoscope? What will happen to me? How am I special? Go deeper, and it becomes an exploration of community and finding what Hunter calls our soul mirrors. "Whoever is in your field of vision, field of feeling, in this moment is helping you wake up to an opportunity to see something, learn something. This is the universe's subliminal nurturing," Hunter writes. The places we choose to live and work, and the people we choose to partner with and befriend, none are bad, even if the choice brings heartache or guilt or both, because it is the experience we were supposed to have just then. We are always right where we need to be.

"If you're present, you are in touch with the past, present, and future. They're all there, at once, equally. It's all informing. It's paradoxical." This is the Tibetan Buddhist perspective of awareness. I asked Hunter about it on one of our weekly calls, and he answered: "Well, they exist in terms of your paradigm. But conscious attention doesn't have to be on it. I actually agree that it is a good idea to be putting your attention on the present moment, but not in a kind of 'moving away from past and future,' but more as like a 'I'm planting myself in this kind of vivid, tactile-y, present immediate world.' But then as a conduit of my attention, other things flood in from behind that I'm also open to informing my experience of the present and extrapolations of where this present is going and my concern for humanity and all these different trajectories, and maybe not as a story but as a felt sense. Maybe none of this as a story but [as] felt-sense past, felt-sense present, felt-sense future. That create bookends around this moment, keep its borders, give it even more focus, like a frame for a picture."

I'm not sure Hunter has ever given a one-word answer to a question.

The idea of the past and the future being bookends around the present implies that the past and the future are supportive rather than in tension with or a distraction from the present. When I get inappropriately indignant, I try to remember to ask myself, *Is this a big deal or a little deal? Will I remember this in five years? Or even six months from now?* I told this to Hunter, thinking he'd agree.

Instead he said, "Another way of looking at it is to see if that part of you can take the accident out. If there aren't any accidents, then every time you're out on the road, on the sidewalk, whoever is in your field was chosen as a destined reunion, confluence. That gets into another Tibetan Buddhist concept, interdependent co-rising: everyone is helping each other wake up all the time not by anything they're intentionally doing, but just by being who they are; the way they're designed to be is to help everyone else wake up. So whoever that person's being at that moment on the street, energetically, how they act, everything, and you, there's an opportunity to wake up to something you couldn't unless it was just those people moving just that way; take the accident out of that . . . Presence means inquiry. I'm with somebody who's acting that way now. What are they supporting me in, how are they supporting me in my own self-remembering?"

In the fall of 2017, in an article for Vox, David Roberts wrote that "the US is experiencing a deep epistemic breach, a split not just in what we value or want, but in who we trust, how we come to know things, and what we believe we know—what we believe exists, is true, has happened, and is happening."

The questions I have asked of psychics and of spirituality are the same questions we are faced with as a nation every time we open the Twitter or Facebook apps on our phones. My mother may have been Catholic, and my father may have been an atheist, but they both, to varying degrees, believed in government, in a system of checks and balances, built and reinforced to support the people. So the first thing I ever put my faith in was government. Only now our government is facing a crisis of faith, and I find myself wondering if I have misplaced my beliefs, if the foundation of my country, which I assumed was surely more solid than any altar, is not. Men built the church, and men built America.

I am circling spirituality as if it were a viable third option. Why do I think that Tibetan Buddhist philosophers and astrologers and shamans who ask me to find my Core Beastie will be more reliable? The difference is that they are not built on the idea of power for the creators, the CEOs of government or religious orders, but on power of the self, power of the practitioner. Astrologers like Hunter, shamanic practitioners like Sarah, and empaths like Michelle encourage doubt. They do not insist on blind faith.

You *can* and you should try this at home. Learn your natal chart. Explore what resonates and what does not. Take a shamanic journey. Find out if it leads you to answers. Have a reading done with an empath. Is it helpful? If it's not, cool. Don't come back. They emphasize the power to let go, the power to release power. What is more powerful than not needing power? They acknowledge power, because they have to. It's real. We all feel it, have it, struggle with it, abuse it, fear it, love it. You have to acknowledge it in order to let it go. When I think about committing exclusively to our government or to a single religious organization, I cannot help but be wary of the history of abuse of power

I am supporting. I am complicit in a lineage that does not mirror or respect my values.

A friend of my dad's majored in religion. He was raised in California as a Catholic but arrived at college eager to understand religion both more broadly and more deeply. He graduated both broadly and deeply mistrustful of all religion. The bloodshed and misogyny of the Catholic Church horrified him. As a gay man, he felt unwelcome in the church of his ancestors. I cannot argue with his feelings or the conclusions he has drawn. Nor am I comfortable with supporting the Catholic Church with my time, my presence, and my money. But I also recognize that as a human being who was born in a particular place, in a particular time, I am by default linked to and permanently tied to my country, my ethnicity, and my ancestors' religion. I am an American. I am Catholic, by lineage, on both sides of my family. I am French. I am Irish. I am the descendent of law-enforcement officials. All of those groups of which I am associated have done things I do not agree with. I could give up my American citizenship because I no longer want to be associated with the country's cruel history and its cruel present, both abroad and at home, but give it up for what? Name a country without blood on its hands. Countries, like the present, come tied to their pasts.

CHAPTER
TWENTY-SEVEN

In the November 12, 2007, issue of the *New Yorker*, Malcolm Gladwell wrote a piece entitled "Dangerous Minds: Criminal Profiling Made Easy." In it, he writes about FBI agent John Douglas's illustrious career as a profiler of serial killers. He also includes quotes from Douglas's book *Inside the Mind of BTK*, in which Douglas recalls a local detective asking if he is psychic after the profile he has just outlined for the officer matches exactly to the information a psychic had already given the detective. Douglas writes, "What I try to do with a case is to take in all the evidence I have to work with . . . and then put myself mentally and emotionally in the head of the offender. I try to think as he does. Exactly how this happens, I'm not sure, any more than the novelists such as Tom Harris who've consulted me over the years can say exactly how their characters come to life. If there's a psychic component to this, I won't run from it."

But Gladwell will run from it. He cites a study done by the British Home Office, which "analyzed a hundred and eighty-four crimes, to see how many times profiles led to the arrest of a criminal. The profile worked in five of those cases. That's just 2.7 percent." Close analysis of profiles written for hundreds of cases finds that they are "so full of unverifiable and contradictory and ambiguous language that it could support virtually any interpretation."

In other words, exactly what happens when you assess your average psychic reading or a horoscope. Most every one of us will identify with it, will see the ways in which it describes us. There are known ways to achieve this effect. Psychic readings can be taught. Gladwell references the book *The Full Facts Book of Cold Reading* by the magician Ian Rowland, who lists and describes these techniques, though, for some of them, the names alone suffice: the Fuzzy Fact, the Greener Grass, the Diverted Question, the Russian Doll, and the Good Chance Guess. "If you make a great number of predictions, the ones that were wrong will soon be forgotten, and the ones that turn out to be true will make you famous," Gladwell observes.

In *The Book of Joy*, Archbishop Desmond Tutu and the Dalai Lama emphasize that they are just two of the seven billion human beings on the planet, that remembering their humanity, just being like anyone else, people who want to be happy and have joy and to be safe and fed and protected, makes it easier to live harmoniously with others, to feel fewer feelings of inadequacy and envy and more feelings of grace and compassion and gratitude.

Somehow, knowing they're part of a seven-billion-person community heightens their personal spirituality.

In the collection *The Moth Presents All These Wonders: True Stories About Facing the Unknown*, there is a story by Christof Koch called "God, Death, and Francis Crick." Koch recalls being with Crick when Crick got the call that his colon cancer had returned. When Koch asked him about his diagnosis, Crick said something about how everything that has a beginning must have an end. Which is exactly the way Archbishop Tutu and the Dalai Lama explain it: every life has a beginning, middle, and end. Nothing could be more natural. The finite makes everything that comes before it more meaningful.

In Koch's telling, Crick's ending comes, and Koch examines the loss of his colleague and friend from his own point of view, believing more in "Spinoza's God than the God of Michelangelo's painting or the God of the Old Testament" and believing that "we have to see the world as it really is, and we have to stop thinking in terms of magic." He concludes, "I'm a highly organized pattern of mass and energy, one of seven billion. In any objective accounting of the universe, I'm practically nothing, and soon I'll cease to be. But the certainty of my own demise, the certainty of my own death, somehow makes my life more meaningful, and I think that is as it should be . . . and every day in my work, I try to discern through its noisy manifestation, its people, dogs, trees, mountains, stars—everything I love—I try to discern the eternal music of the spheres."

Koch's story is about starting life religious and losing his religion along the way, and then losing his friend and collaborator, and the argument he uses to chart these shifts is the same argument the Dalai Lama and Archbishop Tutu use in favor of spirituality and in favor of investing in a belief in something larger than us. Same argument, different conclusion. And yet that same argument and those same differing opinions are what help make it easier, clearer, for all three of these men to live in the world with meaning and with peace. Archbishop Desmond Tutu, Kofi Annan, and other leaders from diverse traditions came together on a UN High-Level Panel and concluded that there is nothing wrong with faiths. Only the faithful.

CHAPTER TWENTY-EIGHT

There are two things and only two things that I like about winter. By *winter*, I do not mean fifty degrees Fahrenheit or even thirty degrees Fahrenheit, when only a chic coat is called for. I mean glove weather. I mean the kind of weather where if you forget your gloves, it's a big deal. I mean the second week of January when the holidays are over, there is nothing to look forward to, and the wind, cold and sharp as ice, cuts through every last layer of clothing. I mean winter when your shoulders curl inward as if you can make yourself small enough not to feel. There are two things I like about this kind of winter, the real kind. I like when it snows so much that entire cities shut down and nothing is ugly because all the ugliness is buried under feet and feet of unblemished snow. The world stops, and there is nothing to be done but race outside and run down the empty streets.

The second thing I like is winter light. The kind of light you get when zero feels like a goddamn victory. This light will never be mistaken for summer light, which is slippery and spreads out uncontainably like lemon Jell-O. Winter light is severe and slices across the floorboards and the wall for a few minutes each day and only those few minutes. If you miss it, it might as well not have happened. You have to look up at the right moment from the right chair. When I see it, it fills me with awe, and, for those few minutes at least, I believe that my soul and the universe are in complete alignment and that everything is, always has been, and always will be exactly what it needs to be in the moment it needs to be. I see then that the only person I need to trust is myself. The only person who can make me feel safe is myself. In the end, it turns out, all I have ever wanted is not to be with someone but to be myself.

It is the sun sign Capricorn, as well as my father's birthday, that falls in the second week of January. Capricorns, with their ambition and their manipulation and their volatility, can be hard to take. But their winter light, if you can catch it, is a chance to see what you're made of. For all of winter that makes me shrink and retract, if I should settle forever in a part of the world without it, I know I would miss those first hours of new snow and that I would miss that light even more. I never had such light as a child in California. Maybe all the things I've seen and done have all been in a higher service to get me to a place where I could know first cold Capricorn's light and now my own.

CHAPTER
TWENTY-NINE

Dr. Lisa Miller argues that her "ongoing research on thousands of entering adults—more than four thousand college students—confirms that a direct relationship with nature or a higher power protects like a parent's love against the perils and sufferings in the first two decades. It also supports formation of the positive traits that have been associated with life success and satisfaction, like optimism and grit."

And this: "Developmental science shows us that infants at birth show care. Infants have the capacity to perceive suffering and distress, and the motive to soothe and ameliorate suffering."

I never meant to write a book about how great babies are, but here we are.

According to Dr. Miller, babies are drawn to prayer. They're intuitive, empathetic, and helpful. They feel innately connected to others. But somewhere between babyhood and adulthood, many of us lose that attraction to and comfort with prayer. We stop listening to our instinctive sense of empathy and intuition. It doesn't leave us, but we have to invite it back. We have to want to hear it again.

I was more than halfway through Hunter's training when M. asked me to stop doing the calls, to drop out of the class altogether. There were still a few weeks left in the course, and I wanted to finish. The class was not inexpensive, and I knew I wouldn't be able to get any kind of partial refund. But I said okay. I chose M. I told Hunter I couldn't continue. But I continued feeling uneasy on Sunday evenings, when I should have been talking to Hunter. Uneasy on other evenings now, too. Nights I shouldn't have been talking to Hunter but I should have been talking to M.

For as long as I can remember, I have liked very little, but that which I have liked has always been, in my opinion at least, superb: I like one pair of perfectly broken in boots that I will keep resoling until my cobbler won't take my money anymore. I like one cup of strong, black pour-over coffee every morning, and some nights I like a single glass of thoughtfully produced, organic, biodynamic, natural wine, preferably one made by a winemaker working her own land and her own vines. I like the smallest house on the nicest block. And, at thirty-two, I have finally learned to apply this philosophy to people.

I will now accept nothing less than a man who knows himself, who doesn't just behave respectfully toward others and to the earth but who *is* respectful, who in treating himself with complete respect is also able to treat me with complete respect. A man who is his own source of confidence and direction, his own cheerleader. Because no one can truly believe in him if he doesn't first believe in himself. A man who loves me simply because he loves me—and not because of how I make him feel about himself. A man who understands that breaking up is just as much cause for celebration as falling in love, because it is an opportunity to stitch your heart back together bigger than it's ever been before. And I will only have a man who has his whole, huge heart to give.

I will only accept a man who is so authentically himself that possessiveness is the last thing he could ever imagine needing. James Baldwin wrote, "Love takes off the masks that we fear we cannot live without and know we cannot live within." Before love is patient, before love is kind, love is an invitation. I will only have a man who is love, who embodies love as an open invitation for growth.

I now understand I will only accept a man with integrity. A man who values creativity and expansion, authenticity and optimism, trust and delight. A man who understands that falling in true love is never a risk, because if you fall in love already whole, you can't lose anything, you can only gain. And I know that I will say to such a man someday, *I choose you. I accept your whole heart and open mine to you. I invite you into love knowing it may not be forever, because I know that no matter how long or short our love lasts, our partnership will only ever be a blessing. At the moment of our separation, whether it comes on the deathbed or in divorce court, we will part as we met: with complete self-respect, self-acceptance, and self-love. I will only have a man who will listen to me say these words and know that they are more loving, full of more truth and opportunity, than any vows of forever.*

And I will know when I meet this man. I will spot him in the crowd without hesitation, without doubt, this man who knows himself, because long before I ever laid eyes on him, I committed to respecting, knowing, and loving myself. I already treat myself the way this man will treat me, which is why I don't need him. And it is the very fact that I do not need him, will never be dependent on him, that empowers me to recognize him, that makes this, the only kind of love and partnership I am willing to accept, possible.

No matter who I am with or not with, when I wake up each morning, before I have my one outstanding cup of coffee, before I put on my indestructible boots, I can, on my own, ask myself, *What is today's delight?* and know that I will always find an answer.

Today the answer is Dr. Miller's research demonstrating that children's spirituality supports all other aspects of their development, that a strong and supported spirituality enhances a child's and adolescent's frontal cortex.

Yesterday's answer was the fMRI research showing that when a participant sees a religious symbol that is personally significant to them, their physical pain is lessened.

But my favorite is tomorrow's answer. Physician and researcher Larry Dossey has done studies on what he calls "the nonlocal mind." A healer and a patient are given simultaneous fMRIs in two different rooms. The healer is instructed to pray for the patient, and as they begin to pray, a distinct pattern appears on their fMRI. Within minutes, the same distinctive pattern appears on the fMRI of the patient down the hall.

CHAPTER THIRTY

"Sounds like a party."

It was ten o'clock in the morning on December 26, 2017, and I was in my apartment building's basement sorting my recycling, which was, I'll be honest, all wine bottles. My neighbor, still pj'd and wearing a peach-colored robe, got off the elevator and stuck her head around the corner. I managed a thin smile at her as I answered, "Yeah, I guess it does. How was your Christmas?"

"Good, good," she said, but she had already disappeared back around the corner, and the second *good* was hard to hear as she walked toward the laundry room at the other end of the basement. It didn't surprise me that she did not ask how my Christmas was. I have known this woman for a long time, and her lack of giving a single fuck about what anyone might expect her to do or say is one of my favorite things about her.

It did sound like a party. Maybe it was. One of those parties that starts strong, builds to a crescendo, and then collapses under the weight of its own expectations. The night before I had broken up with M.` That's right, on December 25. Christmas Day. At, according to the new watch M.'s mother had given him hours earlier, precisely 7:03 p.m.

I swear it was never my intention to break up with M. on Christmas. I had intended to wait until his mother had flown back to Florida and we had time for a real conversation again. But M. knew things were not okay between us, and all day, in front of his mother, he had been pushing me. In the morning, for no discernible reason, he had asked me if I would go back to Italy with him, and I had replied, "We can't afford it." Because that was the truth, but also because I did not want to lie and say yes.

But he wouldn't let me off. "You didn't answer my question."

So I looked at him, aware of his mother's gaze, and said, "Sure. We can go back to Italy."

Later, when the three of us were spread out across the sectional couch, his mother knitting, M. scrolling through Instagram on his phone, and me reading a book about wine, he said, "How ya doing, Victorian?"— using one of his nicknames for me—and when I said, "Okay," he had replied, "Is the baby kicking?" My whole body tensed. M.'s mother had made no secret of her desire for grandchildren. Not that I was pregnant. He was joking. His mother laughed. I rolled my eyes and tried to do it in a funny *oh, M.* way. But all I could think about was when I had been pregnant. I was aware that both he and his mother were staring at me. I said nothing. I wanted not to be there, sitting between this mother and son, both of whom felt like strangers. But I had nowhere to go.

We did not leave the apartment on Christmas Day. M. and his mother didn't want to, and I spent the day feeling emotionally and physically trapped. It didn't help that we didn't own a TV, just an iPad and an eleven-inch laptop, so we couldn't comfortably forget one another with a movie or by binge-watching a television series. It also didn't help that M. and his mom weren't big on meals, preferring instead to snack on coffee and eggnog and fancy cheeses and the rum balls she had brought with her from Florida.

But I like breakfast. I like lunch. I like dinner. By late afternoon, forget hangry. I was farving—fucking starving.

So I suppose that when his mother left to call a friend and take a little walk around the neighborhood, it should not have surprised me that M. immediately began to lay into me. "It's obvious you're not in a good mood. What do you want? What is wrong with you?" I suggested we just try to have a pleasant evening with his mom and that we could talk after she left for the airport the next day. But he wouldn't let up. He texted his mom and suggested she have a cup of tea at a nearby Middle Eastern restaurant, the only place we knew was open. I didn't want to be having this conversation, but I also understood that M. just wanted to know, that he didn't feel good having this impending discussion hanging over his head a moment longer. I understood, and I knew that if I were him, I would have felt the same way.

So, when he asked me point-blank, "But you want to stay together, right?" I told him, "No, I don't. I want to break up. It's over."

And M. replied, "Wow, okay. I mean, no one has ever broken up with me before."

In just that moment, it suddenly felt as though the universe was validating my decision, and it was the best I had felt in weeks.

And then he left. He went to get his mom and then to check into a hotel. The same hotel, as it happens, in whose lobby bar M. and I had met a year and a half before. We had finished our walk.

Which is how I became the asshole who broke up with her boyfriend on Christmas Day while his poor mother waited in an empty restaurant around the corner. Not that I needed a reason to avoid the Sunshine State, but this seems like an awfully good one.

As soon as M. was gone, I broke down and sobbed and ate the rest of the stinkiest cheese I had ever smelled, the one his mom had bought that I didn't even like. The smell had been making me nauseous all day, and in that moment I knew only that I had barely eaten and that I wanted to stop smelling that cheese. Eating it seemed like the dumbest but also the fastest way to kill two birds with one stone. I also wanted a drink. Only we had no wine left, and our liquor cabinet consisted of a nearly full bottle of cheap tequila, an even fuller bottle of Cointreau, and an unopened bottle of Spanish vermouth that my ex B.'s father had gifted me on a trip to Andalusia a few years back.

I thought about going to the liquor store. Christmas seemed like exactly the type of occasion when a liquor store in New York City would not be closed. But I was afraid I would run into M. and his mom on the street, which was one of the few ways the day could have possibly gotten worse. I opened the vermouth. From the first sip I was pretty sure in the time it had taken me to accumulate my two most recent ex-boyfriends, the vermouth had oxidized. I took a second sip just to be sure. Oh yeah. And whether it was the bad cheese or the bad vermouth or the ugly crying or some combination of all three, five minutes later my eyelids were so swollen I could barely see. I took two Benadryls and passed out. Merry Christmas.

I woke up to a full trash can and an overflowing recycling bin and immediately wanted them both out of the apartment. At some point in our relationship, M. and I had taken to saving the empty bottles from wine we had especially liked and wanted to remember. Sure, we could have just written them down. In fact, I maintained a rather thorough spreadsheet of the winemakers and vintages and regions and varietals that I loved. But M. liked the look of the empty bottles. Now, though, almost as an afterthought, I rounded them up and took them out with the rest of the trash.

I placed bottle after bottle into the recycling bin in the basement, and in their clinking and clanging, my neighbor heard echoes of cheers from some warm gathering the night before. What I heard were the echoes of shattering glass from the first night M. came over to my apartment, before it became our apartment.

It had been a summer Saturday evening. It was our second date; our first had been the night before. We were not playing coy. We were already all in. I had cooked for him, and now we were on the fire escape, finishing our first bottle of wine together. We were looking out onto the street below, at the bare legs walking down the sidewalk, at the groups jumping into and out of black Ubers and yellow taxis. M. had emptied his glass and placed it on the ledge, or maybe it was the step. He had his arm around me, but in the course of a story he was telling, he removed it to gesticulate out into the humid air between us. He turned toward me, I think, and his arm stretched to the side or behind him, and I heard the glass shatter. I didn't know what it was at first. But then M. said, "My wineglass." I looked down five stories to the sidewalk beneath us, which was suddenly glittering. It was as beautiful as it was dangerous.

I climbed back through the window and ran down the stairs and out onto the street. There was no one in front of the building. No one had been hurt. I crouched down and picked up the biggest pieces, placing them gingerly in the palm of my hand, wishing I had thought to grab a towel. It was not a good system, but I didn't want to leave them unattended. Should anyone come along, I would be the human caution tape.

And then I went from being alone to having a man standing over me. It was a man I had only recently noticed loitering around a dilapidated town house down the block. He was short and tan. His hair was blond, his eyes bugged out a bit, and he reminded me very much of the actor Richard Denning from *An Affair to Remember* (not Cary Grant, the other guy). He was yelling, "What is wrong with you? What were you thinking? Someone could have gotten hurt! Or an animal, what about someone's dog—its paws? Are you stupid? What were you doing? You're damn lucky no one was standing below when you threw that glass!"

I stayed low on the ground, still picking up shards. But I answered him. "I didn't throw it. It got knocked over. It was an accident. A mistake. We shouldn't have had glass outside. You're right."

He went on. "Don't you have a broom? What are you doing? This isn't going to clean it up. Are you stupid?"

M. appeared on the stoop. Now there were two men I barely knew speaking over me. "Hey, man. We're sorry. We're cleaning it up. It was an accident." They both asked me if I had a broom or a dustpan, and I was embarrassed that the answer was no. The man left and returned with one of each. I thanked him, and M. and I cleaned up all of the glass we could find, walking past my building and around the corner and into the street, as far as we could imagine that a shard might have carried. All the while Angry Richard Denning watched us. At some point, a woman I had noticed him with on a few occasions materialized and stood with him, also yelling. She was drunk or on something or both. She wanted to know my name. The man continued shouting about dog paws.

M. tried to reason with them. "Hey, man. We're doing our best here." They didn't respond, but they did start pointing out shards of glass to us. Eventually none of us could find any more glass, and I stopped sweeping. I gave the man back his broom and dustpan, and M. and I went back inside. While we waited for the elevator, he said, "You just disappeared. One minute we were on the fire escape, and the next you were just gone. I thought you were inside getting a broom or something, that we'd come down together. But you just left me."

I said goodbye to my neighbor and went back upstairs with my empty recycling bucket. My apartment still smelled like a *fromagerie*. I made the bed and swept the pine needles from beneath our dried-out Christmas tree. The alarm on my phone went off, reminding me to meditate, and I recalled another of the last debates M. and I had shared. He had told me that he understood sex to be a largely meditative state. Sex has its meditative moments; Sting and Trudie may have some thoughts here. But a meditative state implies, to me, a certain degree of silence and stillness, and healthy sex is neither silent nor still.

In America, sex is the highly stylized, sensationalized sexuality of our pornography, our blockbuster movies, and our binge-worthy television series. Or it's the #MeToo movement and Harvey Weinstein's couch and Donald Trump's pussy-grabbing. Culturally and politically, we talk about sex *constantly* but always in these polarities. What we don't talk about is the sex many of us are actually having. Or not having.

The writer Leila Slimani once told fellow writer Lauren Collins that, for her, "sex is something very painful, very melancholy, because one sees oneself."

Sex can be painful. It can be melancholy. It can be scary. It can open and leave all kinds of scars. But sex also has the power to heal.

Yes, we face ourselves when we have sex. But sex is also an opportunity to see one's partner, physically as well as emotionally. We rarely acknowledge how fulfilling it can be to see, hear, smell, taste, and feel each other's bodies in the singular space where physical intimacy and emotional vulnerability converge.

We need to tell our children that no means no, but we also need to tell them what yes means.

Sex is vocal and active, demanding questions asked and answered, positions offered and embraced. It is about responsibility—for yourself. When I go on a date, I am responsible for my own good time; I arrive having already decided to enjoy the restaurant or the concert, alleviating the pressure on whomever I am with to entertain me. And if I decide to be physically intimate with someone, I take responsibility for both my own safety and my own fun. It is not my partner's responsibility to give me an orgasm, just as it is not my responsibility to make them come. When I touch my partner, I do so always with the hope and intention that I bring them pleasure, but the touches I choose are those that I know will also heighten my own arousal. I ask them to do the same. I want to learn what makes my partner feel good; I want to teach them what makes me feel good; and I want to discover together new opportunities for more pleasure for us both. It is not about selfishness or even self-empowerment so much as it is about two people embracing an opportunity to see and to know, to be seen and to be known.

The sex I want to have and choose to have is not meditative. M. felt differently. We felt differently about responsibility, too. We felt differently about many things. Which was okay right up until the moment it wasn't.

I turned the alarm off on my phone and sat down to do a *metta bhavana* ("loving-kindness") meditation. And when I was done, I checked my email and realized I had forgotten to read Rob Brezsny's astrology newsletter that week, which included my horoscope:

"ARIES (March 21–April 19): Your life in the first half of 2018 will be like a psychological boot camp that's designed to beef up your emotional intelligence. Here's another way to visualize your oncoming adventures: they will constitute a friendly nudge from the cosmos, pushing you to be energetic and ingenious in creating the kind of partnerships you want for the rest of your long life. As you go through your interesting tests and riddles, be on the lookout for glimpses of what your daily experience could be like in five years if you begin now to deepen your commitment to love and collaboration."

About a week before we broke up, I was cooking dinner, and M. was on the couch scrolling through Twitter. Some tweet or another led him to Joan Didion's famous essay "Goodbye to All That." I first read that essay in the fall of my freshman year of college. I've read it many times since. It's well-known, but probably no more so than among the New Yorkers who have dreamt of being called a writer. But M. had never read it. He had only just started it when I told him dinner was ready. He wanted to finish it before we ate, which was fine. I held dinner and loaded the dishwasher and wiped down the countertop, and a couple of times M. called out from the living room, "This is good. She's really good. Memoir when it's done right is incredibly good." When he finished it, and we sat down to eat, he repeated those three sentences verbatim four more times, and each time I said a variation of, "Yeah, it is. Didion's great."

But when we had finished dinner and I was reading a novel and he was back on Twitter, he repeated those three sentences. This time, I just didn't have it in me to say again that I agreed. All I wanted was to read my book. So I didn't say anything, and he said, "Oh, you're going to ignore me? You don't want to talk to me now?" I put my book down. I looked at him. I thought about the fact that my own next memoir was due to my editor at the end of the month, on December 31, and that I was just a wee bit stressed about it. I thought about the fact that M. had never read either of my first two memoirs, despite my telling him that it would mean a lot to me if he did. It had gotten to the point where I had asked him to just read chapter 12 in my first book. I had resorted to begging my boyfriend to read a single chapter of *me*, and he kept saying he would, but after a year and a half of dating, my hope's heartbeat was awfully faint.

I thought those things, but I said something else. I said that he had already told me his feelings about Didion's essay several times and that I didn't see why I needed to agree yet again.

Now, I definitely did not say that from a place of generosity or compassion. My tone was almost certainly bitchy.

Things escalated from there until we were fighting about a long list of things, the least of which was Joan Didion. I found myself admitting that I wasn't sure about us. I didn't know if we were going to make it. I started to cry, and M. asked me if I was crying because I was being so mean.

"How am I being mean?" I asked.

And he said the things I was saying about ending our relationship were mean. That was not why I was crying. I was crying because I was sad. I was sad, because I had only just begun to realize how little I'd settled for, just how little I was willing to accept. I was sad at my betrayal of myself. My writing is the very essence of who I am, and I was in a relationship with someone who could not be bothered with it.

In the previous summer, three of the psychics I interviewed had insisted on giving me brief readings at the end of our conversations. At the time, M. had been talking about getting married, about our wedding, for months by then. We had discussed where and how and when. He had shown me a ring that he particularly liked. But these psychics, all three of them, wanted more than anything to warn me about narcissists. They were dogmatic on the topic, in fact—a topic they broached, they insisted on. Each of them, in their own words, said that I had a tendency to let narcissists get too close to me. They said I had to be careful about narcissists; I had to watch out for the narcissists.

They didn't say marriage and babies wouldn't be with M., though they didn't say they would be, either. I didn't ask them about marriage or babies or M. even. They mentioned, of their own accord and practically in passing, that marriage and babies weren't happening for me just yet. I was going to be a horse unhitched for a while longer, which, when you think of it like that, sounds pretty nice. It wasn't until the fall, when my work intensified, when I needed M. to step up and emotionally support me for the first time in our relationship, and when he didn't, that I started to hope he wouldn't propose after all and started googling: "How do you know if your boyfriend is a narcissist?"

CHAPTER
THIRTY-ONE

After M. and I broke up, I returned to Montreal, to Catharine River-Rain. I had met Catharine on a warm summer morning surrounded by friends. More than a year and a half had passed, and now I was returning to her as 2017 limped to a close. The last time I had seen her, she had told me about M. And M. had come. And gone. Was I better off for having met him? Did it matter that Catharine predicted his arrival in my life? Would it have changed anything if she hadn't? If I had never seen her? Would M. and I still have met? Still have dated? Would our relationship have lasted as long as it did? Even before I realized that M. must be the "Prince Harry" Catharine had foreseen for me, I was smitten. We really had been "like this" from the moment we met. I do not regret my relationship with M. If I could go back and change it, make it so we hadn't met, I wouldn't. I'm a little wiser, a little more mature, a little better in almost every way than I was before M. I understand that he was a reaction to my ex B. I understand that it was a reaction I needed to have, needed to go through.

But I'm still not sure I want Catharine to tell me anything new. I'm still not sure it was a good idea to come back. I stand in the stairway of the building. The same stairway I stood in so many months before and wondered if I should go back up, ask her real quick if this man she saw coming would be "my marrying man." I didn't, and I'm glad that I didn't. Which makes taking those steps now all the heavier, all the more unsteady.

When I began to write this book, I worked for a large corporate technology company, and I lived with four very alive plants and one very alive boyfriend, my Prince Harry, with whom marriage and babies and commitment were routinely discussed in a practical, confident manner that lured us both into feeling good about the other, better than we ever truly were or could ever be. In other words, I began this book with the makings for the fairytale ending already in place.

I finish this book now with no such happy ending. Which is not how memoirs are supposed to go. They are supposed to start with your life in tatters and end with your life pieced back together again. Not this time. Romantically, I am unattached. Professionally, I am unattached. I am single, and I am freelance. I do not have a dog or a cat or even a succulent.

There is no person or job or responsibility that tethers me to any place. The sole recurring obligation in my life is to my monthly book club.

Would I be happier if I were married? Would I be happier with a mortgage and a nine-to-five job, dizzying with spreadsheets and too many open tabs on my laptop and mandatory meetings at which colleagues speak earnestly of stakeholders and scale? Would I be happier if Elvie were sleeping or screaming or smiling beside me right now? Or am I happier answering to literally no one or anything? Am I happier in the silence of my apartment in New York or in this sublet house in Los Angeles that will never belong to me? Happier getting up and showing up only whenever and wherever I please? The answer is both and neither. Sometimes, yes, I would be happier with all the compromises, all the expectations, all the joys of kissing a man and hugging our child and cautioning my colleagues, *My god, don't forget about scope.* And sometimes I would be happier all alone in the world. And sometimes the former would make me incredibly unhappy, and sometimes the latter would. No one is happy all of the time. There will always be another unhappy moment, another unhappy day, another unhappy week.

It is easy to find someone to be happy with. It is much harder to find someone to be unhappy with.

But I believe I can. Only I am worried that Catharine will cast doubt on my faith. Still, I am here. I flew all this way. I keep going up the stairs, because in the twenty months that have passed since I first saw Catharine, I have learned that psychics don't tell us our futures. The good ones, the ones like Catharine, who are full of empathy, who charge a flat fee and don't want your 401(k), listen. Then they tell you a story. It's a real story, but the point of the story is not the plot, not what happens, and never the ending. The point of the story is the way you hear it, what you make of it. How will you fill in the story's gaps? Your future is in those gaps and how you choose to fill them.

After my reading, after Catharine and I have hugged goodbye, I walk down the stairs without hesitation and for what I know will be the last time. Catharine did tell me a story. I heard it, and I will remember it, but I have my own story to live now. Joan Didion wrote to find out what she thought; M. spoke to find out what he thought; and, for a time, I saw psychics.

CHAPTER
THIRTY-TWO

Philosophy is the preparation for death. —Socrates

We talk about love poems but not about love books. This is a love book.

Socrates got it wrong. Philosophy isn't the preparation for death. Living is. Loving is.

Dr. Miller writes in *The Spiritual Child* that "beyond our natural, biological wiring for it, what makes us spiritual is our awareness that our lives, our relationships, and the natural world both seen and unseen are filled with an ultimate presence. It is our awareness of transcendence, in us, around us, through us, and beyond us, that is spiritual."

The preparation for death is living with integrity, hearts cracked wide-open, and big vaginas fully to the wall every damn day. That is how we come to know what we know. That is how we acknowledge the siren call of epistemology.

I didn't forget that Michelle asked me to come up with a new word to replace *spiritual*.

I am not religious. I am not spiritual. I am in tune.

ACKNOWLEDGMENTS

Of all that I have ever written, the book you are holding was by far the hardest for me to complete. I did not do it alone. I could not have.

Thank you, Jess Regel, for making this book even possible, and Vivian Lee, not only for having one of my favorite Twitter bios, but for understanding the true nature of this project long before I did, and for essentially saying, "Bitch, please," when I tried to return my book advance. Thank you, Merideth Mulroney and Laywan Kwan, for your dedication and your vision.

To the many, many individuals whose generosity of time, knowledge, and trust made the research and writing of this story a reality, I will never be able to thank you enough: Oluseye Adesola, Lanre Akintujoye, Elizabeth Alexandre, Antero Alli, Abdi Assadi, Ariane Brandt, Meghan Boody, Rob Brezsny, Alyson Charles, Dominic Ciccodicola, Andrea Cipriano, Michael Cipriano, Iris Reesha Clark, Timothy Cope, Jennifer Corforte, Gemma Deller, Chris Dukes, Clay Dukes, Maureen Bright Healer, Deborah Hanekamp, Terese Jordan, Nike Lawrence, Lindsay Mack, Sergeant John Magallanes, Priti Mahalanobis, Colleen McCann, Maria McCullough, Lauren Naturale (and Naomi!), Bob Nygaard, Julia Popescu, Anthony Ribera, Debra Saalfield, David Sauvage, Natalie Schachner, Sarah Bamford Seidelmann, Gary Strauss, Isabel Unanue, Cathrin Wirtz, Jaime Wolf, and Sergeant Robert Woods.

The hope of this book first began to take ahold of me when I was still employed at Twitter, and I owe a tremendous amount to my fellow Tweeps. Thank you to every one of my former colleagues, for their smarts and their patience with me, most especially: David Blackman, Mindy Diamond, Sarah Downs, Linda Jiang, Valerie Kuo, and Madhu Muthukumar. Thank you, too, to Katie Jacobs Stanton, for answering my out-of-the-blue email so swiftly and doing a bit of psychic detective work on behalf of one of the mysteries of this book.

To my @TwitterMoments family, because that's what you are, even if that makes me the flaky cousin, who may or may not show up for the holiday dinner—thanks for still setting a place for me.

Cooper Smith, for being (wo)man's best friend, obviously.

It was a privilege to work around the globe with Andrew Haigh, Luke Hopewell, Leandro Mota, Heba Wahab, and Jennifer Wilson, all of whom built incredible teams—teams that continue to stand on their own as well as together.

John Jannuzzi, for being exactly what the US team needed when we needed it and for baking batch after batch of chocolate-chip cookies that were, like their baker, sweet but never too sweet.

Monika Anderson, Jozen Cummings, Laura Franco, Kristina Lucarelli, Chris March, Amelie Meyer-Robinson, Sarah Munir, Quenton Narcisse, Ryan Ocenada, Darrick Thomas, and Jade Williams—I would do almost anything for each of you. You need to borrow a cup of sugar? You need to bury a body? DM me.

Andrew Fitzgerald, Joanna Geary, and Leonardo Stamillo, for giving all the damns.

And in memory of Francisco Rubio, who gave more to Twitter on any given afternoon than most of us give to anything ever, and whose hard work and boundless enthusiasm will forever be an integral part of the past, present, and future of Twitter Moments and every one of us lucky enough to have had Paco as a teammate:

Y en memoria de Francisco Rubio, quien dio más de sí mismo a Twitter en una tarde que lo que muchos de nosotros damos a cualquier cosa, y cuyo trabajo arduo y entusiasmo ilimitado será por siempre una parte integral del pasado, presente y futuro de Twitter Moments y de cada uno de los que tuvimos la fortuna de tener a Paco como compañero de equipo.

To those friends of mine who were there for me as I was writing this book:

Viviane Silvera and Melissa Marks, two incredibly talented artists who together appeared in my life like some kind of wild, gorgeous mirage that turned out to be oh-so-beautifully real.

Dana Deskiewicz, whose artistic talents and kindness never cease to amaze me.

Abigail Downs, because she never takes herself or me too seriously.

Liz Ichniowski, who, like Nancy Drew, has a knack for perfect timing, forever popping up with just the compassionate wisdom I need to hear when I need to hear it.

Alex Levenson, for being my most unflappable friend.

Brooke Slezak, for her open heart, mind, and door.

Amy DiTullio, Jason Del Col, and Neko Del Col, because they let me finish this book at their dining room table and because I love all three of 'em almost as much as Neko loves "copters."

Roshni Naik, who answered a million personal questions about astrology and whose infectious zest for life never gets old.

Amber Latner, for always understanding.

Jill Brenner, because she gets that being an asshole and being nice are not mutually exclusive.

Erin Mazursky, because our friendship really took off the night she let me ask her all the questions about psychics and crystals. And because she has big, important ideas that she wills into even bigger and more important realities.

Megan McGowan, for being so droll, so self-aware, and so determined.

Mary Dain, whose compassion and empathic intelligence are out of this world.

Daisy Freund, because I think she and I might be more similar than we realize, and because she has brought such poetry into my life, both literally and figuratively.

Patty Fels, because she has been a mentor to me at every step of this writing journey.

Hunter Reynolds, for his wisdom and for his grace.

And Michelle Sinnette, for the invitation.

ABOUT THE AUTHOR

Victoria Loustalot (pronounced LOO–STA–LOW) has written for the *New York Times*, the *New Yorker* online, the *Onion*, *Women's Wear Daily*, and *Publishers Weekly*, among many other publications. Her writing has also been acquired by both the Metropolitan Museum of Art's Thomas J. Watson Library and Yale University's Beinecke Rare Book & Manuscript Library. She earned her BA as well as her MFA from Columbia University in New York City and previously worked at Twitter as the global program manager for @TwitterMoments. *Future Perfect* is her third book. She is also the author of the memoir *This Is How You Say Goodbye* and *Living Like Audrey*, a meditation on the life and career of Audrey Hepburn. In the future, according to one psychic, she will call the Scottish countryside home. Another claims she will eventually move to Hawaii. Loustalot is dubiously unopposed to both. Visit her at www.victorialoustalot.com.